A PLUME BOOK

THE DISAPPEARING GIRL

"*The Disappearing Girl* is a meticulously researched, beautifully written, and emotionally powerful piece of work that speaks to the compassion and depth with which Dr. Machoian approaches the topic of depression in girls. She takes an honest and insightful look at the many challenges facing today's girls while providing practical (and hopeful) analysis and advice. As a researcher, and as well as a mother of a twelve-year-old girl, I found this book to be an invaluable resource."

—Jean E. Rhodes, PhD, professor of psychology, University of Massachusetts, Boston, and author of *Stand by Me: The Risks and Rewards of Mentoring Today's Youth*

"Finally it's here: We've been waiting for a book to provide us with a clear understanding of what interferes with the robust development of girls. But more importantly, Lisa Machoian takes us that final step beyond understanding to doing something to change the downward spiral of many adolescent girls. EVERYONE who knows a girl needs to read this."

—JoAnn Deak, PhD, coauthor of *Girls Will Be Girls: Raising Confident and Courageous Daughters*, and author of *How Girls Thrive: An Essential Guide for Educators (and Parents)*

THE DISAPPEARING GIRL

LEARNING the LANGUAGE
of TEENAGE DEPRESSION

Dr. Lisa Machoian

A PLUME BOOK

PLUME
Published by Penguin Group
Penguin Group (USA) Inc., 375 Hudson Street, New York, New York 10014, U.S.A.
Penguin Group (Canada), 90 Eglinton Avenue East, Suite 700, Toronto, Ontario,
Canada M4P 2Y3 (a division of Pearson Penguin Canada Inc.)
Penguin Books Ltd., 80 Strand, London WC2R 0RL, England
Penguin Ireland, 25 St. Stephen's Green, Dublin 2, Ireland (a division of Penguin Books Ltd.)
Penguin Group (Australia), 250 Camberwell Road, Camberwell, Victoria 3124, Australia
(a division of Pearson Australia Group Pty. Ltd.)
Penguin Books India Pvt. Ltd., 11 Community Centre, Panchsheel Park,
New Delhi – 110 017, India
Penguin Group (NZ), cnr Airborne and Rosedale Roads, Albany, Auckland 1310,
New Zealand (a division of Pearson New Zealand Ltd.)
Penguin Books (South Africa) (Pty.) Ltd., 24 Sturdee Avenue, Rosebank,
Johannesburg 2196, South Africa

Penguin Books Ltd., Registered Offices: 80 Strand, London WC2R 0RL, England

Published by Plume, a member of Penguin Group (USA) Inc. Previously published in a Dutton edition

First Plume printing, March 2006
10 9 8 7 6 5 4 3

℗ REGISTERED TRADEMARK — MARCA REGISTRADA

The Library of Congress has catalogued the Dutton edition as follows:

Machoian, Lisa.
    The disappearing girl : learning the language of teenage depression / Lisa Machoian.
    p.   cm.
    Includes bibliographical references.
    ISBN 0-525-94866-X (hc.)
    ISBN 0-452-28710-3 (pbk.)
    1. Depression in adolescence.   2. Teenage girls—Mental health.   I. Title.
RJ506.D4M23 2005
616.85'27'00835—dc22   2004025777

Printed in the United States of America
Original hardcover design by Daniel Lagin

AUTHOR'S NOTE
Most of the girls' stories in this book come from my research project; some are from my clinical
and consulting experience. Names, places, and other identifying details have been changed to
protect the privacy of the girls. (Some of the girls chose their own pseudonym.) Any similarity
between a girl's story in this book and a girl who is known to readers is inadvertent.

PUBLISHER'S NOTE

To the memory of my dad and my mom,
with love

To the memory of my dear friend Michael,
who gave me laughter and joy

For Carol Gilligan,
for always believing in me

And for all the girls,
with love, hope, and faith

CONTENTS

ACKNOWLEDGMENTS

I want to thank the source of my strength, hope, and faith—God. My spirituality has been the foundation of my life. I am ever grateful for my health and the opportunity to write the book that for so long was in my heart and soul to write.

Carol Gilligan has been and continues to be a brilliant inspiration in my life. Carol was my dissertation advisor at Harvard, which is where I began the research for this book. Her consistent belief in my work and her insistence that I write about my research has compelled me to follow my heart and my vision.

My agent, Gail Ross, wholeheartedly and enthusiastically believed in this book from the moment we first spoke, and she made sure it happened. I am grateful to Jane Isay for her expertise and talent. Thank you to Jenna Land Free for being there at several critical moments.

Trena Keating, my editor at Dutton/Plume, has been wonderful from the day we met, carefully keeping her eyes on both the vision and the details of this book. Her ideas have been terrific; her patience, I gratefully appreciate. Thank you to Emily Haynes, Jake Klisivitch, Robert Kempe, and Kathleen Schmidt at Dutton/Plume and to copy editor Anne Newgarden; it's been a pleasure working with you, and I am grateful for your help.

The funding support that helped to make the research possible came from several sources: Carol Gilligan helped to fund the initial phase of this research during my dissertation through the Harvard Project on Women's Psychology and Girls' Development. When I continued as a postdoc at Harvard, Carol Gilligan and the Gender Studies Program at The Harvard Graduate School of Education, the American Foundation for Suicide Prevention, and The Harvard Suicide Research Committee helped to fund this research. Bessel van der Kolk and Gil Noam were involved in my dissertation research and cosponsored my postdoctoral research with Carol; Bob Kegan at Harvard also served as a research sponsor. I appreciate their support and all that I learned from them.

I thank Gil Noam, Michael Hollander, Michael Rater, Sharon Weinstein, Gina Murphy, Terry Bragg, the teachers, clinicians and everyone who helped orchestrate the project. I want to thank all of my former students at Harvard who helped with this project (far too many to list). Thank you to those students who participated in my year-long research seminar: Jennifer Bateman, Stephen Chow, Suzanne Duke, Jamie Howard, Lionel Howard, Connie Scanlon, Tara Tatelman, and Travis Wright. Megan Costello, Lissa Dutra, and Jennifer Smith worked with me in year-long independent studies. My students' enthusiasm about my work, and their genuine desire to help young people, was a source of inspiration.

Thank you to everyone in the Atamian, Beck, Brox, Guillott, Kolligian, and Machoian families for their love as I was writing. I am grateful to Allen M. Beck for his love, encouragement, and support. I am ever appreciative and deeply grateful to my friends who sustained me all year as I was writing: Thank you to Blair Barone for her love and uplifting spiritual messages; to Amy Blitz for positive support and kindness; to Barbie Brox for talking with me and the generosity of her ideas; to Betsey Brox O'Reilly for her insight, support, and conversations about the many issues in the book; to Jacque DeSisto for always being there and for listening; to Holly Gelfond for reminding me to take care of myself during a grueling process; to Tamarleigh and Don Lippeygrenfell for being there; to Jill Rubin for her optimism; and to Steve Sherblom for his perspective, encouragement, friendship, understanding, love, and constant support across the miles. I thank my brother Stephen Machoian for his brotherly encouragement. Thank you to Gork Kluzak for always believing in me. I am grateful to Leslie Korn for "divine intervention." As I began writing the book, my very dear friend Michael DeSisto died. He was so excited about the book and so very proud of me; I am eternally grateful for his love, encouragement, and support. The love and life of my cousin, Ginger Atamian, gave me cause for my research. I thank my cousin Terry Atamian for his love, help, and generous spirit. I am ever grateful to my parents, both of whom passed on in my early adolescence, for their love and for giving me strength and hope. I thank Allen M. Beck and the late Kitsy Beck for giving my brother and me love and a home. I am grateful to Michele Kolligan for her friendship, love, and support. I thank my cousin Robyn Atamian for her positive spiritual support, encouragement, and love.

Thank you to my friends and neighbors Ray Castagnola, Karen Motley, Sue Rushford, and Vikram Savkar, who encouraged me and discussed the book with me every Sunday on my weekly outing to brunch across the street. Friends, family, neighbors, and colleagues encouraged me as I was writing this book. Thank you to Angie Arkin, Terry Atamian, Robyn Atamian, Sheryl Ricco Atamian, Tim Bedel, Mindy Bier, Nancy Cardwell, David Castellvi, Jed Clark, Thomas Cordima, Ernst Françoise, Jonathan Goh, Diane Grimaldi, Donna Guillot, Nan and John Guillott, David Halevy, Michael Humphrey, Gus Kaufman, Michele Kolligian, Susan Lynch, Peggy Machoian, Martin Machoian, William Maykel, Susan Mirow, Rose Najarian, Holli Neilson, Kate O'Neill, Paul D. O'Reilly, Susan Peppelman, Mignonne Pollard, Elizabeth Rice-Smith, Deborah Rose, Norman Sadowsky, Rachel Simmons, Brian Swinney, and Denise Guillot Vansant. Tamarleigh Lippeygrenfell, Karen Motley, and Steve Sherblom read chapters, for which I am extremely grateful. Thank you to Vikram Savkar for his kindness, generosity, and trust. I am grateful to Michael Kimmel for his friendship and support in making this book happen.

Thank you to Lori Allison, Sharon Broll, and Emily Hass for their help. Professionally, I wish to thank Kevin Becker, Dodi Cole, Carrie Pekor Jasper, Roslin Moore, Michael Nakkula, Frank Pescoloslido, Carol Scheppard, Joan Sedita, Meryl Sheriden, and Caroline Watts. Thank you to Katie Wheeler and the Boston Girls' Coalition for help with statistics on girls, and to William Maykel for help with the nutritional aspects of depression. I thank Beverly Sangston, Gerald and Lisa Vesper, Andy Ziencik, Betsy Furin, and Jim Beck. I am ever grateful to Tim Bedel for his love, friendship, and support. Thank you to Owanza. Thank you to the Armenian General Benevolent Union for their support during graduate school.

I did almost nothing but write for over a year, and there were several moments of inspiration for which I am grateful: The sunset over the ocean on a train ride en route to New York for a meeting and the respite and joy after the meeting, hearing Jackson Browne and Bruce Springsteen together singing "Take It Easy." A by-chance visit with Meryl Sheriden kept me connected to the roots of my work—being a teacher. In the last week before submitting the initial manuscript, I was walking hurriedly home through Harvard Square, and standing at the top of the steps of the First Parish in Cambridge stood Toni Morrison, my favorite writer. I bounded up the steps to tell her how I loved her work and how *The Bluest Eye* deeply touched my soul. I told her I was a child psychologist finishing my first book, and with kindness and warmth she graciously took my hand in hers, looked deep into my eyes, and said, "Go to it." I walked home deeply moved. The weekly sermons of Joel Osteen helped carry me, as did the prayers of Unity.

I've loved baseball ever since I was a little girl and, unbeknownst to them, the Boston Red Sox were my constant companions on the lonely writing journey; from opening day in April through October 2004, they have no idea how their hope and resilience inspired and helped me as I was writing (as did the hope and resilience of the fans). For months, my life was writing and watching the Red Sox games on TV. I did attend one game during a mini-break in August. There was no greater culmination of happiness than to bear witness to the amazing and historical comeback that took them to the World Series. I'll never forget the evening that I finally finished, e-mailing off the final manuscript; and then moments later Johnny Damon hit a grand slam, which literally had me jumping for joy. The Red Sox and Red Sox Nation never lost hope. Then I watched with anxiety, thrill, and sheer delight. It was a double celebration! I was finished with the book, and the Red Sox won the World Series! I officially reentered the world by attending an ecstasy-filled parade. For years, I had signed cards to the children and teenagers with whom I worked with the phrase "*Keep the faith*," which serendipitously emerged as the slogan of Red Sox Nation. The power of the Red Sox's hope, teamwork, and love for one another and their fans was extraordinary. The 2004 Red Sox story is a poignant, important story and the theme of this book: Never lose hope, no matter what. Believe. You can do it. Anything is possible. Thank you, Red Sox.

Some parts of this book appeared in earlier versions in journals. I gratefully acknowledge these journals as original publication sources of earlier presentations of some of the ideas and clinical material in this book and thank the publishers for their permission to reuse the material: "Cutting Voices: Self-Injury in Three Adolescent Girls," *Journal of Psychosocial Nursing and Mental Health*, 39, no. 11, (2001): 22–29, and "Learning to Speak the Language of Violence: A Relational Interpretation of an Adolescent Girl's Suicidality," *Studies of Gender and Sexuality*, 3, no. 3, (2002): 321–40, which was coauthored with Carol Gilligan.

Most important, I want to thank the girls for their courage in telling me their stories, their help, their passion to make a difference, and their inspiration. I thank their parents from the bottom of my heart for giving them permission to participate so that together we all could be of help to others. Without the girls, this book would not exist. It's for the girls themselves that I felt the stories in this book had to be told. I remember all the girls I have listened to over the years. I thank you all for your hope, your courage, your strength, your love, and your trust. I love you all. Keep the faith.

INTRODUCTION:
A THOUSAND FACES

"The number one positive thing about girls is that we are resilient. It may take us a while, or a long while in my case, but
when we fight back, we fight back, dammit."

—Nicole, age 18

What I know about teenage girls comes from listening to them.
I've listened to girls for over twenty years in different
capacities—as a psychotherapist, a teacher, a researcher, a school
consultant; working with families, facilitating groups; doing educational, learning disability, trauma, and psychological evaluations. I've
worked with girls in private and public schools, boarding and day
schools; in community settings; in outpatient and inpatient clinical settings; and in juvenile justice settings. I've trained teachers and clinicians
working with girls. I've spent my career working with children and
teenagers and, regardless of the setting, I've learned that they want to
be taken seriously; they want people to listen.

After working with teenagers as a teacher, I went to Harvard to
study with Carol Gilligan, who was conducting pioneering research on
girls, and to earn my master's and doctoral degrees. I was interested in
adolescent development, particularly girls who were struggling. *The
Disappearing Girl* is the first book ever to focus on teenage girls' depression, and rests on the foundation of that research. Depression skyrock-
ets for girls during adolescence, which raised the important question in
my mind: "Why now?"

At Harvard, I was interested in developmental psychology. It had always seemed to me that the impact events and opportunities have on people can depend on where they are in their lives. A developmental focus is especially important in understanding teenagers and their struggles. In fact, I conceived of the project on which this book is based because of my question, "Why now?" Why do we see a rise in depression and a peak in suicidal behavior in early adolescent girls? Why now and not when girls are eight, or when they are twenty-seven? As a teacher, I observed that adolescent girls who were depressed and suicidal did not, deep down, really want to die. This led me to wonder: What, then, was their intention?

What I found missing from the research on girls' depression and suicidal behavior were the perspectives of the girls—what they thought, what they had to say. What did girls have to tell us about their depression and about why they hurt themselves? No researchers had directly asked girls struggling with depression about their lives, their stories, or their perspective on depression and suicidal behaviors. My questions and curiosities became the basis of my doctoral dissertation, postdoctoral research at Harvard, and *The Disappearing Girl*. As I was conducting this research, I was working as a psychotherapist for children and adolescents. What I was hearing from girls in therapy was similar to what I was hearing from girls in research interviews.

After I completed my dissertation, Carol Gilligan asked me to continue this project as a postdoctoral researcher at Harvard and to include boys, which I did (there are so many issues for both girls and boys that boys also require their own attention). During the process of this research, I was also teaching about risk and resilience, and students at the Harvard Graduate School of Education asked me if I could develop a course specifically about adolescent girls that would go beyond research and theory into practice. They wanted to know what to do to help the girls with whom they were working. I created the course and for five years taught a class on risk and resilience in adolescent girls' psychological development; that course provided additional background for this book.

The Disappearing Girl is based on my research interviews and is informed by my psychotherapeutic and other types of experiences working with girls; it brings you the real stories, straight from the girls themselves, who told me about their lives, struggles, and hopes so they could help other kids and the people who love and want to help them. They felt it was important for people to know.

Ali on the Roof

Ali trudged home from school thinking middle school was no fun. She missed her friends. They were all split up now. There were all these cliques and groups. The teachers even seemed a little different, too. She got in the house and looked around the kitchen. Usually she had a snack, but today, like other days lately, she didn't feel like eating. After school used to be fun; now it was a lonely time of day. In the old days, in elementary school, she'd be outside playing kickball with kids in the neighborhood, or at soccer practice. School changed, kids changed, teams changed, everything changed with middle school. She went upstairs to her room and dug out a journal she never used. Ali hadn't written in a journal in about a year, but in late October, she started writing:

> *I was always happy before middle school. You grow up and you go to middle school and you don't really grow up, you just move up. It's totally different. Girls wear tight shirts and bell-bottoms and lots of the guys wear baggy pants and baggy shirts. They call you a boy, or whatever, if you don't have long hair. I like short hair. I have it long now, but I used to have it short. Now they just seem to single out all the people who are different. They make fun of them and make them seem worthless, like they couldn't do anything. I miss my friends from elementary school. They were good friends. We used to hang out. All the girls are worried about what they look like. I think I'm fat. I don't like life anymore. I miss my good friend Tim. We're not on the same soccer team, we're not even in math together and we always sat next to each other for years. People piss me off when they are disrespectful to other people and make fun of other people. I even hate it when kids are disrespectful to their parents. I'm still in a lot of pain because my best friend Laurie made friends again with Brianna who betrayed her before. Laurie won't talk to me. It makes me really upset. She's mad at me because I told her Brianna isn't a true friend and only cares about herself, and I didn't want Brianna to betray her again. Everything really hurts me. I'm worthless and fat. If something happened to me, no one would even know I existed.*

Ali put the journal under her pillow. Her bedroom was on the second floor and adjacent to the garage roof. She opened the window, took out the screen, and climbed onto the roof. She inched her way closer to the edge and sat down. Her dad was home from work early that day and was downstairs. He felt a cool breeze so he went upstairs to see what was going on. His heart pounded when he saw the open window and his daughter on the roof. Taking a deep breath, he calmly said, "Ali, honey, come on back in, get in here." She looked up at her dad with tears in her eyes and climbed back in.

You're Not Alone

If you are reading this, you, like me, are concerned about your daughter or a girl you love and care for, or you want girls and women to be able to live their lives to the fullest. I wrote this book for you because I care about girls, and the women they will grow up to be. I do believe that together we can make life better for them.

If we can begin to notice the difference between teen angst and signs of depression, and if we discern when angst is spiraling into depression, we can do something very important. Not only can we save girls from unnecessary suffering when they are teenagers, but if we help girls at this point in their lives, we will also help them to become happier, more fulfilled adults.

I made a wonderful discovery in my research of and psychotherapy with teenage girls struggling with depression: No matter how despairing they may feel, there is always a spark of hope within them, and the energy to make their troubles visible to themselves and others. In doing so, they can feel better about what is troubling them. That is the promise of this book. Hope manifests in teenage girls in ways we don't always recognize, just as teenage girls' depression does. From the stories in this book you can learn to recognize the many faces of girls' depression and girls' hope—how both make themselves visible in our society. Adults experiencing depression often lose hope. In teenage girls, as seventeen-year-old Harmony says, *"There is always a tiny speck of hope."*

Because hope is alive in teens, this age is the prime time for intervention. We need to do something now. We know that cultural forces are responsible for the preponderance of depression in women—and for many women, depression begins when they are teenage girls.

The Numbers Tell a Story

Here is what happens. At the edge of adolescence, around age twelve, the rate of depression in girls rapidly rises, which stands in contrast to childhood, when boys outnumber girls in rates of depression. By age fifteen, girls with depression outnumber boys by a ratio of two to one, a statistic that mirrors the adult population. Some surveys report that teenage girls are seven times more apt to be depressed than teenage boys and two to ten times more likely to attempt suicide. Boys, though they attempt suicide less frequently, are more apt to kill themselves when they do attempt it. Surveys tell us that 25 percent or more of teenage girls report depression. Teenage girls report high rates of suicidal thinking, a common symptom of depression. A survey reports that 29 percent of the teenage girls said they think about killing themselves but would not do it. Suicide is the third leading cause of death among fifteen to twenty-four-year-olds.[1] Researchers found a peak in girls' suicide attempts at ages thirteen and fourteen.[2]

Eating disorders, cutting, and risky acting-out are different faces of teenage girls' depression. The epidemic of eating problems has been with us for years and most often coexists with depression, but the overemphasis on food and the body can distract parents and professionals from seeing and addressing the underlying depression. Diets precipitate eating disorders. Forty-two percent of first-through-third-grade girls want to be thinner. Fifty percent of fourth-grade and eighty percent of fifth-grade girls have dieted. Ninety percent of junior- and senior–high school girls diet regularly even though only 10 to 15 percent of girls are over normal weight percentiles. Fifteen percent of adolescent girls and young women have disordered eating. Nearly 4 percent of teen girls and young women have anorexia; 3 to 4 percent have bulimia, and up to 19 percent of college-aged young women are bulimic.[3]

Cutting has become more common in girls than in the past. Girls with depression tell me it's important to let people know how many girls are cutting. A survey in a suburban high school in Massachusetts found that one in three sophomore girls reported feeling so sad or angry that they cut or burned themselves. Statewide, 29 percent of the girls and 19 percent of the boys surveyed said that they harmed themselves on purpose.[4]

Mental health problems in kids are much more common than we think, and affect one in five children and adolescents. But only 30 percent of those who need help get help, which means the other 70 percent do not.[5] This is not because no one cares, but rather because we often don't know how to distinguish real trouble from the seemingly inevitable teenage blues. Prior to the 1970s, doctors and researchers did not think children and adolescents experienced depression. Since then, there has been a flurry of research, but none before this book that specifically interviewed girls about their experiences and understanding of depression.[6]

Most girls in emotional distress pass beneath the radar, their depression unrecognized, mistaken for typical teen development or teenage angst. Lack of recognition during adolescence can have a negative impact on the development of a girl's positive identity. This creates the risk that girls will grow into women with depression and, often, a lost sense of who they really are, what they really want, and what they are really capable of doing with their lives. If girls don't learn how to understand and cope with the issues that contribute to depression, they may never learn to do so. In *The Disappearing Girl*, I suggest ways you can help the girls in your life cope with the pressures they encounter.

Since depression can come and go repeatedly, many girls think the recurring waves of distress and negative thoughts or subtle low-grade dissatisfaction with life and themselves is just how life is. They don't know that they are contending with depression. They grow into women thinking this is simply who they are, and how they must live because they have felt this way since they were thirteen or fourteen.

From the Blues to the Depths

There is quite a range from mild depressive symptoms to major depression. Many teenage girls exhibit symptoms of mild depression—irritability, boredom, and feelings of worthlessness—but do not have all of the symptoms required to be officially diagnosed with "major depression" (which I discuss in Chapter One). That doesn't mean they're not depressed, or not at risk. Many girls may have partial, moderate, or subclinical depression. As many as 20 percent have moderate depression, which can persist for years in girls and is linked to problems in school and peer relationships. (Similarly, in adults, it's linked to problems in work and interpersonal relationships.) Research indicates that girls run a multitude of risks when partial symptoms go untreated (no therapy, no help, no sympathetic ear or shoulder to cry on). One of the biggest risks is that without any intervention, girls with some symptoms are two to three times more likely to become depressed than the rest of the population.[7]

It's crucial for us to have early detection methods and to make sure there is appropriate intervention. Women's risk of osteoporosis is increased by depression, as is their risk of heart disease, the number-one killer of women. Women with depression have to work harder at everything they do, because everything feels like a great struggle.

From the girls' stories in this book, we will see how one symptom of depression can wreak havoc in the life of a teenager and how teen angst can move along a continuum and turn into depression. We will also see how girls resist disappearing into the black hole of the teenage blues, and what you can do to help.

I am not trying to make girls or women out to be victims, nor am I looking to find a problem that does not exist. I am calling attention to a serious problem in women's lives that has been endemic in our society for a long time, and is getting worse.

To help us understand the context of girls' vulnerability to depression in early adolescence, we need to understand the dynamics of girls' psychological development in our culture and then consider the current social context (I explore the current social context in Chapter One).

Girls' Psychological Development

Close to twenty years ago, my colleague and friend, psychologist Carol Gilligan, found that little girls are amazingly strong and sturdy in their sense of themselves. Their childhood resilience is linked to their relationships and their relational strengths: their ability to say openly what they are thinking and feeling and their ability to distinguish fake relationships from real relationships. As they approach middle school and early adolescence, girls absorb cultural messages about femininity telling them how to modulate their voices and behavior so they can become "good" women: "On a daily basis, girls receive lessons on what they can let out and what they must keep in, if they don't want to be spoken about by others as mad or bad or simply told they are wrong."[8]

Because they are discouraged from honest self-expression—saying what they genuinely think and feel in their relationships—girls subtly begin to disconnect from what they think and feel. At first, they may not say something out loud if it diverges from their peer group. It may be a conscious choice but, slowly and insidiously, not saying what they think can lead to disconnection from what they really do think. When girls give up being authentic in order to stay connected to others, they give up being in real relationships. This renders them disconnected from themselves and others and vulnerable to psychological distress. This paradox is central in women's psychology, and for girls it begins in early adolescence.[9]

Some girls begin equating isolation and loneliness with independence and autonomy. Many girls stop raising their hands in class and clam up about saying what they believe. Many girls resist conforming, fake relationships, and disconnection, and they try to fight back, which is healthy, but far too often they are told implicitly and explicitly to be quiet.

Finding Hope

The most powerful finding in my research has been this: Girls who are depressed and thus start acting out and hurting themselves are doing so in the desperate hope of being listened to and understood, getting help, finding real relationships, and being true to their real selves. In that effort, they discover they are taken more seriously when they endanger or hurt themselves with violence than when they communicate with words. As a society, we pay lots of attention to violence—just watch the news.

Girls' healthy resistance to disconnection in early adolescence sustains their hope;[10] "the possibility of love," meaning connection with friends and family, spurs them to reach out. Through their actions—

their suicide threats, risky behaviors, and self-harm—teenage girls are actively seeking help. Unlike many depressed adults, they have not given up. Neither should we. Parents can learn to help their daughters navigate and think critically about the pressures, the images, the messages, and the unspoken rules of today's adolescence. Girls grow up both too quickly and not quickly enough to readily cope with the pressures of today's adolescence.

As you read the chapters that follow, I hope you will come to understand what I see—that a pattern of events, some big, some small, can push girls from ordinary teen angst into depression. I hope that we will all see how important it is to listen to girls' voices and not panic, and to pick up their signals of distress. Adolescent girls are full of hope, though sometimes that is not how they appear. If they are not flourishing and thriving, it's not because they are lazy or bad. Something is amiss. If they have the "wrong" friends, there may be a reason underlying their choices and it's up to you to find out what it is. If their grades plummet, if they are spending too much time alone, if they are acting out—listen. What you may hear is a small voice, in its own little (or loud) way, speaking out and asking for help.

If you respond and help an adolescent girl navigate the world's messages and support her in building good relationships and increasing communication, you will not only be making her feel better today, but also may be preventing a lifelong pattern of self-hate and depression from taking hold. Things I love about adolescent girls are their resistance, their hope, their grit, and their spunk. They can get on with their lives—but we need to take the first steps and pay attention—to their words as well as their actions.

Organization of This Book

In Chapter One we look at the current social-cultural context and the expectations and pressures girls face as they enter adolescence. In Chapter Two we explore how the everyday changes of adolescence—big and small, external and internal, can create risk and vulnerability. In Chapter Three we explore the heart of the matter, how girls lose themselves and their identity in an effort to conform and belong. Chapter Four explains how depression is not just about moods and emotions, but also about thinking, and how negative thinking is dangerous. We look at ways to know if your daughter is slipping into such a quagmire. Chapter Five covers trauma and loss, common risk factors for depression, and how to help girls manage.

In Chapter Six, we explore how girls' depression is masked by acting out and unruly behavior. Chapter Seven follows Elizabeth as she spirals into depression and keeps reaching out for help while everyone around her thinks she has only normal teenage problems. In Chapter Eight, we listen to Olivia, as she literally disappears from the world around her, with a simultaneous deep, ongoing inner struggle and resistance to losing herself. In Chapter Nine, we meet Grace, who with a spirit of hope realizes that she has to endanger herself to be taken seriously by larger societal systems.

The final section of the book, Chapter Ten, helps you to learn more of what to look for, explains some of the differences between angst and depression, and includes the *Emotional First-Aid Kit* all girls can use. In Chapter Eleven, you meet the reappearing girl, Rachel, who shines with resilience, epitomizing the hope inherent in girls that I want us to sustain and keep alive. And in Chapter Twelve, the girls speak about what they think adults and schools can do to help, and give their words of wisdom to other teenagers who may be hurting.

This book is a call for women and girls to change this epidemic of depression in their lives. We all know women who are quietly depressed, defeated, not living up to their fullest potential. Just think how different their lives might be if they had been helped as teenagers. If we intervene in the lives of girls, they may not have to suffer with depression for the rest of their lives. We need to defeat depression in girls' and women's lives, and we can. Think of this book as a call to help us understand and listen to girls, and take them seriously so we can move toward eradicating the widespread depression encompassing so many women's lives.

THE DISAPPEARING GIRL

1. ENTERING DANGEROUS TERRITORY

Dear Diary,

I'm not the way I should be. If I could explain how I feel or justify my emotions I would in a second. I want someone to understand what it's like to have something dissolving your confidence, your happiness, trapping your true self—whoever that may be, behind a wall. All I know is I'm falling, suffocating, yet I have no reasons, no words to explain why, no reason to feel this way. Everyone wants me to act and smile and say I'm super but on days like today it doesn't work. The things kids do to buy popularity are things I don't want to do. Some days I think if I could just disappear . . . See you later, Olivia

As girls become teenagers, it's as though they are suddenly hapless tourists in their own lives, dropped in a strange uncharted territory without a compass or a map. The whole experience of trying to meet the new demands of friends, school, and family can be confusing, and girls can lose a sense of who they really are. It's not news that culture, peers, and social expectations play tremendous roles in the lives of teens.[1] What is new is that the mass media are more seductive than ever; teenage millionaire celebrities are on magazine covers weekly; expensive designer labels attempt to define girls; technology provides new ways for teenagers to communicate—and be hurtful to one another; and the social pressure to engage in sexual behaviors is falling on younger and younger girls. We have known about these cultural pressures and stressors for decades, but they are becoming so intense that they are having an impact on the rate of depression in teenage girls. When the expectations and standards around them shift so quickly, girls don't have the life experience to guide them on their way.

Parents tell me things have changed since they were teenagers and that the landscape looks different from how it did twenty years ago—or even just five or ten years ago. The following story is that of an ordinary mother's "education."

Whatever Happened to Romance?

My friend Merry calls me, distraught. It all started when her daughter Amber came home from her friend Doug's party totally wasted one Saturday night a month ago. Merry is an extremely responsible mother who is trying to hold back the tide of drink, other drugs, and conspicuous consumption that is threatening to drown Amber. In fact, Merry had spoken to Doug's father to make sure that the party would be supervised. Otherwise Amber, just fourteen, would never have been allowed to go.

Amber came home at 12:30 A.M., thoroughly drunk and miserably sick. What had gone wrong? Amber swears she never saw Doug's father. She said everybody was drinking. When they ran out of liquor, the kids went out and bought new supplies. Kids were both inside and outside of Doug's house, and on the patio, around the pool, drinking and smoking cigarettes and pot. Merry couldn't bear to ask Amber about hard drugs.

In a rage she called Doug's father. "You promised you would be there," she complained. "I was," he said. "I was home the whole damn night. But I had to promise Doug that I wouldn't leave the bedroom. So I don't know exactly what happened during the party." Merry's silence traveled along the phone lines while she thought, "Since when do parents make such promises to their children?" But before she could finish her thought, he continued, "Look, I figured it's better to have them drinking at home than at some dangerous place. I can't do better than that. Can you?"

Merry didn't have a good rejoinder for Doug's dad (ironically, a day after she tells me this, there are news reports talking about making parents legally responsible for underage drinking in their homes), but she had a great idea for Amber: She was grounded for a whole month. Go to school, come home, that's it. Amber cried for two days and then calmed down. She was as pleasant as she could be; in fact, she didn't even get into any fights with her younger sister.

The last few days of Amber's grounding were on a weekend, so, pleased with Amber's good attitude over the month, Merry and her husband let her go to a party on Saturday night. This time they dropped her off and then picked her up at 11:00 P.M. A month before, these strictures would have elicited tears and moans, but by now Amber was thrilled to be allowed to go out and grateful to her parents for being so flexible. Merry said she suspected that Amber was kind of relieved to be grounded.

Just before the four weeks of grounding were up, Merry brought up that drunken party again. She knew about the drinking, cigarettes, and pot; was there more Amber had to tell?

Here's the scene Amber painted: Four fifteen-year-old boys are leaning their backs against the radiator, drinks in hand. That's how guys stand around at parties, right? But there's more to notice. There are four girls on their knees, giving the boys blow jobs! To Merry's expressions of shock and disgust, Amber was adamant—"It's not sex, Mom, don't you *know* that?"

Merry called me right afterward and said she could only shake her head in dismay, explaining that she had feared she was going to hear about more drugs, which would have been bad enough, but not this. As other parents have said to me, when it comes to their daughters and anything about sex, Merry emphatically proclaims, "I don't want to know about these things." She pauses and before I say a word she continues, "I know, I know; it's good that she told me, and I need to know what she's dealing with even if I don't want to."

A few days after Merry's phone call, it's Thanksgiving night, long past dessert, and I'm with close lifelong friends. Several of us are sitting around the kitchen table. Beth, a mother of three, sighs, shaking her head, and marvels, "I can't believe I'm actually a suburban mom. Get this—all the sixth-grade parents have to attend the annual middle school meeting on the oral sex epidemic next week." We all sit up a bit.

"What?" Ellen loudly exclaims.

"Oh yeah, haven't you seen it on *Oprah*? She always knows the scoop. Haven't you read about it?" replies Barb, home visiting from Florida.

Betsey, a mom with two young teenagers, says calmly, "Yes, it's very common, and the boys tell the girls it's not sex."

"And the girls believe them?" Ellen exclaims, loudly, once again.

We talk about the misnomer—that the media refer to this as an oral sex epidemic—but it's not an oral sex epidemic, it's a fellatio epidemic. Having been friends since we were little girls, we reminisce that this was not a typical preteen issue or pressure when we were eleven- and twelve-year-old girls.

We worry about why young girls are servicing and pleasing boys—to be popular, to be hip, to be cool, to belong and be accepted, to gain high status, and to fit in. An important part of this story is that girls who are feeling insecure and not strong enough in their sense of themselves, and who really want to be accepted and feel wanted, are especially vulnerable to coercion and exploitation and going along with what their peers do. Every human being wants love and acceptance, but some girls, feeling uncertain in the new teenage terrain, are at risk to do whatever it takes to be part of a group or clique, and to have friends, even if it means giving up their own values, desires, and feelings.[2]

On the teen love scene, romance is waning and rapidly being replaced with "hooking up," "rainbow parties," and "friends with benefits" ("FWB")—friends with whom you have sex or do sexual things. It has become socially acceptable for girls to be sexually active at a younger age, but young girls have not typically developed the coping skills for the emotional aspects of these experiences, or the decision-making skills to think about the consequences. Preteens and teens may be physically ready, but psychologically many are not.[3]

Last fall I held a focus group with teenage girls. I asked: "Is there pressure to be in a romantic relationship?"

Emma, age fourteen, one of many bright girls, answered, "I think it's the opposite. I think there is more pressure to engage sexually with guys without being in a relationship, because guys don't want a relationship. A relationship is mainly what girls want. I mean, some guys do, but I think it's more that they want sex and sexual activity."

"Guys don't want to be romantic most of the time, they want to do something sexual," says Victoria.

"There's a lot of pressure to do stuff with them even if you're not ready or if you want to be in a relationship or you like them and then if you don't do something sexual, someone else will," says Carrie.

Kristy explains, "You don't know what to do. You are confused. You end up doing something because you want to make them happy, and then you feel guilty and go into feeling depressed."

When girls are in romantic relationships, breakups can leave them brokenhearted and vulnerable. Too often their pain (and often it's their first time dealing with such a loss) is trivialized and their love not taken as seriously because they are teenagers. If you remember how many people marry their high school sweethearts, suddenly teen love isn't necessarily so trivial.

But, despite Merry's story, it's not just sex and romance that create new social pressures for girls; it is also the world of friends.

Friends and Foes

There's nothing more important in a teenage girl's life than her friendships. This can make or break her psychological health. As girls reach middle school, the importance of girlfriends is heightened, and friendships often begin to change. Here's another instance in which girls' social worlds become vastly different from what they experienced when they were in elementary school. "Everything starts to shift in middle school," explains Carrie. "People, especially girls, start becoming so much more aware of how they are supposed to fit into the culture. When kids were younger, they didn't pay attention to stuff on TV. You run around and play. But then, a lot of my friends started watching MTV all the time and reading *Seventeen* magazine and looking at all the pictures. Once that started, it shifted their focus. They started to think more about fashion, and how they're too fat, or too thin, they want this color hair, or whatever. I noticed a lot of my friends shifting, and I never really cared. That started separating me from the friends I had for a long time. Then I eventually had the typical seventh- and eighth-grade fights with my friends."

Friends are central, and so disconnections are fraught with hurt and anger. "It's the end of the world when you're in eighth grade. Friends are everything—that's what your life is to you at thirteen—your friends," says Carrie. A girl experiencing the meanness from peers described by Rachel Simmons in *Odd Girl Out* is beyond unhappy. If other girls are shunning her, and if she's sitting alone in the cafeteria, she's at risk. Researchers find that good friendships help protect girls from depression. As they move into middle school, they become increasingly vulnerable to rejection and exclusion. When things are going well with their friends and peers, they tend to get along better with their parents and to feel good about themselves.

Technology adds an unusual twist to the pressures and importance of friendship. The advancements we all appreciate have made life easier, but also increasingly treacherous. Teenagers are using the Internet as a present-day tool for bullying, harassment, and sexual betrayal. Male classmates rank girls' attractiveness on the Web. Girls worry that something private—a confession, a response, a picture or video, or even a made-up rumor—might be spread through their whole school and community via the World Wide Web. More sweeping forms of public humiliation exist today than ever before, and this is true for both girls and boys.

The good news is that friends can also be a tremendous source of help. Girls often first reach out to their friends when feeling bad, knowing that their closest friends will be most likely to listen to them and most likely to understand them. Given the importance of social and emotional skills for navigating teenage life, I think it's important to talk with girls about what healthy and real relationships are. A real friendship is one in which there is trust and loyalty, one in which she can be herself, in which she feels safe saying what she is thinking and feeling without fearing she will lose the relationship.

How Do I Look?

The emphasis on looks as the determinant of women's value in our culture has a pernicious effect on the self-worth of girls, as well as that of their mothers. We have known this for a long time. Research shows that when seventh- and tenth-grade girls are exposed to idealized female images, they become less satisfied with their bodies and more likely to feel depressed, anxious, and angry. And the numbers are worse, not better, for the tenth-grade girls.[4]

Young girls experience the celebrity culture like everybody else. But the impact of this really hits girls when they are old enough to compare themselves with the teen celebrities creating billion-dollar empires and setting expensive trends. All of a sudden, it can seem like quite a shock. "Celebrities are everywhere," says eighteen-year-old Nicole. "No matter where you are you see them—TV, ads, magazines, news, the Web—entire shows and magazines gossip about what they're doing and who they're sleeping with. When something is always in your face, it's going to influence you. You want to look like them—and when the standard is that high, it's not humanly reachable, so you don't feel good enough. It's impossible to have any self-esteem if you don't feel good enough, or good enough for anyone. Society and celebrities set the standards, and the problem is that the standard they set is impossible. And adults wonder why we have problems." Nicole has clarity now; she did not understand it this way when she was twelve.

Girls tell me that the emphasis is more on image and status than ever before; a mother tells me the story of how a thirteen-year-old girl went from the inner to outer circle of friends because she had an imitation Coach purse.[5] So it's harder than ever for your daughter to feel she is worthy and valued for who she is as a person, rather than how she looks and what labels she sports.

The Perfect Storm

It's difficult for girls to find themselves and grow their very own identities if they are trying to emulate an image or be something society tells them to be. If they live like this, girls end up disconnected from their real selves, from their souls, and from figuring out who they are. Without knowing who they are, it's harder for them to find their direction, where they are going, and their purpose in life. This inevitably leads to emptiness and loneliness.

I have come to think that what we know about girls' psychological development in our culture,[6] mixed with the current social context of our culture and youth culture, are in place, like the right weather combinations, to lead to the perfect storm of teenage girls' depression. What is happening for girls is that instead of feeling they can expand and grow into the world, they have to shrink themselves back and away, or contort themselves into something and someone they're not. Far too often, the gradual and essential process of growing and discovering their identity is cut short, cut off, and squelched. This is tragic, since it may limit the richness of their personalities throughout life. Girls need a safe place in which to experiment with who they are and what they want. Girls' identities can become negative in a world where they feel they're not good enough because they never measure up to the images and messages all around them. Rather than being able to focus on the adolescent identity questions of "Who am I?" and "Where am I going?" as teens always have, girls today are more worried about "Who am I supposed to be?" and in the process can disappear as the person they are.

When We Just Don't Get It

One of the problems teenagers face is that in our culture we expect teens to be sullen, irritable, moody, bored, anxious, and uncommunicative. From time to time they may be pleasant, we think, but not for long and not often. Then comes the time when they are being difficult— upsetting us and themselves. Too frequently, we dismiss these behaviors as typical teenage behaviors, and the problems are minimized. It takes an escalation to catch our attention. This common misunderstanding and mishandling of girls' depression, even when it is recognized (in many instances it is missed altogether, or not given attention, or diverted onto eating and food), contributes to what has become a runaway epidemic.

I want to emphasize that it is not up to you as a parent or teacher or friend to determine or diagnose depression; a mental health professional trained to work with teens should do this. But it is up to you to know if a girl needs to see someone. And if you take her to a clinician who does not think there is a problem, and you think there is, listen to your gut and get a second and third opinion. I also want to say that I wish we could send our society to therapy, not girls, but given the cultural toxins girls encounter, we have to intervene.

Sometimes, even well-meaning clinicians can miss the boat. Fourteen-year-old Emma finally told her mom she was having suicidal thoughts. It was at night and her mother, frightened, did exactly the right thing and took her to the local hospital emergency room. But because Emma is bright, articulate, and calm, she was sent home and was not referred for any kind of intervention. "I talked with the psychiatrist about three hours, told him everything, completely honestly. I wasn't in hysterics. I was just talking like this. I have a sense of humor. I'm not going to have emotional breakdowns. At the end of three hours, he said, 'You seem like a really nice girl, pretty smart. I don't think you have that much reason to be depressed, so I'm going to put you on a waiver. Make sure you sign not to hurt yourself in any way, and I'm going to send you home now.'"

Emma says, about the experience, "It reinforces that I'm not good enough and that I'm not important enough, and that even my problems aren't big enough to be dealt with." Emma's friend, who had been through a similar experience, told her and her mom where to go, and the second hospital she went to did not send her home. Pediatricians and even some clinicians may not know what to look for, not because they don't care, but because they lack the appropriate training. Many were even trained in an era when the experts didn't believe that children and adolescents got depressed.

"No Reason" Girls

"Understanding what a girl is thinking and feeling is just as important as taking care of her," explains Carrie. "Sometimes there aren't any signs or symptoms, but that doesn't mean the girl isn't depressed. It's scary sometimes. I hid it from everyone. There was absolutely no reason why I should be so upset, so I thought everyone would think I was a freak."

Some girls don't think there is a concrete or tangible reason for them to feel bad or be depressed, so they don't tell anybody if something is wrong. They pretend everything is fine. Even when they think they have a tangible reason, many girls don't want to upset or hurt their parents, so they keep it inside. Girls don't want their parents to think it is their fault, because it isn't. They don't want other kids to think something is wrong with them. In the minds of many girls, there is "no reason" for them to feel blue, and that makes them feel even worse about themselves.

They understand that the culture wants them to grow into happy, good women. "A big part of hiding it was that I'm supposed to be happy. I'm a girl—I'm supposed to be nice and sunny and smiley," Victoria tells me. And Crystal says, "How could I tell anyone I was depressed? My nickname is Sunshine!"

Nicole explains, "I was so mad at myself. I just kept thinking, 'I'm so stupid for doing all of this.' My one train of thought was: 'I live in a nice house, in a rich town. My family gets along really well. I even get along with my brother—most people don't. I get good grades. I'm fairly smart, and I don't struggle in school. I don't even have to think about it that much; I just do the work. I have everything that you could ever really ask for and so much more than most people ever get. So this is pathetic. Why am I doing this? This is so stupid. I'm so ungrateful.' I would yell at myself for that, and I'd hate myself for it."

There is a reason for feeling blue, but girls are not consciously aware of it: Their identity is disappearing. Nicole says that around eighth grade, after fighting with her friends, she stopped speaking up and just went along with what everyone did, "because you can't be alone; you have to have friends." She explains, "I knew something was wrong, in that quiet source of knowledge about yourself in the back of your mind, but it wasn't like I was thinking, 'If I do this, I'm giving up my ability to assert myself.'"

Why We Need to Get It

Girls who do hide do not hide forever, and some girls don't hide at all. When pretending becomes too difficult, they may eventually try to communicate with their families and friends, teachers and schools. Often they are not heard or taken seriously. As I've said, their words are brushed aside as normal teenage problems, mood swings, exaggeration, dramatics, or hormones.[7] Many girls have been doing well for so long, no one really believes them when they hit a rocky stretch.

Or maybe it's something unspeakable. And everything and everyone around them conspires to hide it too. But eventually, when their voices fail to elicit a helpful response, and they can't hide their pain any longer, girls find other ways to make people notice and take action. Instead of being understood as another symptom of depression, however, their acting-out behavior—skipping school, drinking, or doing drugs—

too often is seen as the problem itself. It draws attention, just not the right kind. Instead of getting an adult to explore and understand why a girl is doing these things and what she is trying to communicate, her behavior gets her labeled as trouble. Girls tell me people and institutions don't listen to them.

When their spoken words are ignored and behavior is censured instead of acknowledged, understood, and addressed, struggling girls discover other ways to get people to hear them and take them seriously. All too often, they learn that this includes hurting or endangering themselves. Although some girls direct anger outward into the world and get in trouble, lots of girls turn their pain inward by starving and cutting themselves and exhibiting suicidal behavior, in effect making it visible, making it tangible.

Noelle: "An All-American Girl"

Noelle's story illustrates how culture and everyday events can create distress and how, as a society, we tend to think subtle signals of trouble are simply typical teenage strife.

Fifteen-year-old Noelle is friendly, vibrant, and bright, alert and quick-witted, beautiful, though she says otherwise, with sparkling green eyes and a winning smile, and long, straight, shiny, dark-auburn hair. She wears bell-bottom blue jeans, a dressy sky-blue T-shirt under a white oxford shirt, and wedge platform sandals; her earrings are small silver hoops. She's a little more dressed up than usual, and wearing a little more makeup, and I think she is excited about our interview, as she exclaims, "Today we're going to talk about my life story with Lisa, hooray!" Noelle wants to help me help other kids.

We sit outside in the warmth of the sun and she shows me her necklace—a silver rune on a softly worn brown leather cord. She turns over the rune and on the other side it says "Protection." I tell her that I like her rune. Proudly, she shows me her silver ring with a beautiful stone, telling me that it was her dad's when he was a teenager.

Noelle lives with her mom and stepfather and two younger brothers in a middle-class town. Her parents divorced when she was in preschool, and both have remarried. She has lots of cousins and a large extended family. Her cousin Johnny is like a best friend, and she is close with the brother who is nearest to her in age. Her best friend is Stephanie. She said she's always been close to her mom. When Noelle was ten they moved a couple hours away and she missed being so geographically close to her cousins and old friends. She felt hurt that her friends promised they would always be friends even after she moved, but they didn't keep the promise.

A bright and intelligent girl, she did well in school until eighth grade. When she was little she loved dancing, ice-skating, and team sports. She loves going shopping and likes baby-sitting.

I ask Noelle what gives her hope and she explains, "People who want to help you and when you're around kids who can relate to you, and who share so much in common with you, who may also be struggling, then you start to develop close relationships, and you feel good about yourself. There are so many more people out there and you realize you're not by yourself. You're not alone. That's the most important thing to realize. And you don't hear that. So, something like that should be said in books so other kids know."

"Do you want to say that again, so I make sure I get it loud and clear?"

"Yeah," she says with a growing smile. "You're not alone! There are plenty of people with problems.

"Having relationships and love, that's the most important thing in life," she says, and explains that without friends you feel like dying when you're a teenager. Not surprisingly, she follows this statement by emphasizing the importance of family. "Kids can be so cruel these days. A lot of the time, they'll do anything to get back at you if one slip happens. So knowing your family will be there, no matter what you do, gives you a good feeling. You've known them your whole life, and you can trust them a hundred percent. It's nice to have people there for you, that's what I like about life."

I ask Noelle to describe herself and she says, "I'm depressed and I'm confused. I'm also articulate and pretty artistic. I have done poetry and writing, and dancing, soccer, and ice-skating. So basically, I guess, I'm an all-around American girl."

Depression, she says, comes from "just all kinds of things."

"What kinds of things?"

"All my friends started making other friends in middle school." She explains that all her friends started becoming sexually active, and that in time, she felt she was losing her self-esteem.

"Did you ever have self-esteem?" I ask.

Sighing heavily and squinting in the noonday sun, she nods her head and says, "Yeah."

"Where did it go?" I wonder out loud.

"When I was around eleven or twelve, I thought I was getting fat, and I felt uncomfortable in my body," she explains, putting on her sunglasses. Even though she's slender and below weight percentiles for her height, she started dieting, which no one thought was a big deal, since most girls her age, and women, are on diets. "Then I was anorexic and bulimic for a while too.

"I started worrying about everything," she explains. "There's a certain way you're supposed to look. You don't even know if you're wearing clothes because that's truly your style or if you're wearing something because that's what you're supposed to wear." She worried about being perfect. She worried about having friends and a boyfriend. She worried about school. She was already worried about getting into a good college. She worried about the food she ate. She worried about what she looked like, comparing herself to pictures. She worried too much about boys.

Her first real boyfriend was Blake. Noelle believes the end of her relationship was a catalyst. "I guess the whole boyfriend thing triggered things getting worse. My boyfriend didn't leave me; well, he did in a way, but I was the one who had to get out of it—just the things he would do." He didn't harm her physically, but emotionally she was getting hurt, so she finally broke up with him.

The fact that she missed him and still wanted to be with him even though she knew he was not good for her perplexed her, and she asks me, "Why would you want someone like him back?" Adults and other teenagers thought her heartbreak and strife was an adolescent rite of passage, which would pass in a matter of time. She spent more time alone in her room, listening to really loud music with headsets on, and at her computer, alone. If she had done that when she was seven, everyone would have worried, but this is what we think teens tend to do.

Noelle dropped out of modern dance lessons and never wanted to go ice-skating anymore, which just seemed like a teenager losing interest and moving on to other things. She had friends in school but worried what would happen if she made a mistake or if she didn't go along with everything.

"What happens when you don't go along?" I ask.

"You're not accepted."

"And then?"

"You're all alone."

Noelle got negative about herself and began muttering things like, "Life sucks." She was irritable and was constantly arguing with her parents.

At school, she had lots of testing because her grades dropped, but everything was fine cognitively. Because there were no learning problems, she was referred for counseling and began seeing a counselor. Still, it did not seem that her depression was really understood.

Noelle got back together with Blake for a short time, and they broke up again. This time, she sat in her room and thought about carving the word *heartbroken* into her foot with a razor. She explains that girls with depression do many things that signal trouble, such as cutting. "There are other behaviors that show girls are depressed and self-destructive," she says. "Having sex and being promiscuous, doing a lot of drugs to drown out their problems, or just taking high risks."

"What do you think about girls and unprotected sex?"

"I've had unprotected sex. I'm being a big hypocrite. But I don't sleep around, that's the thing. I was with the same boyfriend for nine months. I knew him pretty well," she says.

"Why do you think you or other girls have unprotected sex?"

"I didn't think I was worth protected sex until this year. I didn't think I was worth being safe. If you have sex, you end up thinking you're a slut. It had to do with my self-esteem. Everything leads back to your self-esteem, no matter what the issue is."

Noelle was at a party with her friend Lily, and things got out of hand. "That's when I went into drugs, and then I felt disgusted with myself so I wanted to destroy myself."

One day, after school in the bathroom at home, she took out a razor and impulsively cut her wrist in a suicidal gesture. She didn't think about it, she just did it.

Noticing the concern in my eyes, she says, "I didn't cut too deep at all, I was fine." She told her best friend, Stephanie, who starting telling people at school. She figured on Stephanie telling.

"Did she tell any adults, did your parents find out?" I ask.

"My mom did and then everyone did. We got in a real bad fight and I said look what you made me do and put the blame on her, even though it was wrong. It really hit something with her."

"Can you say more?"

"Well, my mom loves me, but she never took me being depressed seriously. She just said it's normal adolescence but after that she made me go and see a new therapist and the therapist said, 'It's not normal, something is wrong here.'"

"Did you really want to die?" I ask Noelle.

"In a way. I was in so much misery, so much emotional pain. It was too much to bear, too much to take. I've seen too much; I'm only fifteen."

Because I hear her say, "in a way" I ask: "Would you say all of you wanted to die?"

"Part of me did," she replies.

"What was the part of you that didn't?"

"The part that had succeeded in doing things when I was little, like dancing and soccer and ice-skating and things like that."

I ask Noelle what happened after her suicidal behavior.

"Everyone noticed, they thought I was the perfect kid," she says, explaining. "People started taking action."

I ask her to put her suicidal behavior into words.

"I wasn't planning anything. It was a random thing. I guess I needed people to notice me. 'I have a problem here. Help.' I think I wanted people to pay attention to what I was going through. 'Look at me. I'm hurting. Please do something about it. I can't function. I can't manage on my own.' It's a natural response. People aren't listening. Our culture has a lot of hype about adolescence being overly tumultuous so that kids who are in trouble have to go to the extreme to get noticed, to get help."

Figuring Out Depression

The problem parents and professionals face is that many symptoms of mild depression—restlessness, boredom, surliness, irritability, anger, sleeping too much or not enough, self-loathing, aches and pains, teens crying in their rooms all the time—are thought to be normal teenage angst. Just as Noelle's mom thought it was normal adolescence, many girls said their mothers and even some professionals had similar reactions. As a parent, you need to pay attention to the duration and intensity of anything that seems like an unusual or uncharacteristic change, anything that causes you to look or think twice. (I know this is hard when so much is changing.) Mild or moderate depression can persist for years in girls, keeping them from reaching their potential during this crucial developmental stage. Over time, it can turn into severe depression.

There are ways to differentiate teenage angst from teenage depression, but even the National Institute of Mental Health reports that most physicians and families don't distinguish between adolescent depression and normal teenage experience. Adding to the problem is the fact that adolescent girls' depression has a thousand faces and can exist alone or in concert with eating disorders, cutting and other forms of self-hurting, substance abuse, trauma, anxiety, and conduct problems. Making it even more difficult to catch is the fact that girls' depression may not fit the "mainstream" definition of depression, which is based on adult symptoms. In fact I think teenage depression can be very different from adult depression, and statistics show that depression in teenage girls, if it is ignored and untreated, can turn into lifetime depression in grown women. That is one of the reasons it is so important for us to understand and recognize depression in girls.

Here are the criteria for depression, according to the psychiatry profession's authoritative diagnostic manual:[8]

A person is considered to have a major depression if, for two weeks, she or he is sad or down, with a depressed mood all day and loss of interest in activities that bring pleasure, including sex.

The person also must show four of the following symptoms:

- Weight loss or weight gain (in children, this includes failure to make expected weight gains)
- Sleep problems—sleeping too much or too little, insomnia, physical agitation, restlessness, lethargy
- Daily fatigue and no energy
- Feeling worthless and guilty

- Difficulty thinking, concentrating, and making decisions, nearly every day
- Recurrent thoughts of death (not just fear of dying), especially recurrent thinking about suicide, a suicide attempt, or a specific suicide plan

These symptoms cannot be caused by the death of a loved one in the past two months (I discuss distinctions between depression and bereavement in Chapter Five).

Because teenagers' behavior is different from adults', it's easy to miss mild depression in girls. Teenagers are in a different phase of development. Just as these traditional or "classic" criteria don't always work for men, as Terrence Real pointed out in his book *I Don't Want to Talk About It*, they don't always work for teenage girls.

Most teenagers don't lose interest in sex. If feeling sad or depressed, they may have sex to make themselves feel better, to fit in, to be popular, or to feel loved and wanted. In fact, depressed teens may even have more sex, or sexual activity—and the aftermath of sex, especially if it was impulsive, can trigger feelings of despair. Or the opposite can happen: A mother told me the story of a thirteen-year-old girl who attends a private girls' school who fell into self-loathing and distress because she did not know how to please a boy with her hands in a dark movie theater.

Teenagers have a lot more physical complaints than adults do—they have stomachaches and headaches and body aches.

They may not appear to be sad; they may appear agitated.

They may show irritability instead of despair.

Sleeping too much may seem "typical," as may not sleeping enough.

They may be considered moody, or thought to be going through "a phase."

Far too many girls, when they reach the adolescent pressure cooker, feel worthless, as though they don't measure up.

Teenagers have energy to burn and don't lose that energy unless they are seriously depressed.

They may pretend everything is just fine all the time. And we all know that can't be the case with a teenager.

If they always say everything is OK, think twice, because teen life can be filled with stress. Be aware that there may be things they don't want to tell their mom or dad. Be aware that they know they're supposed to be happy.

At lunch with a small group of girls ages seventeen to nineteen, I ask for their perspective on the standards for diagnosing depression. One says, "It's so much more than what the diagnosis says it is." Another girl agrees, and adds that depression is hard to pin down.

Some girls are just especially sensitive when it comes to the changes and stresses that arrive in full force during adolescence. The latest research on depression shows that our genes do not cause depression, but rather that there is a gene that renders some people more vulnerable than others to developing depression following stress or the accumulation of stress.[9] For some girls the developmental changes of adolescence in and of themselves become stressors that put them at risk for depression.

As Kristy at age fifteen explains, "I think depression has a lot to do with the inability to deal with all the pressures that are brought on by adolescence. A lot of people have a hard time dealing with all of them—pressures with guys, pressures with school, pressures with parents. A big one is change. Adolescence is a big time of change, and that's hard. Personally, I can't deal with change. A lot of people are the same way. Being depressed can be a result of change, of pressures, of everything you have to deal with during your teenage years. There's no guide."

Not only is there no guide, there's no simple way girls can satisfy all the demands that are made on them because so many of the demands are contradictory. On the one hand, they are supposed to speak their minds and have integrity—but not if they disagree with the kids they desperately need as friends. On the other hand, they are under strong pressure from their families to do well at school, because these years can make a difference—but if they do that, they can lose popularity. They know what they like, but dare not express it. And heaven forbid they're close to their parents, which is a strong protective factor for this phase of development—that's frowned upon in teen culture. There are many paradoxes. If girls can't meet all the demands, they blame themselves. No wonder girls are at risk.

2. HURRICANE WATCH

O n a summer day in late August, when I was eighteen, I went to Nantucket Island with friends for the day on a large ferry from Hyannis, Cape Cod. It was not the first time I had gone over for a day trip and though there was a storm warning for the following day, we embarked, as it was calm and clear. We spent the bright sunny day at beautiful Surfside Beach. In the late afternoon when we went back into town to catch the ferry back to Cape Cod, we saw that the town had boarded up all its windows, and we learned that the storm was now a hurricane and that the path of the hurricane had changed and intensified and was heading toward the island. No ferries would return that day; everything closed and there was not a room to be found. We slept on the floor of the gym at Nantucket High School, which opened as an emergency shelter. Friendly neighbors gave us blankets to keep warm. The winds whipped and trees crashed as the storm made its way over the tiny island that night. The following day people began picking up the pieces; it was not as bad as it could have been, and the next evening the ferry once again set sail even though the sea was still rough. I'll never forget that rocky, tumultuous boat ride back to Cape Cod, with enormous waves crashing over the bow of the large ferry, or the entire experience.

In many ways, the changes of adolescence are similar to hurricanes. Just like hurricanes, some changes are small, some large, and others huge. Some are mild and others severe. Some come crashing into teens' lives with a force so powerful that their lives are forever changed, while others are subtle, like a storm merely hovering over the sea. Though all the factors are in place when a hurricane rises to the level of severity that it is named, the path remains unpredictable, and so does the damage; there are too many changing factors to make it easy to predict—just like the storms of adolescence.

I've written that girls enter an uncharted land, socially, as they reach adolescence. To make things even more volatile, girls' bodies, minds, emotions, and morals are changing during these years. In this chapter you'll read about many of these internal and external changes that can put girls at risk. And you'll see how Harmony, who began coping with the storm of depression in early adolescence, later became devastated—though not obliterated—by a hurricane named tragedy.

Physical Changes

Girls' bodies change. This is something they have no control over. They have no say in whether or not they turn out looking like a pop star at age thirteen (some try to reach that goal, with bad effects, as we know). Girls usually experience puberty two years before boys (though it varies by girl). Take a look inside a middle school classroom and you can see the size and body differences in boys and girls; peer relationships are different and are awkward at this stage. With puberty, girls' breasts and hips develop, and genitals change. Their bodies develop more fat. Girls notice that both peers and adults look at them and relate to them differently once they have breasts. Some girls might welcome the changes, while others resist. Some girls miss the more lithe-and-quick-moving body they knew as little girls, and the change is experienced as a loss. Then, seeing all the media's images of female bodies, they start wondering if they measure up.

Large breasts are idealized culturally, and now more girls are flocking to get implants in high school; but when girls are preteens, those who physically mature before their peers may feel self-conscious. In fact, early pubertal development is considered a risk factor for depression in girls because they feel so self-conscious. Girls with small breasts also bear the brunt of put-downs. We know it's not just breasts that get targeted. One girl tells me people called her "thunder thighs" once she started developing. Girls harbor inner concerns about their bodily changes.

We need more places for girls to talk about their body changes, feelings, and questions, and about how relationships can change as a result of a changed body. Research consistently shows that body dissatisfaction is a risk factor and is highly correlated with girls' depression. And the dissatisfaction typically emerges and heightens when their bodies are changing. See how a normal change in the life cycle can become a risk in our society?

Cognitive Changes

It's not just girls' bodies that are changing. Inside their bodies, their brains are changing, too, just not nearly as fast. Teenage brains take longer to develop than teenage bodies. Once, it was believed that after puberty, the brain was fully developed. Now we know that's not the case. We've also learned that teens are ruled more by emotions and impulse than adults are, because that part of their brain still has quite a bit of growing to do. Teenagers' impulsivity often leads them to make snap judgments, to do things and then wonder why; it also explains why they are suddenly convinced that their teacher hates them over one slight.

Time magazine reports that the latest research tells us that the last area of the brain to develop is the part that carries out "executive functions," such as suppressing and containing impulses, thinking through the consequences of one's actions, cause-and-effect thinking, setting priorities, planning, and organizing thoughts: "In other words the final part of the brain to grow is the part capable of deciding, I'll finish my homework and take out the garbage, and then I'll IM [instant message] my friends about seeing a movie."[1] Sound like any teenagers you know?

This is not an excuse for teens' behavior, but rather serves to help us understand their reality and why they do the things they do. It gives us clues about what they need from adults. In fact, it teaches us that we need to set limits with them and keep them consistent, and let them know the consequences ahead of time (for instance, if they miss their curfew by so much time they will be grounded for so long). We need to follow through with all the limits we set.

Teenagers need support in learning how to prioritize and judge. As we all very well know, developing judgment is an ongoing process. It's something I talk about with girls. It's hard enough for adults to do ourselves, but we need to help kids learn to manage urges and impulses, and to think about the consequences of their choices and actions: *If I make this choice, these are the things that could or could not happen.* I suggest that the kids I work with make lists of the pros and cons every time they have to make a tough choice. It helps them organize their thoughts if they can see it on paper.

Emotional Changes

It's no big surprise to those who have been around teenagers that the brain's emotional center becomes quite active during adolescence: "Not only do feelings reach a flashpoint more easily, but adolescents tend to seek out situations where they can allow their emotions and passion to run wild."[2] Teenagers are on a quest for thrills, excitement, and sensation, which historically may have emerged to encourage exploration, but in our world of raves, fast cars, hooking up, and a drug called ecstasy, ordinary teen passion can derail into extraordinary risk. And remember, teenagers are also known to take more risks in the presence of other teenagers.

This doesn't in any way mean we should squelch our girls' passion. We want to encourage it. But we need to find ways to provide opportunities for passion and wildness that do not lead girls to endanger or hurt themselves. It's normal for them to want to have fun and be wild and dance and have excitement, but they need to be in the process of learning that most things are better in moderation. These brain fireworks may also be part of the reason teenagers' symptoms of depression get missed or look different from those of adults. This part of their brain is excited, giving them a vibrant get-up-and-go—which is terrific when channeled in a positive fashion.

Smart Girls Are at Risk

As abstract thinking develops, girls can observe and reflect on themselves and the world in new ways. On the one hand, this is terrific; but if they end up being too self-critical, it's a problem. Believe it or not, high intelligence becomes a depression risk factor for girls during adolescence. Research finds a high correlation between intelligence and depression in girls, but not in boys, because girls are more likely to be rejected by peers for being smart,[3] which puts restrictions on girls' ambitions and independence. Friends and peers are vital for psychological health, and girls define their sense of self through their relationships. "In high school," says Debbie, now age twenty, "I didn't want to be too much of a brain because I wanted guys to be attracted to me. If you're too smart or too successful, girls won't like you either." With the onset of adolescence, many girls begin concealing their intelligence and their strengths. As a parent or teacher we want to provide opportunities for girls' talents to shine.[4]

Morality Changes

Ironically, the developing capacity to reflect upon the world as well as on themselves can raise other problems for girls. It's as though they wake up one morning and all the hypocrisy of the world is suddenly staring them in the face. What they once knew to be true is now false. Adults tell kids to do one thing and then we do another. And now, as teenagers, they see it, and call us hypocrites, or think it inside. They also see the hypocrisy in the world—which bothers them—so we need to give them opportunity for community activism, so they don't feel helpless, angry, and powerless to change the world.

Now some might say girls see the hypocrisy and problems because they are experiencing depression; but spending time with teenagers, I'm left believing that their eyes are newly wide open, so they watch and observe, and they don't miss a beat. Carol Gilligan described adolescents as the "truth tellers of society"—which captures, for me, the stalwart seeing and naming so inherent and blatant in teenagers.[5] Part of being a teenager is to question authority. I know it's hard when they are in your face questioning you, but it's a timeless aspect of adolescence and part of their development.

So here is the mix: great physical, emotional, cognitive, moral, and social changes; pressure to be just like everybody else, no matter who you really are; pressure to say things you don't believe just to keep friends; pressure not to say what you really think and feel; idealism that develops for the first time, teamed up with clarity of vision that now sees all the bad things as they are; and a sense of powerlessness over one's self and the world.

Girls who are perfectionists, girls rigidly conforming to gender roles, girls who ruminate,[6] girls who are smart or more independent than their peers, girls who are just a little bit more sensitive than others, girls who are strong-minded and nonconformists who are trying to conform, and girls who are having trouble in school may be at heightened risk.[7] One symptom of depression can set off a ripple that turns into a tidal wave. It can start in any aspect of life.

The Law of Small Changes

All it takes is one thing for depression to upset the stability of a girl's life. Let's say she has trouble concentrating. That one symptom will affect her schoolwork, and her grades will start sliding. She starts worrying about getting in trouble. She stresses out about not keeping up. She falls behind and can't get caught up. She starts feeling anxious and scared. If she comes from a family in which education matters, academic success is central. She has to make good grades and is expected to go to a good college, and her ability to withstand the academic pressure wanes. If her grades are going down, she worries about letting her parents down or getting in trouble at home or in school. There may be arguments and conflicts, creating tension in relationships. If she's been successful in school all along, she may be told she's not trying hard enough or being lazy. She starts to feel guilty and stupid. Or if it's just a slight drop in grades, no one might notice. If she's never done too well, she might get by, depending on the size and resources of the school.

She doesn't know why she's having trouble concentrating and is doing so poorly in school. She can't do anything right, she wonders what's wrong with her, everything's her fault, and soon it feels like no one cares or understands even though at some level she knows they do.

She skips a class, skips a day or two, hangs out with kids who skip a lot and do drugs or other things to fill the empty hours. She feels like a failure. She's let everyone down. She starts to hate herself. If she doesn't talk about it, it's going to come out somehow, usually through behavior of one sort or another. If she's feeling miserable for too long, she takes drugs, has sex, and/or stays out late, doing these things so she doesn't feel miserable all the time. Her sense of efficacy can deteriorate. She thinks she's dumb and lazy—which is not true. Going to school is her "job," so to speak. Imagine if you felt as though you were doing terribly every day and could never catch up at work. But you're only thirteen and don't know things can get better after they get worse. It just feels endless and insurmountable. As if there is no way out. Girls slip quickly out of feeling good, and they may slide downward fast.

Other ordinary aspects of everyday life, when disrupted, can have serious repercussions. Take sleeping and eating. It surprised me how much the changes in sleeping and eating that get ushered in for girls in adolescence can create a domino effect. My colleague and friend Jean Rhodes told me, over iced coffee on a hot and humid August morning, about her latest research.[8] When kids start middle school in sixth grade, girls get more sleep at night than boys do. By eighth grade, the number of hours of sleep per night decreases for both boys and girls, but the drop is steeper for girls. Girls and boys have similar bedtimes on weekdays, but girls get up much earlier before school than do boys. The kids who did not get enough sleep were the most at risk for depression and low self-esteem.

Girls may get up earlier than boys for personal grooming because they worry that they have to look good, or to prepare for school, or to do household chores. A girl's personal grooming can take well over an hour if she is trying to blow dry or flat-iron her hair, put on makeup, and make sure her outfit is just right—whereas boys generally simply shower, get dressed, and are ready to go in twenty minutes. So while lack of sleep is a symptom of depression, we're learning that not sleeping enough sets teenagers up for depression. If we don't get enough sleep, we feel lousy, down, unfocused, and irritable—especially over time.

Teenagers need about ten hours of sleep a night, which is more than adults need. We know it's unlikely teens are getting that much sleep. After the loss of just one night's sleep, attention, mental flexibility, and creativity are affected. Chronic lack of sleep can increase the levels of stress hormones in our bodies, which adversely affects learning and memory. It doesn't take long before all of this has an impact on school performance. So it's important that girls get adequate sleep and that sleep be considered when diagnosing depression.

Then there's food. This is not just about anorexia or bulimia. Many girls don't eat enough to get the right nutrients. Today 80 percent of eighth-grade girls are on diets, which means most of these girls are nutritionally deprived. A diet is usually what opens the door to disordered eating. The coexistence of eating disorders and depression is common among girls. Girls with anorexia and/or bulimia are not getting the correct nutrition, nor are girls who binge. And girls who binge may have sugar surges and sugar crashes. Girls who don't eat enough can also experience low blood sugar. Glucose is the brain's primary fuel, so if sugar levels drop, a person may feel tired or cranky, have trouble thinking clearly, or feel depressed.

Girls are eating poorly in order to look good, and this has an impact on their overall health. Bodies, minds, and hearts are connected. The high-school vending machine is usually filled with sugar, soft drinks, aspartame, and junk foods. Girls who are eating a lot of junk food and sweets made from refined carbohydrates, or girls who are not eating enough, are depleting their bodies of the B-complex vitamins that their bodies need to create the brain chemistry necessary for a healthy mood.[9]

This is not to say or guarantee, by any means, that stable eating and sleeping will protect a girl from depression if a boyfriend breaks up with her, or if she doesn't have any friends, starts losing her sense of self, or is struck by a trauma or other stressor. She can eat and sleep perfectly well and still get depressed, but not eating and sleeping right can make everything worse. I think it is important to take a whole-girl integrated approach: mind, body, heart, and soul. Basic needs have to be addressed, and we need to teach girls to take good care of themselves and help them to understand that they are worth taking care of. They need to be reassured that they're not sexual objects or merely conforming consumers.

Few of us acknowledge that many of the changes adolescents undergo are experienced as losses. This may help us understand their vulnerability. Freud pointed out that loss—and not just loss from death—leads to depression. There is loss of childhood; of their body, as they knew it; of the previous school they knew; and of the way they spent their free time. They have lost their old playmates, the sense of how they fit in, and some of their former beliefs.

Strong Winds

Then in this unsettled environment, something happens. But it may not be something that everyone can see. It might be subtle. A girl starts to feel miserable and it gets worse, but there's no apparent reason. All kinds of events can set off mild symptoms of depression: A comment someone makes about her or her looks can make her feel useless; a disagreement, fight, separation, loss, or disruption in a relationship could set it off. So could boyfriend troubles. She feels heartbroken and thinks it's stupid because she's only a teenager, and therefore her strong feelings of love are never taken seriously.

She has sex, but the emotional part of a relationship can be hard, especially after a breakup, though she thinks it shouldn't bother her for too long. People might snicker and whisper about her in the hallways. She agonizes over being the perfect girlfriend. She agonizes over being perfect.

She gets into a fight with friends and has no one to eat lunch with in the cafeteria. She sits alone, feeling shamed, obvious, and mortified. In the shift from a small intimate school to a huge one, a girl can become lost, anxious, invisible—a lonely girl in the crowded mass of teenagers.

She worries she's not pretty. She doesn't fit in with any crowd. She don't have the right designer label clothes, which leaves her left out and feeling "lower," as many girls call it.

She's not popular, or popular enough, which when you're thirteen can be the most important thing in the world. She compares herself to others.

Someone says, "You're getting a little pudgy." "That's an awful lot of pasta you're eating." "Young ladies don't do that." "Quiet down." "Can't you do anything right?" She begins to feel awful about herself. She's convinced she's too fat. She thinks she has to look and be "amazing and perfect," just like a celebrity.

A girl falls behind in school, and she can't catch up. This has never happened before, and she doesn't see a way out. She has an argument or doesn't get along with a teacher, and feels bad about school, or she is made fun of or bullied.

If she does not make the sport team she was trying out for and her friends do, she is left out. An injury stops her from playing her sport and this disconnects her from the group of friends, which is a source of identity and efficacy.

A girl may start hanging out with a different group of kids. If her parents are divorced and she doesn't see one parent as much, it upsets her; she wants more time and attention from Mom and Dad, but it's hard for her to come out and openly ask for it. Or that yearning may not be so conscious.

A little anxiety keeps all of us on track, but when there is too much a girl can become revved up or immobilized by it.

Harmony: Weathering the Storms

Harmony is bright and intense, with long blond hair pulled up high in a ponytail, and large bright hazel eyes; she is slender, and is wearing bell-bottom blue jeans and a white T-shirt and smoking a cigarette. I tell her I wish she could stop smoking. She is like many seventeen-year-olds: strong-minded and vulnerable at once. She loves vintage shops and hates malls because the clothes in malls all look the same. She's a little shy and is easily embarrassed. Friendly and interested in helping others, she likes to try new things. She loves nature—ponds, woods, and the outdoors. We take lots of walks together. As the sun sinks into the western horizon and the air cools she tells me she loves the Native American Indians because of their respect and connection to the earth, and because they did not destroy the planet. She loves music, is very interested in fashion, and loves hanging out with her friends.

Harmony's story begins like many girls' stories. She lived with her mom and dad and two older brothers in a suburban town. When she was little her dad took her on kiddy roller coasters and he always took her to the store with him and would buy her a candy bar. When her friends came over he made them soup and sandwiches.

Harmony and her mom were always very close. Even though they have had their disagreements, Harmony thinks they are a lot alike. She would be lost in the world without her mom. "We always had a good relationship, but then of course, I got into high school," she says, implying that I understand all that high school means to a girl.

Her brothers never did anything wrong. They were always quiet, got good grades. "So I was always the one that got into trouble," she explains. It was "normal stuff at first," but compared to her brothers, it was a lot.

Her symptoms of depression began around the end of eighth grade and the beginning of her freshman year in high school. "I started getting really conscious about my looks. I had so much pressure to be like everybody else with the hundred-dollar sneakers, designer labels, and rap music." Harmony takes an apple turnover out of our little snack bag and says, "I of course wanted to fit in, like everybody."

When Harmony started high school, the pressure she started feeling in eighth grade got worse; with this change, her whole life started getting more difficult. "I went from a little school to a huge high school, four thousand kids, and my anxiety rose, and I started getting depressed. And then I would skip school. I had really bad self-esteem. I think that's when I started feeling it. Then I started failing all my grades, which made my depression worse. And then I started getting anxiety. That made the depression worse. And then it just escalated."

Harmony began feeling irritable, she had trouble sleeping, and before long, not being herself bothered her. "I got aggravated because being the same was all anybody cared about. I wanted to be free, to be able to express myself, because I was putting on a front. Who I was, it was plastic."

Taking a gulp of milk, she says, "If you're not like everyone else, then you are out. Everyone is scared to just do what they want because they won't fit it and then they will be called a freak." For a while she colored her hair purple, then blue, and for a moment she felt like she wasn't "suppressed like everybody else."

She wonders why anyone would want a world all the same and says, "Racism bothers me. Because nobody is born racist, it's like a little circle, they get taught." Other things in the world started bothering her too. "All these actresses, actors, models—they're making a plastic picture of what a woman looks like, which is totally not true, because most of it's airbrushed. It's not like she's naturally like that, she's on diets and all that crap, and tons of makeup. They pay her ten million bucks and

there are people starving on the streets and schools don't have books."
She felt angry over the beer commercials: "Like the stupid beer commercials drive me crazy. They're advertising drinking; they glorify it
and romanticize it like you'll have the best time of your life. But after
twenty drinks, you're puking all over the place and you get in fights and
do stupid things. You'll regret it."

At home and school she started getting in trouble for her falling
grades. Everyone thought she was being lazy. She was having trouble
concentrating, and was secretly frightened that she might have a brain
tumor. "My emotional thing gets in my way. They say I'm pretty smart,
I'm intelligent," she says with a sigh and shrug, scrunching her face.
Her "emotional thing" was getting in the way; she felt it inside her body
like a fog, taking over, filling her with anxiety and heaviness.

Into the storm of depression that Harmony was experiencing came
a hurricane, when she was fifteen. Her dad's health was failing rapidly.
He had emphysema and then had a heart attack. Under stress, he began
drinking and smoking, which caused tension as everyone in the family
worried and started fighting. His condition got worse and he ended up
in the hospital.

When Harmony was visiting him he was in pain. He could no
longer smoke, which had been a way he coped. He said, "I'm going out
to have a cigarette," and began pulling out his IVs. "I was screaming,"
says Harmony. "I was crying, and he yelled, 'Just get the hell out!' And
that was the last time I saw him. That's why I still have problems today."

Harmony's heart broke when her father died, and her depression
was made worse through grief: "After my father died—well, I had depression before my father died, and then it escalated. And escalated, and
escalated. And now I never got rid of it, so things just kept weighing on
top of each other. And now it's like a big tower."

She felt like she was in a much deeper "fog" than ever before. She
felt removed, "like I'm looking at the world, but I don't feel like I'm
here. It's like this big cloud in front of me. Do you know what I mean?"
She began to dissociate, although she didn't recognize it at the time. "It
came on, like a static in my brain," Harmony explains. She began skipping school much more frequently.

Her mom began dating about eight months after her dad died.
One relationship became serious and she was remarried in about a year

and a half. Harmony says she was still numb, still in shock over her dad. "I was in pain." Her mom's remarriage was too quick; it was yet another big change for Harmony, and that's when, she said, "I was in rebellion."

She would stay out later than she was supposed to and began drinking and smoking pot, and then she would rub it in her mom's face. Her mom would ask, "Have you been smoking grass?" Harmony would say, "Yeah." She grew irritable and thought she had "anger problems." Performing worse academically now than ever before, she was getting yelled at in school and at home all the time. She was sent to a psychiatrist, but "he never got anything right." He didn't seem to understand her, or what was wrong with her, or that her behavior was anything other than teenage rebellion. She started hanging out with kids who did drugs. If she felt depressed she would look to drugs; if she felt bored she would do drugs; for a while she thought she was depending on drugs.

Now it seemed that she and her mom, who used to be so close, never talked. When her mom remarried, Harmony said their relationship got "bad, really rocky." "I was bitter," she says. "I admit that I did take a lot of things out on her, but sometimes she was wrong." And even though her stepfather was nice to her, she wouldn't give in, although she did recognize his kindness. She liked him, but she didn't let on. She felt sad and lonely, scared inside. Her stomachaches got much worse. When really nervous she felt like she might throw up. She missed her dad. She was failing in school. At times she didn't see a point to living and would lie in bed for hours filled with despair. Then "a tiny speck of hope" always seemed to come back, whispering to her, you can get through this, you can deal with it.

Sometimes she thought about dying. She used to say to her mom and stepfather, "I feel like killing myself," and never did anything so she thought that was why her mother didn't listen. Once she even tied a rope around her neck and sat in the kitchen, but because she was ignored she didn't think anyone cared, and she didn't want to die if no one cared. "I just wanted to get a reaction. I just wanted it to be noticed that I needed help. I didn't want to be screamed at constantly. I wanted sympathy." She began moping. Because of her Christianity, she would never kill herself, and besides that, she didn't want to die. She just didn't want to be miserable. (Whenever a child or teen threatens suicide or has such thoughts, always take it seriously and have him or her see a professional immediately.)

Harmony began scratching herself. Then one day, using a scissor, she cut herself right in front of her mother. Soon she began cutting her arms. "I did it when my mom was there—because she wouldn't listen to me, so I cut to prove a point that I was so aggravated. And then they'll be like, 'Well, don't cut, talk to me.' And I'll be like, 'OK'; cutting gives me a reason for people to listen to me. But I don't think about it consciously; it's subconscious. If I cut, I'm not saying, 'Gee, I want them to talk to me.' "

She found that people listened to her in way that they hadn't before. "I cut when people don't listen. And then of course people are going to notice it, and of course people are going to ask why. I mean, nobody really looks at somebody with scratched-up marks on their arm and ignores it. Of course they're going to ask you why. It's obviously a sign of trouble."

The psychologist Rollo May explains the teen's thinking: "If I cannot affect or touch anybody, I can at least shock you into some feeling, force some passion through wounds and pain; I shall at least make sure we both feel something, and I shall force you to see me and know that I also am here."[10]

Although her cutting began as communication, now she also cuts to change how she feels, to regulate her unbearable emotions: "When I feel like nobody cares, I cut myself because I think I'm not worth it, and then I take everything out on myself." She also cuts to punish herself. "It's so they know that I'm punishing myself. But sometimes I want them to see them so they can see that I'm not all wonderful. I don't do it for pity. I do it so they'll know, so I can get some understanding."

Her cuts and scars have meaning. "And people will look at them and say, 'What happened?' And I say, 'Well, that's when this happened, when I was really depressed, when I was fifteen. Oh, that's when I was seventeen, and my boyfriend broke up with me. Or I was depressed.' So it's like a sign to others, and it's part of myself."

Harmony also tells me about sympathy cutting, when girls cut together, or cut when another cuts. Cigarettes are sometimes used too. These girls have empathy for one another; we just need to channel it into something positive. On a walk one day, Harmony spots a piece of glass, picks it up, and hands it to me, a poignant gesture that she is not going to slip it into her pocket in case she wants to cut herself later.

The thought of getting over depression gave Harmony hope. She had hope that therapy would help her. She found hope in her future. "I want a family. I want to have a good job. I want to make a point. All these politicians don't make any points. I either want to make a point about women's rights or civil rights."

One day Harmony is very distressed. She hasn't cut herself in weeks, but has a huge urge. She runs up to me when she sees me, "Lisa, I want to cut." I look into her eyes; she looks at me, her eyes filled with tears.

"What do you think is going on?" I ask.

"I don't know," she wearily replies.

"What are you feeling right now?" I inquire, suspecting deep down that she does know.

"Oh, Lisa, I'm obsessed with love, I want to be loved. I just want to be loved, not romantic love, intimate love. If no one loves me there is no reason to live. I can't live without love, I know people say they do, but I don't know that, I don't feel that. I have to show them how much pain I'm in, it's not that I'm doing it on purpose," she says, tears streaming down her face. "I'm afraid . . ." she collapses into my arms and I hold her.

Harmony's journey embodies a teenager's vulnerability and the characteristics that make daily stresses very hard to take, and render her weakened in the face of tragedy.

Still, Harmony wants to feel better, get well, and live a full life. And I believe she will. Teenagers are effervescent fountains of hope. But we must listen when they need it, even when we don't have time, and give them some positive attention, even when they are misbehaving (kids often get attention when they act out, but it's usually negative attention). Maybe then they will develop the inner strength to weather the storms that they may have to face.

Picking Up the Pieces

As teenagers, girls equate listening with caring: If they think someone is not listening, they may think that person doesn't really care.[11] This is a significant finding from research on girls, and something I have heard repeatedly. When girls feel like they are not being listened to, they become increasingly distressed and are at risk for depression.

Having one adult they can talk to helps strengthen girls' resilience and buffers both children and adults during times of stress.[12] Little girls' resiliency is linked to their relational strengths, their ability to know what is going on in their lives and to talk about it.

When girls are younger, they go to Mom and Dad for help and support, or when they're uncertain, upset, or frightened. Going to their parents is a way children cope with stress. But teenagers get society's message that they are supposed to separate, become independent and autonomous. They're supposed to do things on their own. And they feel pressured to do many things. Then, to top it off, the norm, in order to fit in with other teens, is to not get along with their parents—that is, unless their parents let them do anything they want and have no rules, and we know that's not a good idea. Only then, I'm told, is it cool and socially acceptable to get along with Mom and Dad.

Teenage girls might act like they don't want to get along with their parents but deep down most do, and they can't show it because it could jeopardize their fitting in. They're "supposed to" have a rocky relationship with parents, and we know how teenagers are prey to teenage "supposed to's."

Or, teens may actually be talking with their parents but not saying what's really going on in their lives because they worry they aren't living up to expectations. They fear they will deeply disappoint them. They don't want to hurt their parents. They're scared their parents are going to be mad or ground them, not trust them, or blame themselves. They get snappy and irritable and sassy and surly. They may be quietly or not so quietly seeking Mom or Dad's help and attention without words. Some may just constantly be mad at their parents. It helps for parents to ask specific questions, *not* just "How was school?" But "Who did you sit with in the cafeteria?" Kids need to know it's OK to tell you if they are all alone.

Parents are often uncertain about how much space to give girls. Now that they aren't little anymore, parents don't have to physically watch them or have someone else watch them. Thus parents may give them too much space when they should be more vigilant. Parents are encouraged to give teens plenty of autonomy, but finding the balance between giving too much space and being overly involved is tricky. The goal is to help them develop a positive, strong, and healthy sense of self, help them grow and develop sound judgment and decision-making skills, help them become independent while staying genuinely connected.

A push-pull often exists: Girls want space to do their own thing, but they also really want their parents' attention. Even if they "know" you love them, they want more attention, but don't dare ask for it. They want you to leave them alone yet also spend more time with them. Ambivalence tugs away at them.

Research reports that even parents with good communication skills with their kids cannot detect depression in their teenagers.[13] The good news is that researchers found that parents' increasing their good communication with their daughters helped them know if their daughter was experiencing symptoms of depression.

The teen years are a time when girls are exposed to a great deal. Get them used to talking with you. Let them know they can tell you anything, and you won't freak out and feel like a failure as a parent, or think they are terrible, bad, or ungrateful. Even if they don't talk about everything they think or feel at least they know there is someone there they can talk to.

Harmony's story is one of a teenage girl already vulnerable with depression when a hurricane of tragedy hit. (A significant loss does not necessarily lead to depression; I explain the differences between depression and grief, and how grief can lead to depression, in Chapter Five.) Already experiencing depression, Harmony's father's death and her mother's subsequent remarriage left her isolated and lonely. Still, Harmony is here to tell her story. The hope that kept her alive, the strong desire to be herself and feel better, and the determination to be understood all worked to help her.

Staying Out of Storm's Way

Clearly, we don't have control over many of the storms and hurricanes that life hurls our way, but there are things we can do to help shelter girls from ravaging winds, hail, and rain. (In Chapter Five I discuss grief specifically, and how to help grieving teens.)

Try to make sure your daughter has someone to talk to and doesn't keep things bottled up inside. Talk to her yourself, and make sure she has others to communicate with, both friends her age and adults. Talk with her about the many pressures and changes in her life. Make sure she takes part in some kind of regular physical activity to help keep her feeling connected and comfortable in her body during a time of bodily change. Bear in mind all the changes that too often don't get talked about. Remind yourself that her body is changing, and she has no control over that: hips, breasts, genitals, height, weight. Younger girls are anxious about getting their periods. Talk with her about what it's like to be in middle school and no longer have your own desk all the time, to have many teachers. Notice if all her friends dress alike. What kind of music does she listen to? Does she feel free to like what she likes? Does she have to keep it secret from her friends? Can she tell you? Do things side by side; sometimes it's easier to talk about harder things if you're not face-to-face. Harmony and I often went for walks to get ice cream or a slice of pizza.

What were her coping strategies as a little girl? What changes do you notice? Did she come to you when she was upset? Did she talk? Did she cry? Did she express anger? Did she pout? Yell? Run and hide? What do you see her doing now? The same things? Different things? Do you see continuities? Discontinuities? Let her know you acknowledge that there are lots of changes that come with adolescence and that they are big stressors and can feel scary. Talk about how we grow up and have teenage- and adult-type stressors, and how girls need to develop new coping skills that go along with them. Talk about coping skills— that they can be positive, but that there are also coping strategies that can hurt. Tell her that we can also cope through having someone to talk to, listening to music we love that makes us feel better, a physical activity, a team, arts, or a hobby. Let her do volunteer work to empower her, or something that builds self-efficacy.

Every day, say something positive about her, something that does not have to do with looks, hair, body, nails, etc . . . find some good in everything. Ask her to tell you a positive thing about herself every day, and/or a positive thing she did. This is the time to bolster her sense of self as strong and capable and competent. Make a ritual out of doing this. It's best to begin when she is young, but it's never too late to start.

Ask her if she is worried about anything: On a scale of one to ten, how big is the worry? What is the worry? What is she doing about it? How can you be of help to her? Who could help? Can she figure it out? Let her know you're there if she wants to talk. Normalize and validate her feelings, and then work to see what she can do to manage them or how she can do something proactive.

Teens definitely want to be "normal." In the next chapter, I look carefully at the ways in which the culture commits identity theft on teenage girls, and the price they may pay.

3. WHO AM I?

"Doesn't anybody miss me? Don't you miss who I was?"
—Autumn, age 14

Walking down the street in Harvard Square on a beautiful day in mid May, on my way home from the gym, I passed a group of lively teenage girls, moving quickly, excitedly, but not hurriedly. They looked to be about fifteen. I noticed their tan faces; these girls all appeared happy in the moment, with long straight blond hair; a couple of them still had braces. I thought to myself, they almost look like sisters, but I could tell they weren't. We passed and I heard one say, "You all look so pretty, and I'm disgusting." I stopped in my tracks and turned around to look at them, their backs to me now. I could tell from the fragments of their conversation and by looking at them that the girl who said she was disgusting was wearing jeans—the others had on short skirts.

I wanted to run after her and tell her she was beautiful. I put my gym bag down, and standing there for a moment between Harvard's Kennedy School of Government and the Charles Hotel I contemplated doing an intervention. Then I came to my senses and walked on. I know there is more to the story than I heard in this one comment, but it seemed she thought she was disgusting because she was dressed differently. Then, I couldn't help but wonder if she was dressed differently because she didn't know what everybody was wearing or maybe because she was in clothes that cover her body rather than showcase it, because she was ashamed of her body.

Treacherous Messages

Teenage girls are under tremendous pressure to hide parts of themselves in order to fit in with their peer group. Often this leads to giving up parts of themselves. This has been a theme in adolescence for a long time, but the pressures from the culture continue to build, and the need to belong, the desire for popularity, leads girls to accommodate. In this environment, girls are prey to identity theft—not the kind involving credit card fraud, but more catastrophic, involving the loss of themselves.

Whether it's how to look sexy, how to behave properly, when and where to express their thoughts and feelings, the straitjacket gets pulled ever more tightly. No girl is immune, regardless of race, class, and ethnicity, just as no woman is immune to feeling fear when she walks down a dark street or in a parking garage, alone, late at night. Girls are asked and are tempted to give up their values, virtues, and ideals, their ethics and their self-respect, precisely at the time when these characteristics need to be developing and flourishing. Adolescence is a time when our identity is forming, and our beliefs and values should be developing and growing stronger, a time to invest in finding out who we are. And right at this point, instead of girls' values being able to naturally evolve and grow, that growth is cut off or pointed in a different direction. It's as if girls are little plants that have a bud blossoming and society is pouring on bad fertilizer and spraying harmful pesticides.

In this unfortunate process, girls learn to focus on those aspects of themselves that the culture values: their looks, body parts, and subordinate or passive behavior. They get the message: You're only as good as you look. Your value lies in your attractiveness to males.

Cultural images reinforcing this message abound. "I think a lot of adults forget what it was like being bombarded with these pictures," explains Nicole. "It makes adults have a hard time identifying with what teenagers are going through. It's hard to feel like you're going through so much and you're not understood. 'That's the icing on the cake,' as my mother would say. See, my mom's words come out of my mouth."

These messages lurk around every corner, not just the hallways of middle and high schools. Olivia says, "We're soaked in them our whole lives." Well-meaning adults, peers, parents, schools, and institutions unwittingly or purposefully reinforce these messages. We are all embedded in the dominant culture and have been repeatedly exposed to these "unspoken rules," as Kristy (who you will meet in this chapter) calls the cultural messages and peer group rules. The more teenage girls give up of their core selves, values, virtues, and passions, the more they lose the sense of who they are. With time, the burden of having to live as an impersonator may lead to depression.

When girls internalize these messages the underlying values become part of their belief system, affecting who they think they are and who they think they "should" be. We all adapt ourselves to our subculture's expectations; it's part of being human. But when we internalize negative or oppressive messages, we hinder the possibility of genuine growth. We stifle our ability to find our purpose in life and diminish the chances that we will reach our full potential. To believe that you will be valued if you look a certain way and act a certain way is highly motivating; people long to be valued, especially children. But hiding the real you in order to be accepted is an oxymoron—what is accepted is not you; the real you is carefully hidden, rendered invisible. This leads girls to believe that "It's not important who I really am" and "What I really think and feel is of no interest to anyone." This leads to depression.

"When girls reach adolescence they become subjected to a kind of voice and ear training, designed to make it clear what voices people like to listen to in girls and what girls can say without being called, in today's vernacular, stupid, or rude," explains psychologist Carol Gilligan.[1]

"There are some feelings that you don't express in certain ways. You're taught that through everything: your magazines, TV, culture, and stuff," Nicole observes. As a result of trying to transform themselves into something they are not, girls' relationships eventually, inevitably, begin to feel false—and it's true, they are being false. Girls are transforming themselves and losing themselves in the process.

Women know all too well what it's like to give up your self in service of others, to please someone else, to take care of someone else, to not rock the boat, to keep your mouth shut, to not lose your job, your friends, your boyfriend, your partner, your husband. This dynamic is a central dilemma in the psychology of women, and it begins to wreak its havoc on females in adolescence (just as depression does).

"It really wears you down. It also wears away at you," laments Car-

rie. "You become so much less of a person when all you are doing is trying to please others. You're not being who you are, and after a while,
you lose who you were. You become that other person. So nothing ever
feels quite right, because some part of you knows that's not really you.
So, you're never happy."

I ask about the "some part that knows," and she explains: "I think
there's enough to make you realize you're not happy being something
that you're not. But if too much time has gone by, with all the wearing
away, even if you realize that force is there, a lot of times people lose
the ability to say, 'OK, I'm going to go back to who I really am.' It's like
you turn into that person. You become that person. When you pretend
to be something twenty-four-hours a day, then eventually you're going
to turn into that thing, you know?"

Carol Gilligan describes how girls take their feelings and thoughts
into an "underground world"—a place in which girls continue to know
what they know, but with a keen awareness of the danger of expressing
it. Carefully and cautiously, they choose when and where to speak, how
to speak, what to disclose, and when not to speak at all. In doing so, girls
may outwardly appear to be adhering to cultural conventions, or going
along with their friends and not disagreeing, but they do so in order to
protect themselves and their knowledge from disbelief, dismissal, inval-
idation, criticism, or loss.[2] But with the passage of time, they can forget
this was a conscious choice.

This loss of their authentic voice, and giving up the expression of
their real selves in order to safeguard superficial surface relationships,
leads girls to sudden shifts between knowing and not knowing, between
feeling and not feeling, caring and not caring, meaning and not meaning what they say. The phrases "I don't know," "I don't care," "whatever," "I mean," and "you know" become verbal markers of girls' moves
in and out of knowing what they know and sharing and not sharing
what they feel. This signals their presence or absence in the relationships in which they engage, with others and with themselves.[3]

The story of Autumn illustrates how shutting down feelings and
disconnecting from relationships leads to a deeper loss—her self, as she
wonders "Doesn't anybody miss me? Doesn't anybody notice I'm
gone?" It can happen quietly right in front of our eyes.

Autumn: Too Old to Cry and Too Young to Be Strong

Serious, pensive, pretty, appearing both strong and apprehensive in a nonchalant way, with long straight blond hair parted in the middle and blue eyes flecked with green, Autumn is wearing a pale lavender T-shirt and off-white bell-bottoms. We hang out together eating fruit, bagels, and cream cheese. It's a slow Saturday morning—lazy, cloudy, a little chilly with a sight drizzle. Asking for the veggie cream cheese, Autumn tells me, "It's like there are two mes, the cheerleader people me, and the drug me. The drug people friends know about the cheerleader people, but the cheerleader people don't know about the drug people." She sighs, I nod. We finish our apple juice. Autumn and I decide to sit somewhere cozier after eating. She takes me to her room and offers me a nice chair to sit in and plops down on her bed, wrapping a sky-blue blanket around herself and clutching a worn brown teddy bear that looks like a beloved lifelong friend.

Autumn is fourteen, "almost fifteen," she says, is in the ninth grade and lives with her mom, dad, two brothers, and their beloved dog Snuffles. Her oldest brother, Justin, is one of her best friends. Both parents are working professionals, and they live in a middle-class town. She was an avid reader during childhood, almost a bookworm, and loves to snowboard and ski and swim, and is on the track team. She loves art, poetry, playing the guitar, listening to music, and talking on the phone with her friends. Her best friend is Julie, and they talk about everything.

Highly skilled in computer science, she can easily fix computer problems and glitches. She loves animals. She likes it that life is interesting and unexpected. All the hate in the world upsets her, and she believes loneliness is at the center of everything that is wrong. She keeps a journal and likes to write.

"I'm a pretty laid-back person," she says. "I like to think of myself as open-minded, and I can't stand people that are racist. I'll accept things that come along, it doesn't really matter to me, and I just kind of go with the flow with everything."

I ask if the way she described herself would have been different five years ago.

"Obviously, I'm growing and changing, but five years ago I was really outgoing and didn't care what people thought about me."

"Now it's different? How come?" I ask.

"When I got to middle school, it changed, everyone started to care about being popular, and I was into reading and stuff. It just hit me, 'Wow, everybody's changed,' and it really made me self-conscious to speak up in class to say what I thought."

So she began to shut down and stopped raising her hand in class. "I went through a stage where I totally cared what people thought about me, but it's kind of a waste of time because if you're worried about what people think about you then you can't be who you are. And you're not being true to yourself." She didn't arrive at that conclusion in a day or even a month; it took her a couple of years, and a lot of heartache, and a fair amount of soul-searching.

But she still shows the aftereffects as she talks about anger. "I don't get angry; I get annoyed."

I ask her how she would show that she was angry. "I'd shut down on you," then she hypothetically asks herself a question and in an emotionless voice says: " 'Yes, no, I don't know, I don't know, I don't know,' that kind of thing, and my body language would change." She demonstrates a more closed-off posture, with her arms folded, protecting herself. "I wouldn't come right out and be like, 'I'm angry with you,' because of that whole thing about pleasing people my whole entire life, you know. So it would be hard for me."

When girls are conditioned to please others they know that expressing anger is not pleasing and not pleasurable to the person on the receiving end. She does feel safe expressing such feelings to her brother. They had a big fight a couple weeks ago, and she yelled and screamed at him. "I don't often get angry so when I do have a chance all the anger that's been stored up just kind of comes out." Usually, though, she says, "I can keep it under control. Like I don't get angry, but when I do it shocks people."

It's not that Autumn doesn't feel anger. She just doesn't express it. Sometimes she expresses it indirectly, but largely she has learned how to cut herself off from those natural feelings. She will deny it because she's not supposed to feel it. The internal contradiction is that she does get angry, but she keeps it under control, and it only comes out with those with whom she feels safe—the brother with whom she is so close.

When I ask Autumn, "What's important to you?" her eyes fill with tears.

"You know, no one's asked me that in a really long time. I think that's kind of why I got myself help because I lost sight of what's important. I'm still trying to find out."

"Do you want to say more?"

"I was confused about who I was, where I was going, how I thought about things. And my life was kind of empty. It had been going on for two years and I was like, 'This is enough,' you know, it's time for this to end, I've got to find some stuff out about myself, so I ended up getting help," she explains. Being a teenager is challenging because "you're too old to cry and too young to be strong."

When I asked Autumn what she likes and doesn't like about life, she sat up a little bit and said, "These are hard questions because I've been trying to avoid them for so long. It's just kind of hard for me to look into myself. What I don't like about life is how people judge people and how there's so much hate in the world, and there is such a potential for love but we don't use it. And that kind of upsets me. Like maybe at one time we were all connected as one and we're lost and we don't know how to get back to that point, and it hurts. Maybe we're all just going along waiting for the time that we can be connected again."

She explains, "Like our minds were emotionally connected, and we could all help each other out, and for some reason maybe it was too painful to have everyone emotionally close, so maybe they cut themselves off. Then they're all alone. I think loneliness is at the center of every human soul. I think everybody needs somebody to be with, maybe not like a guy necessarily, but a friend, a girl—they just need people. That's why I don't get hermits. I think every human being needs someone. We're not living in the moment. We can never really enjoy ourselves. Well, maybe I'm saying all of us, but maybe I'm just saying me."

Her language shifts from them, to we, to me, as she talks about disconnection in the social world, her own life and relationships, and her emotional connection to others. Sometimes, for teens, it's easier to talk about difficult or painful subjects by projecting and displacing their feelings onto someone or something else, onto the world.

The most important people in her life are her family. Her dad is a complex person who doesn't talk much about himself. He jokes a lot, which is fun, but she has begun to wonder if it is a cop-out. She and her mom have always been very close. When Autumn was eleven, her mom took a new job, which was much more demanding of her time. Because they were so close, her mother's sudden absence was disconcerting. Autumn explains, "I lost a sense of who I was. And I felt like my mom was never there. So I tried so hard to please her and everyone and be the perfect child so she would notice me. But she took me for granted, she just started to expect that I'd always get all A's and be the perfect child and do all my work and stuff like that. It made her expect so much of me then, it kind of backfired."

In middle school Autumn began to shut down, and this changed her relationships. Confused about the difference between who she used to be and who she was becoming, she began to have a hard time concentrating in school. Sometimes she had bad headaches. Worrying about what people would think, she was not herself in school. She felt disconnected there just as she did at home, constantly trying to be perfect. Her grades sank right along with her sense of self. Not really being herself with people was painful for Autumn, and she felt emotionally cut off from others. Suddenly, she didn't want to get too close to people, and began disconnecting from them. So she hurt inside more and more because she felt so terribly alone. Carol Gilligan explains, "If psychological health consists, most simply, of staying in relationships with oneself, with others, and with the world, then psychological problems signify relational crises: losing touch with one's thoughts and feelings, being isolated from others, cut off from relationship,"[4] which is exactly what was happening with Autumn.

Trying to be the perfect child "backfired" on Autumn, as it often does, because when things began to go badly at school and she couldn't concentrate, her grades dipped, and her beloved mom was upset with her, exclaiming, "What's wrong with you? You used to be such a good kid!" Something was wrong. Autumn's confusion and disconnection was leading her toward depression, and nobody knew it.

At the end of seventh grade, Autumn's mother, suspecting something was off, went through her room and read all her journals. Reading Autumn's journals led to a huge fight and created a rift between them because Autumn felt so violated.

It was getting harder to concentrate in school, where kids sold Ritalin, among other drugs. Her friends did not do drugs but when she was offered Ritalin she thought because it was legal, she was safe. Since doctors prescribed Ritalin for many kids, she thought it was all right for her to take it, because it was supposed to help kids concentrate. She heard it didn't have any lasting effects on the brain; her grades were getting so bad that she began buying and taking Ritalin pills in school. This felt peculiar to her, because her friends did not do drugs at all.

Before she knew it she was snorting it in the bathroom, even skipping a class here and there. The lovely Autumn became such a regular that she got a discount. Her friends who didn't use drugs yelled at her constantly, but she didn't think they could understand what she was going through, and Autumn genuinely believed the Ritalin would help her concentrate. It didn't. It made her worse. Soon she turned to other drugs, which were everywhere and easy to get. "I didn't deal too well with emotions. I'd space out and it would be a way of bringing me back, or I'd be so upset that I couldn't deal with the pain and the angry feelings." The drugs helped with the emotions she felt prohibited from expressing, as she gradually moved away from the person she was and the people she loved.

Then she was involved in an incident in which some kids brought drugs to school. They got caught and were nearly arrested. Her parents were called in, and it shocked them, but she was able to convince her mom and dad that she was not doing any drugs. Autumn had some Ritalin on her, but she didn't admit it: "I was too embarrassed," she says.

Teenagers are highly sensitive to shame. Autumn didn't want to upset her parents, and she was afraid that they would never trust her again. Surprised that they believed her, Autumn concluded that her parents, coming from another generation, were deceiving themselves. "They believe what they want to believe; it's so amazing when a person believes what they want to believe." If her mom really knew what was going on with her, their whole relationship would be a "lie." But what Autumn didn't quite see at this moment is that the relationship was already a lie since her mom didn't know anything about what she was doing.

She was no longer the good kid she used to be. Lost, she felt like no one was listening, no one was noticing. She told me she often wanted to shout, "Doesn't anybody miss me? Don't you miss who I was? Doesn't anybody notice I'm gone?" No one but Autumn noticed she was gone. And this made her feel even more uncertain about who she was. She reads to me from a poem she wrote: "Do you know who I was? Do you care? I miss myself."

Hiding in Plain Sight

The major task of these turbulent teen years in Western culture is identity development. The important questions become: "Who am I?" "Where am I going?" "What is true?" "What is love?" "What is of worth?" "Where do I belong?" "What will I be?" Autumn was grappling with these questions.

Over the course of my years of research and working with teens, I have found that the primary questions of adolescents are shifting. In 2004, I'm hearing new questions: "Who am I supposed to be?" "Who should I be?" The key teen question: "Who am I?" is being overwritten by the cultural concerns of "should" and "supposed to." It's as though their chance for finding themselves and their purpose is being stolen, eclipsed by the lurking shadow of what they must become. In our new millennium, the girls tell me it's more about status than ever before. One girl said, "Lisa, it's all about money and status."

Development is about unfolding, imagination, creativity, and the courage to explore, not simply about surface appearances. We need to encourage development, exploration, and efficacy in girls, and not allow them to be oppressed by stereotyped expectations.

"I'm waiting in line at CVS," says Victoria, "and all the magazines' covers have women plastered all over them in skimpy dresses, and they say 'twenty-five ways to lose weight,' 'One hundred and one better sex tips to please your man,' 'Forty-nine ways to look hot,' 'Ten minutes to flat abs,' and you're like, oh . . ."

A girl is subtly asked to give up her taste—in clothes, music, hair, what she watches, and reads, her own style; to wear the right labels; to fit in with the "in group." Deriving her sense of self from things outside of herself—social approval—leaves her empty inside and dependent on others to make her feel good about herself.

One mother told me that after she finally bought her thirteen-year-old daughter an expensive pair of jeans she had been pleading for, her daughter had breathed a huge sigh of relief, exclaiming, "Now I feel confident" once she pulled on the jeans. Her mom is worried that materialism has become the value system operating in her daughter's social world, and that status is now bought with designer labels and the achievement of a certain "image," the media-defined "look." Peer feedback on her success at achieving "the look" has become the basis of her daughter's self-confidence.

Their group or clique can monitor a teen's taste in music. Emma explains: "I define myself as a punk-Goth. I do like to wear black clothing. I listen to punk music, because otherwise I wouldn't associate myself with that name. But that's not all I am. When people hear me listening to Norah Jones, Tracy Chapman, Sarah McLachlan, and Ani DiFranco, they're like, 'What are you listening to?' I'm like, 'These are my girls! They're calm, they're mellow, and they're smooth. It's beautiful.' That kind of music really touches me in a completely different way than punk music does, which is good, because I like to have multiple sides. If I want to be energetic, go out with my friends, or I'm in the mood to, as my favorite band, Pennywise, says in one of their songs, "Fuck Authority," stand up to the government and strive for something better for the youth of America and the outcasts, that's great too. Sometimes I feel like being emotional and hearing a soothing female voice. I have a whole range of emotions and a whole range of music to fit it. But people say, 'I would never guess you listen to that!' What, because I dress to associate myself with punk music doesn't mean it's the only thing I listen to."

So girls diet, give up or hide their taste and style, cast their values to the wind, and buy, beg, or steal the right labels. Teenagers may be nonconformists to their parents, but they are perfect conformists to their peer group, even if they have to be a contortionist to do it. Teens want to know what the standard is—what to wear, the right labels, how to look, what to eat, what music to listen to, and who to hang out with. The rules can vary by group. There are subcultures within subcultures. Teens are sensitive to shame, and they don't want to stand out in the wrong way with their peers. Their overpowering need to know these rules gives us a clue as to why celebrities have so much power.

Celebrities also have the potential to influence teens in positive ways. The *New York Times* reported in an article entitled "Punk's Earnest New Mission" that there is a trend for punk rock musicians to compose songs and then videos in collaboration with several suicide-prevention organizations, which are shown on MTV. One example is Good Charlotte's "Hold On." Described as "therapy rock—that uses the language of punk music to address and sometimes even to attempt to assuage many adolescents' powerful feelings of alienation and despair"[5]—the music has met with wonderful success. While music has historically spoken to the emotionally bereft teen, this is a concerted and directed effort that is working. Many kids quoted in the article said the song and video had saved their life.

Friends at Any Cost

Often, girls don't say how they are feeling because they're scared their friends won't like them anymore. If they stand up for themselves they are labeled a feminist, which is bad in high school but cool in college. Nicole explains: "If you say too many things about women's empowerment or about typical gender roles in society, if you talk about those things, people start to label you a feminist, and at least in high school culture, there are no good feminists. If you're a feminist in high school that means you're moody, bitchy, overly reactive."

"Because I'm vegetarian and liberal," says Emma, "at my school people consistently think I'm some kind of radical who is going to run out and start protesting, and flip out whenever someone says something that's not totally PC, and go with all the typical feminist stereotypes. It's hard to stick with the feminist ideals of women taking control of their own lives without being daunted by the male patriarchy thing."

If girls speak up for themselves, then "Guys look at you funny." And this is when society is teaching them to look pleasing to attract males. "It's not just how you look, it's what you do and say," Kristy says.

A big rule, says Carrie, is "being the good girl, one that everybody likes. To make sure you have a lot of friends you have to be nice, optimistic, and pretend that everything is just a nice piece of pie. You're not supposed to be angry, moody, or pessimistic at all. Nobody likes that. If that's not who you are, it tires you out twice as fast."

As girls make their way through the adolescent years, these "unspoken rules" may be more obvious to them at eighteen than at twelve or thirteen. They can also get so far into the forest that they can't see the trees—or get habituated to them, so used to them, that they lose their awareness.

We need to talk with girls from the moment they learn to speak, in an age-appropriate fashion, about what it is to be a person with feelings, social expectations, peer standards, and conceptions of what's cool. Women know all too well about the insidious effects of keeping it all inside, and no one is in a better position to talk with girls about this than mothers who were once little girls themselves, and who faced these same confusions about what friendship really means, about who you really are, about how people can be hurtful. Girls are asked to restrict the expressions of any strong feelings, such as sadness, anger, desire, and sexuality. Powerful questions regarding their dreams about their future and career are often not articulated. Girls who see or feel that they have no agency against the tide of what they are supposed to do are more inclined toward depression. Believing that their life and social world is mapped out for them and that they have no power to change it, they give up. This is why promoting the development of self-efficacy is so important in girls—so they won't give up.

"You're allowed a better range of emotions than guys in many ways, but it's even more tight," says Nicole. "Guys are allowed to be angry and tough and whatever. But with girls you're allowed to be kind of sad and moping if your boyfriend dumps you, and everyone dotes all over you, but normally you're supposed to be happy. You're allowed a little bit of a spectrum but it's very tight. And if you wander out of it, it's only in certain situations." The negative emotions are ones girls particularly have to disguise.

Scrambled Signals

Girls say they can show their sadness under very specific circumstances. "It's not like you can feel sad whenever you want because women are allowed to feel sad. It's only when things happen. Like when someone dies," says Nicole, "or when your boyfriend dumps you, but only then. And on all those things, you're only allowed to be sad for a short period of time, and only for those instances. That's it."

The crying rules relate to the sad rules. "Some crying is allowed for girls," explains Nicole. "It's not deep, emotional sobbing. Not a cleansing-your-spirit kind of crying. There are very few times that you're sort of allowed and/or expected—the two really go together, allowed and expected—to cry a whole lot. If a serious boyfriend dumps you or something really terrible happens, you're allowed to really cry, and not just sad-movie cry. But you're only entitled to a little bit of that, too, for a little period. Deep crying is not really allowed. I know a lot of people who cry only when they really need to, because they need it to release and express emotions. When you do that kind of thing, you feel cleansed. You've cleansed your spirit. You've let out some stuff that was trapped in you." Too many girls are taught to keep too many feelings trapped inside.

Autumn's disavowal of her anger shows just how hard it can be for girls. Many girls talk about how they express anger only to their mothers or someone else really close—for Autumn, to her brother. Teresa Bernardez writes, "Women's problems with the expression of anger are traceable to cultural prohibitions which emphasize as ideal a feminine prototype devoid of anger or aggressiveness and characterized by self-lessness and service to others . . . anger silenced contributes to the most ubiquitous 'symptom' of women today: depression."[6] But now, mixed messages about anger and aggression can come from the celebrities who have a tough and angry, "I don't care," bad-girl attitude. And the age-old split still exists: good girl/bad girl, slut/prude, and nice girl/mean girl.

The signals are just as scrambled when it comes to sex and sexuality. There's abstinence-based sex education and TV shows in which people have sex on the first encounter. Girls say that they shouldn't be prudes, but they shouldn't be sluts. They are told they should be sexy, but they should not be having sex. Have sex. If you do, you're a slut. If you don't, you're a prude.

"It's a ridiculous double standard," says Carrie. "Guys are praised for having a lot of sex and girls are looked down upon."

Emma replies, "It's been like that forever. I was watching *The Breakfast Club* the other day. That was made in the eighties and they were talking about that stuff! You'd think by now things would have changed."

Nicole chimes in, "A lot of adults like to think things have improved so much and we are more aware of the issues. It's true. But they're not quite in touch with the reality of how, despite the fact that we may as a society discuss it more and be aware of these issues, really it hasn't actually changed." Girls think about sex more than they say, because good girls aren't supposed to.

Sex and sexuality in our culture, unfortunately, can increase the stress, distress, shame, name-calling, and ostracizing already too prevalent in preteen and teenage life. This inhibits the natural development and exploration of girls' own desire, passion, and sexuality. When we don't talk with girls about their sexuality, we don't let them learn about their own desire. Another part of their true selves is lost. Sex education does not explore learning about what they want, what is best for them, what helps them to feel good, confident, and respected.[7]

Romance is another area where girls run the risk of hiding themselves: "I've tiptoed around who I really was so guys would like me, so I wasn't real about my views, or even real with myself because I wanted a guy to like me," explains Natassia, nearing the end of college.

Some girls end up thinking their identity is predefined and prescribed by society and that they can't create their own identity as a woman, which can steal another huge part of who they are, or who they want to be. Olivia explains, "I could see it all. I could see I'm going to go to this fancy private high school that my parents think is going to solve all my problems. I'm going to graduate and I'm going to go to some Ivy League college and get a degree in something that I don't even know if I'm really going to care about. I'm going to get a job, and I'm going to try to take on the world, and just end up getting married, having some kids, maybe getting divorced and by fifty, what am I supposed to do? I'm just going to get older and older and older and then die, and I didn't want to do any of that." We need to encourage girls to see beyond the prescribed roles to which they think they must adhere and help them develop agency against all the things that they think they "should" and are "supposed to" be and do.

Relationships with parents, friends, peers, and romantic interests are affected by the unspoken rules girls encounter in the passage to womanhood. They may feel called to give up many important relationships, as well as themselves. Parents have a big challenge. "It's not cool to get along with your parents, unless your parents are the types that let you do whatever you want," says Kristy. And we know that is not healthy parenting for a teenager; they need teenage limits. Relationships with moms get especially strained, as we heard from Autumn. Often the girls who are closest to their parents struggle as they attempt to stay connected and to develop their own identity at the same time. The culture is leaning on them to individuate, so it's hard to stay close, and it may feel easier for them to individuate, at least initially, by fighting and not getting along. (And as I've said, fighting is a way to engage.)

Kristy: Would He Even Like the Real Me?

Kristy's story exemplifies the hiding of her real self to have friends, have a boyfriend, and be the perfect girlfriend. Her "self" was so false, she wondered if her boyfriend would even like the real her. That is, if he ever got the chance to know her, which might only happen if she felt safe enough, loved enough, and accepted enough, to be who she really was—a catch-22.

Kristy, fifteen, has intelligence, insight, kindness, and beauty. She has golden brown hair to her shoulders and warm brown eyes that are deep and penetrating, and she wears a gray T-shirt, blue jeans, and stylish black flip-flops. Her earrings dangle and her fingernails and toenails are beautifully French manicured. Kristy lives with her mom, dad, and sisters in a lovely town.

She says, as most girls do, that being and finding yourself feels nearly impossible in peer culture, and she explains: "Everyone wears the same clothes or does the same thing. You have to do what people want you to do; conformity is a big thing, so it's hard to know who you are. You have to act a certain way, act cool. You can't care too much about school and grades. That's uncool. You can't care if you're in trouble with your parents; you have to act careless. If you don't do what you're supposed to, you're rejected, you're all alone."

I ask Kristy how she knows all these things.

"I observe my friends and none of them get along with their parents or their legal guardian, none of them. And I observe that. And none of my friends put school first. They always put friends first. If a friend is having a problem they'll go to them first before worrying about school. That's just what you absorb and what you're around and what you get to know—an unspoken rule." If she were to break those "unspoken rules," she would be alone, and for a teenager few things could be worse than that. Friends are the world. She thinks teens want other teens to do the same thing as they do because it makes them feel confident about themselves and what they are doing.

When Kristy arrived at junior high school, there were different groups of kids, diverse groups—popular kids, jocks, preps, punks, conformists, alternatives, Goths, skaters, nerds, freaks, and so on. But she noticed she had parts of herself that came from "different ends of the spectrum," which could fit into different groups. At first, she was wary and uncertain. She thought there was nowhere for her to belong because she didn't fit neatly into one of the groups. She learned what to do. She had to pick the group to belong to and then says she "repressed the parts of my self" that didn't fit in with the group.

Then she began liking Kevin, a gorgeous, popular guy. Every time she saw him in school she felt excited, her heart pounded a little faster, and she would get a little flustered. She worried about whether she looked pretty. When they would pass in the hallway she hoped he would glance at her. If he did she was thrilled. When he began looking at her more frequently and then saying "Hi," she was *really* thrilled.

She didn't dare make the first move—she couldn't bear the consequences of "looking stupid," explaining, "The guy always has the power, people would think, 'Why would she make the first move? She's a girl.' Usually the guy makes the first move and that's how it's always been."

Their "Hi" in the hallways turned into little conversations, and being around each other in the cafeteria, they talked more. When he asked her out she almost couldn't believe it. Once they started going out, she was really worried about what she was doing. She didn't want to do anything wrong. There were ways you were supposed to be and things you were supposed to do to be a good girlfriend.

"Girls have strict rules they have to abide by every day," she says with conviction. "Boys have rules too, but not as many consequences. One of the biggest social pressures for boys is that if they do not have sex they are considered a loser." This is not true for girls, says Kristy: "You can't do too much too soon, because you want them to respect you, but if you don't, they're going to dump you. You've got to figure out the right amount. You don't want to be a slut but you don't want to be a prude. You've got to be right in the middle."

It could affect her friendships, too. She told me what happened to her friend, Heidi, when she broke up with her boyfriend. Heidi was also friends with some of his friends—male and female—until they all ditched her. Some kids, even the girls, she says, "talked trash about Heidi and she never even had sex with him. Sometimes it takes the girls longer to let it go." I ask her if she wants to say more.

"If women held more power in relation to men, they wouldn't have to take it out on themselves, on each other. That's what happens. Women don't fight back against the male society or whatever it is, so they fight it out on their own," she explains.

Then she tells me there are all these rules about being the perfect girlfriend.

"What are they?" I ask.

"You have to be laid back. You can't call them too much, but if you don't ever call or you don't call enough, you're being a bad girlfriend. You don't want to seem, 'Oh she is too needy; I am going to dump her. It's too soon for her to be calling me every second.' You don't want them to worry they have somebody who is going to be on their back all the time. So if you really need them and really need to talk to someone, and you can't call them because you don't want to seem too obsessive, it's hard."

It began to make her sad. "It's depressing. It's like, 'I already called him once today, I can't call him again.'" When she genuinely wanted to call, to share something, or when she needed a friend, she couldn't just call, the way she could with a regular friend; with a real friend she could pick up the phone and call and not worry whether it was OK to be calling, she could just be herself. She didn't like feeling that she had to hide. She had to always look good and be happy and nice and sexy. It felt fake and tiring.

She explains that there are relationship consequences across the board if girls don't follow the perfect girlfriend rules: "If a girl calls a guy too much, it'll get around that she's needy, and guys won't like her. But if she's laid back and does what the guy tells her to, does sexual things with him, totally disregarding what she is ready for in the relationship, guys will like her, but the girls won't. If she's really needy and obsessive about the guy, the guys won't like her because they also know she doesn't do stuff sexually, she's just needy. They won't get anything out of the relationship sexually, so why should they bother?"

Kristy noticed she was snapping at her mom and dad a lot more than she ever did before. She snapped back "No" when they told her to do something new.

She began worrying about what Kevin was thinking and what he was going to do. In fact, it began dominating her thoughts. She says she felt like she didn't have much control in the relationship because she was a girl.

She worried that if he didn't call that meant he didn't like her anymore and was going to dump her. If he didn't call, she was convinced everything was falling apart, certain it was over. She had no intention of breaking up with Kevin.

Kevin broke up with her and she was completely heartbroken. She started to feel sad and have bad thoughts about herself. She told me, "I was depressed about it."

"Do you think it triggered depression for you?" I ask.

"Definitely." And without hesitation, she adds, "I think it definitely triggers depression because that's what girls worry about all the time: other guys or other girls. They worry about their relationships with other people, and when it doesn't go right, they get depressed about it and it makes us really sad."

Kristy felt like she wasn't even herself with Kevin, explaining: "You end up being someone you're not. You twist yourself around to make them like you more and to be the perfect girlfriend, and it's not you, because you're being somebody else. And it makes you unhappy because you don't want to be someone else. Then you start to wonder, 'Would they like me if I didn't act like this?'"

Even more important than boyfriends, girls at this time need friends. Kristy gave up some of the richness of her interests so she could be part of a group, even before Kevin appeared on the scene. Friendships are often the foundation for happiness and unhappiness during these years.

"If you're a teenager, having no friends is a punishment worse than death because friends are what's most important to you," explains Crystal. During adolescence, teenagers learn that friends are a central part of their lives, and a vital part of their journey through their life ahead. Teenagers learn to depend on and to be there for friends in a fashion that is different than when they were children, and in a more adult fashion.

You Have to Have Friends

Since having friends, popularity, belonging, and fitting in are so important, teenagers are extra vulnerable to being different and can be shamed for it. Girls can very easily lose themselves in friendships. Adolescence is not the time when girls can easily say to peers, "This is who I am, take me or leave me." Think of all the adults we know who never get to such a self-confident place!

Things can be great at home, but if teenagers don't have friends or are shunned and left alone, the repercussions can be intense. Carrie tells us a story that is an example of what can happen.

Myra was the leader of Carrie's group of friends. Myra tried to tell Carrie what to do. Carrie couldn't believe Myra really thought she would do whatever she was told. She almost thought Myra was joking. Carrie spoke up and stood up to her and didn't obey her, which made Myra mad. And because Myra was mad at Carrie, the other girls had to be mad at her too. "So I'm sitting at the other end of the table eating lunch by myself." This went on the entire year of seventh grade. "What I think it did is it really kind of broke me. I was such a strong person, before that year. Even to this day, I have trouble being assertive and I have trouble being a strong person, because I was just so worn down by having to sit alone, all by myself, when I was twelve years old. Having to lose my best friends. That wears on you. It teaches you that being strong makes you lose your friends." This is not a lesson we want girls to learn.

During eighth grade, Carrie was back with this group of friends and just followed along, and the school year went fine, no fights. On the surface they were all happy and so was she. But she says, "I felt like a zombie for the whole year. I did whatever anyone told me to do."

"What is that doing to you and the real person you are inside?" I ask.

"You kind of let go of yourself. In the mind of a teenager, it's all about your friends. So sacrificing a part of yourself to have friends is nothing. You have to have friends."

I asked what happens to the strong part of her.

"You kind of learn to depress it a little. You learn to be quiet. That's what I did."

Lily, the teenage protagonist in *The Secret Life of Bees*, describes girls patrolling and policing one another and the effect it had on her: "There was nothing I hated worse than clumps of whispering girls who got quiet when I passed. I started picking scabs off my body and, when I didn't have any, gnawing at the flesh around my fingernails till I was a bleeding wreck. I worried so much about how I looked and whether I was doing the right thing, I felt half the time I was impersonating a girl instead of really being one."[8]

This is the time in girls' development when conformity causes them to stop saying what they are really thinking and feeling to their friends, their family, and in school.[9] They want connection, but they end up feeling disconnected from themselves and from others when they contort their personalities. Dana Jack writes that depression in women arises from "silencing the self," which means censoring the self, deferring to the needs of others, repressing anger, judging the self against a selfless ideal, and censoring self-expression and experience to establish and maintain safe intimate connection.[10]

"The depression comes from keeping everything inside," says Carrie. "When you keep something inside, it doesn't go away, it just sits there, and more and more things come in. It's like a snowball effect—it builds and builds until you can't handle the pressure anymore."

The loss of authentic relationships with friends and boyfriends causes girls to be sad and depressed. In the desire to have social relationships, girls relinquish themselves for the sake of relationship.[11] Carrie continues, "If you just sit back and let people take control, then you'll have lots of friends. You don't even quite realize what you're doing. You just know you can't be alone."

We've all seen the commercials on TV about identity theft, which are intended to get people to insure themselves against the financial costs incurred when their credit is stolen. Teenage girls need a new kind of insurance, lest they become willing accomplices in the theft of the inner core of self. What keeps people healthy and able to mature is the security of knowing yourself, the ability to rely on your own sense of what is right and wrong, and trust in the stability of your world. Teenagers naturally come to rely more on their peers, but they are being pushed unnaturally to separate from their parents and themselves. They give up their interests and tastes, silence their natural responses in school, and rely too much on friends and boys. When girls have given everything away in the desire to conform and belong, the emptiness can cause them terrible pain.

Identity Exercises

Girls can do activities that focus on who they are—in a group, with friends, or with you. They can make a book about themselves, their life, and their changes. A girl can make a collage, using magazines or whatever she wants, that symbolizes who she really is. Have her use a poster board for a big one, or frame a small one. Many girls like making collages. They like bright-colored magic markers and nice paper to draw on.

Go on a nature walk with a girl and gather things to make a nature collage that represents her. Have her make a list of everything she likes about herself. Make a list of everything she wants to do. Have someone hold the light and make a silhouette of her, and she can collage her silhouette.

Make a list of favorite things, including books, movies, sports, TV, and music. Can she say what song symbolizes her? Does it change day to day?

Girls I have worked with often like completing sentence stems, which means that they are given words to begin a sentence and then they get to fill in the rest. They can keep it private or share it. Some starter sentences might be: "I wish . . ."; "What I like most about being a girl is . . ."; "The hardest part about being a girl is . . ."; "I think the hardest part about being a woman is . . ."; "I think the best part about being a woman is . . ."

Girls can make lists and drawings about: The things I'm proudest of; Things I believe in; Things I care about; Things that are important to me. Have girls write or tell a story about how they give and receive love. Have them make a personal time line or river of their life till now and mark the things and moments they feel are important, significant, or changing. Have them talk or write about how they express sadness, anger, power, desire, and sexuality, as well as joy and hope. Make sure they are involved in some physical activity to keep them connected to their bodies.

Empower girls and remind them that they do not have to do what others say and do. The best way to ensure that they don't is to help them develop a strong sense of self.

Knowing Her Baseline

Nicole, whom we met earlier, says the best way for parents to know that their daughter is slipping away is by paying attention—knowing the "baseline" of your daughter. She explained, "As far as recognizing signs and symptoms and diagnosing things, I think that is wonderful. But too many people think depression is signs of hopelessness—they have to show all these signs of hopelessness. It's not about that. It's about the baseline."

So just what is the baseline? It's genuinely knowing someone in a real relationship well enough to notice when things seem to be a little off. It's about being attuned to her typical patterns of behavior, expression, and interaction; her rhythms, little things such as whether she's a light sleeper, what she does when stressed or when happy. Nicole continues, "Any given quality of a person is bound to change and grow when you're going through your teenage years, but there's a baseline. The baseline may move along with that, but you can definitely tell, if you think about it, the difference between the baseline slowly changing with maturity and the baseline shifting on its own—because of trouble.

"It is knowing someone well enough to see something changing gradually over time. It's not usually a big abrupt change, although for some, it can be. Trust your instinct. What's the worst thing, you're wrong? OK. But if you ignore your instincts and you were wrong to ignore them, that's not OK. Bad things can happen," she says.

If you see changes that give you pause, "Listen to the little thing in your brain that says, that's a little different. Listen to that instinct and think about what else has been going on. Notice those subtle changes and don't brush them off. Listen to that voice that says something is wrong, even if she seems fine," says Nicole. And even if she says she is fine, if she seems gone, she may not be fine.

Good advice from a girl who figured out how to make it appear that she was fine when she wasn't. Despite the changes adolescence brings, know what you know about the daughter you love, and if you're the slightest bit concerned, take yourself and your daughter seriously.

It's important that we help girls hold on to who they are and that we help them foster positive identity, because if they have symptoms of depression, negative thinking can start seeping in and start wedging itself into their growing identity.

4. I MUST BE DOING SOMETHING WRONG

"Stop looking at yourself in the mirror in the morning and saying, 'I'm ugly,' or 'I'm not worth anything,' or 'I'm stupid.' You're not, you're beautiful, you're smart, you're strong, you can do anything you put your mind to."

—Jessie, age 15

Caution. Take heed. You are about to enter the danger zone of girls' negative thinking about themselves. Please do not take these thoughts to heart. They are dangerous to girls' mental health, identity, and future. Thoughts such as these are not just bad medicine, they are toxic.

I'm not pretty enough. I'm ugly. I'm fat. I'm worthless. I'm not good enough. It's all my fault. I'm no good. I'm a failure. I'm useless. Nobody cares. I'm a troublemaker. I'm terrible. I'm bad. I'm rotten. I'm not perfect. I'm lazy. I'm stupid. Nobody likes me. I don't deserve to eat. I can't do anything right. I can't do it. I'm a bitch. I'm a slut. I'm a ho. I'm too hairy. I smell. I'm disgusting. I'm so awful even Jesus couldn't love me. I don't deserve help. I didn't do well enough. I'm to blame. I must be doing something wrong. Now I'm doing everything wrong. Everything is all my fault. What's the use? I hate myself. I'm not perfect.

Depression is not just about moods and feelings; depression also has a lot to do with thinking (cognition). Girls' thoughts have a big impact on their developing sense of self, their relationships, and their experiences. Thinking, or cognition, affects what girls believe about themselves as well as their abilities, their expectations of accomplishment and success, the way they interpret what happens to them, and the meaning they make of their experiences in life.

Nicole explains, "Depression is a lot more than just emotions. It affects how you think, how your brain functions, how you interpret the data that all your senses give you, and also what you do with all this stuff." Carrie says, similarly, "Sometimes you get this logic, I've talked to other depressed kids and they'll say things that are way out there, but when you think about what they are saying through their eyes, they make perfect sense. It's strange how depression changes your entire train of thought. I was depressed, I had to hide it from everyone, but in my mind it didn't exist. That made perfect sense to me. It didn't exist, but I had to hide it from everyone."

Maura: If I'm Not Perfect, I'm No Good

Maura, at age fifteen, is quiet and shy, smart and pretty, reserved and tentative. Wearing jeans, a pale pink sweatshirt, and sneakers, she has long golden hair that tumbles down her back in big loose waves. She lives with her mom and dad and two younger sisters, three cats, and two dogs. She thinks she spends too much time with adults and too much time reading: "All I ever did was schoolwork. It's been my entire life." She loves poetry. We spend a lot of time together. When I ask Maura what gives her hope, her beautiful hazel eyes light up. "When people that I don't think would actually care about me reach out, that makes me feel hopeful."

Maura is a dancer. She's danced since she was three years old—modern, jazz, tap, and ballet. Since she turned ten, she's focused primarily on ballet.

I ask Maura to describe herself and she says, "I don't know. I think I'm stupid, and bad, and hurtful, and a troublemaker." I've spent a lot of time with teenagers, and I love kids who are troublemakers and I love kids who aren't, but she didn't strike me as a typical troublemaker.

When I ask her how it is that she has come to think of herself that way, she says, "I don't know, just because I am."

When I ask her how she makes trouble, she says, "I don't know. I just do."

"Can you give me an example of how you make trouble?"

Again, she says, "I don't know, I just do."

I ask, "Is it something you would say or do?"

"I have this overwhelming thing inside me that tells me I'm a troublemaker. I just don't know how to explain it. I just do bad things."

"Can you give me an example of a bad thing you do?"

"Like not fitting well into my coat, not cleaning the litter boxes, you know, stuff like that. Not being more helpful around the house."

I ask what happens if she's not more helpful.

"I just get mad at myself. It's like my responsibilities and I don't do them. It bothers me that I don't do them. So why don't I do them? See that's the thing I don't understand."

"What do you think?" I ask.

She tells me what the doctor thinks now that she has learned she was experiencing dysthymia (low-grade chronic depression) and now depression. "Well, I've been told by one of the doctors that it's because I am so exhausted or angry that doing a little thing like that after the things I've done all day gets to be too much. But I don't see it that way."

"How do you see it?"

"I just see it as being lazy," she says, explaining lazy as "not doing much, not doing what you're told. Not doing schoolwork and homework."

Remembering that she described herself as "stupid," I'm honest with Maura and ask, "I've been around you quite a bit and my perception of you is that you're very smart so I'm curious as to where this comes from—you said you think you're stupid?"

"I am," she says definitively.

"What makes you think that? Where does that come from?" I wonder out loud.

"Well, I never do perfectly, therefore I'm stupid." Being perfect would mean "getting one hundreds in every class at school, unweighted, stuff like that. Always doing what I'm told at home and not making everybody sad or hurt or anything."

This has been going on her entire life. She says she doesn't know where the perfectionism comes from, and says, "A big aspect of dancing is working towards perfection." Then she adds, "I can only connect it with having a dance teacher that was verbally abusive."

Once in a while Maura's teacher said she had talent, but most of the time she said, "You're never going to have a future because you are so bad, and you're too fat, and you can't do anything, so just get out of the room. Some people, like me, were never fortunate to get positive things from her." This was her teacher for ten years, until a year ago. Hearing this made me cringe and I ask her if other adults knew of the teacher's abuse, and she said yes.

Maura says, "For a long time, I was one of her little followers, you know. She taught us to think she was God, the highest being of God that there is and we're like a little army of little dancers."

She was focused primarily on tap because that was her teacher's specialty. When she was ten Maura studied with another ballet teacher, and that made the mean teacher furious. "I was always in the back row, either that or I wasn't in it." But, after studying with a ballet-only teacher, she discovered she had talent in ballet.

Every so often Maura thought her mean teacher was wrong, that "she shouldn't be doing this to me," but explains, "I've always had a self-esteem problem, so it ended up as being a thing I deserved. Obviously, I must have provoked it or done something. You could never please that lady and I always tried. I thought I deserved it. It was stuff I was saying to myself anyway, so just having someone else say it was like an affirmation of it."

The teacher's reputation was for being tough and "everybody always knew it." Her teacher telling her she was too fat drove Maura to diet. Feeling down, depressed, and having dysthymia started a couple years ago when she was twelve. She felt tired, without much energy, and didn't eat much. She felt spaced out a lot and when she danced she never felt pain, though she would feel it later that day. She was very sad inside.

And along came what she calls the "real me" and the "fake me": "The real me is really down and sad. I don't smile because I don't feel that. But I always have to become this happy person so that people won't ask me what's wrong or I won't seem to be weak." Maura thought, "I had to look strong and I had to look like I could help people and so I pretended I was happy so people wouldn't have to ask me questions."

She felt stupid when people asked, "Oh, why are you so sad looking? Why are you so depressed?" The hiding became a friend. "It's like the secret of hiding it has been this companion for me. The secret was to make me look like I was a normal person, so just by deceiving everybody into thinking that I'm OK, it was like a triumph, I guess." Her depression became her secret companion.

To punish herself she didn't eat, and then ate too much and threw up. This is another secret companion. "I'm just a bad person and I need to punish myself." She was heading to anorexia and bulimia.

She didn't want anyone to know she was in such despair because she didn't want to hurt her parents. "I knew how they'd feel. I knew they'd feel like failures as parents and I knew they'd feel hurt they couldn't stop it, but I knew I couldn't stop it and I knew they hadn't caused it." Now her parents are hurt, just as she expected. "I knew that would happen; that's why I had to conceal it." She loves her parents but didn't love herself, which is why the old saying "you can't love someone until you love yourself" confused her. "The advice I would give parents is, try your best to understand the motivation of your daughter's behavior instead of automatically thinking you're the cause of it. Parents should try to control their feelings, talk about them, and in the process they can learn more about themselves as well."

Maura worried that if anyone knew she was thinking of hurting herself, she could be put away in some hospital. She didn't know suicidal thoughts were part of depression. It was never because she wanted to die. Instead, she thought, "I don't deserve to live. All I do is hurt people and make trouble. I'm so bad." Or the other reason was, "because I want to rid them of me, you know." If she could be a "good person, someone who does everything that they're told and doesn't hurt anybody and isn't bad" it would help her feel she deserved to live. But she could not understand how she could not be bad. "I know I'm bad. Because why would I feel like I'm bad if I wasn't?"

It is hard for Maura to express her real feelings and she says she puts her anger, "down where all my sadness hides. I don't deserve to be angry because I probably provoked someone else's anger, which would make me angry." She gets most angry "if someone's treating another person in a disrespectful manner. It doesn't make me feel bad when I'm treated in a disrespectful manner because I deserve respect." Her experiences at school give her the feeling she doesn't even exist. "I swear I'm invisible at school." One day she had a terrible headache, and later she fainted during class. "I was laying underneath my desk and all the desks were in a circle and we were doing this group activity with the teacher in the middle and nobody noticed. And I woke up and had to get up off the floor and sit back in my chair." What this means to Maura is, "Well, it tells me that I'm really invisible to people. No one really cares."

The Danger Signs of Negative Thinking

Have you heard your daughter making comments or muttering negative things about herself? Listen carefully. Negative remarks often start around looks and the body, because in our society that's how a woman's value is determined. A comment such as "I'm too fat; I better go on a diet," or "I can't do anything right" may sound like a typical or normal teenage girl thing to say, but this is where we have to stop and take notice. Even though it seems many girls talk and think like this, it doesn't mean it's OK, and it doesn't mean it should be ignored, dismissed, or written off. This is often how negative thinking and depression start. Negative thoughts about the self can set off psychological problems. They prime a girl for increased risk of depression, eating disorders, and other methods of self-harm, because they precipitate a big decline in how she thinks about herself. Do you hear her mumbling under her breath? Are there self-deprecating comments, derogatory or denigrating remarks about her self, abilities, looks, body, intelligence, or talent?

Is she ridden by the words, "I should" or "I have to"—words that create extra anxiety and worry about measuring up? A girl with anorexia is emaciated but thinks she's fat, which is a distortion of thinking; similarly, I've seen smart girls convinced that they are stupid, and highly talented girls certain that they're worthless and useless.

You may not hear the words; girls may not openly articulate these types of inner thoughts, and that is how they fester and grow—in isolation. So to make certain she isn't harboring horrible thoughts about herself, listen, but also pay close attention to behavior. Observe, be present, and watch.

Missed signals of depression are sometimes misinterpreted as "laziness." When girls are told they are lazy, it makes them feel worse, and they start integrating that into their identity. If you start thinking your daughter, who has a lot of potential, is just being "lazy," think twice.

What appears to be "laziness" or "boredom" may actually be a signal of depression.

Does she tend toward ruminating? Can she let things go and move on? Is she thinking and talking about something over and over?

Behavior can be subtle. It can be as simple as having to do everything right all the time. Perfectionism is often a red flag. How does she respond to success? Are accomplishments something to be proud of, or are they insignificant and short-lived? ("Well, it wasn't perfect. I got one wrong.") Is she discouraged by setbacks? Is it the end of the world?

To teenagers, many things seem like the end of the world. Does she wind up discouraged, defeated, not wanting to try again, not wanting to take a risk? Can she bounce back from a setback or does it become the ruination of her life? Is an A- the end of the world? Yes, she may be capable of an A, and it's important for her to know that you believe she is capable of an A, but an A- need not turn her into a stupid loser who can't do anything right, who now will never get into the right college, whose entire life is ruined. Negative thinking steals away the joy she could find in daily accomplishments.

It would be so much better if she were thinking, "I didn't do as well as I'd like. Next time, I'll study more. Next time I'll get help," or even, "The test wasn't fair."

Does she have a sense of self-efficacy and the conviction that she can accomplish whatever she sets out to do, that she can learn new things and reach her goals? Is this waning with the onset of puberty? Do you see changes?

Does she take too much responsibility? Is everything that happens all her fault? As one girl explained to me, "My semi-normal sense of logic says that everything isn't always my fault. If it rains, it's not my fault—directly. Or if someone does something, it's not directly my fault; I didn't hit her in the face and that's why she's crying. But I always thought of it as, 'If I was a little smarter, if I was paying more attention . . . If I was *something*, I could have done something more right, something better to have made something happen.' So therefore, because I didn't potentially do that, I'm at fault."

Does she understand and see that some things are in her control and others are not? Ruth tells me her friend, Tia, said she would call at six, but she didn't; does that mean, "I must have done something wrong.

She doesn't like me. She hates me" rather than, maybe something came up. Why does that have to mean "She doesn't like me anymore"? How does she interpret things that happen? Can she hear and accept a compliment, or does she disavow, say no, deflect it, and become uncomfortable? Self-hatred and disdain don't fit well with compliments, and praise may not fit with how she is thinking about herself. If she can't take it in, if she doesn't know where to put it, there may not be a place in her mind for thoughts such as, "I'm successful and talented."

Jamie: Confident for a Millisecond

Jamie, a slightly Goth-style girl, lives in a prestigious suburb. At age fifteen, she playfully threatens to shave her head, for no other reason than just because she knows it would bug her dad, whom she loves. I always get a kick out of the antics teenagers come up with. Jamie is astute and graceful, bright with short dark hair, tall and lithe with several piercings in her ears, fine features, penetrating bright, clear blue eyes, and dark eyelashes. Dressed in mostly black—black T-shirt, black jeans—she's serious and intelligent.

Jamie lives with her mom, dad, sister, brother, and two dogs in a beautiful town. She is steamed at her mom for reading her diary. She loves her mom, but at the moment she feels humiliated. She loves her dad, her sister, and her brother. She's close with her uncle and aunt and loves her mom's best friend, saying sometimes it's easier to talk to them than to her parents. She loves music, especially from the eighties. She likes her friends, and art, and loves shoes; she shows me her new boots. She values and loves freedom. She doesn't want to be depressed, and wants to be able to appreciate things around her again. In the past, just simply taking a walk, seeing waterfalls or a brook, would bring her pleasure, but now that she's depressed that is no longer true. She wants to walk down the street again and enjoy it, the way she once did. She says her childhood was happy. She has two very close female friends and a close male friend who's gay. She loves photography, sketching, and writing when she's not feeling bad. She doesn't write about spring flowers; she goes for the disturbing side.

Curious about her writing, I ask Jamie how she feels when she writes.

"I feel like I'm working on something and I feel determined to get it perfect, get it right, and after I write it down, I usually feel proud for a millisecond and then it's just OK, well, whatever." The same is true about her confidence. "I feel confident for about a millisecond." I ask her why she thinks this is so. "Self-esteem issues. You know I've been against myself for the longest time." I ask Jamie what she means by self-esteem.

"For the longest time, even my parents have known and recognized it in me that I just can't feel like I do anything right, and you know taking compliments is so hard for me." She explains that she read a ten-page paper she wrote about depression to a group. They said how excellent it was, but Jamie says, "I had like an anxiety attack. I couldn't handle it. It was so revolting to hear all that stuff—compliments—you know, and I was so embarrassed. I don't know how to take it, and I know in my heart I hate myself, no matter what, because all my actions return to that."

I ask her what "that" is. "The self-hatred, and the fact that I don't feel like I'm going anywhere. It's just basically part of the depression. I don't know anything about myself and I don't know myself anymore. I don't actively hate myself. It doesn't show in the ways that you would think. It just shows in my own inside. Just something that I know."

She doesn't know what caused her depression, what the reason is, but said it started two years ago, when she was thirteen. "Depression is something that really takes over your whole body and your whole self; it stops you, it literally stops you. You can't be nostalgic because happiness is so far away. You don't feel like you're moving forward because you're worthless and you can't get anywhere, so where are you going to end up? And people are always better than you. When depression gets bad, it restricts you from being able to do things."

"In one way I have ups and downs, but I always feel the same." She places her hand on her solar plexus, saying, "I always had the depression right there," showing it somewhere between her stomach and her heart. "It's hard, because I don't know why it's happening. I don't know how to fix it, and I don't know what to do. And I know that I'm missing out. I know what I want to be like."

For nearly two years she quietly hid how she felt. "Back then, I was masking it, keeping it from other people." At first, depression, this "deep empty intense feeling" was her own "little secret." Sometimes at night she would light a candle and stare into it. "I was feeling dark and empty. It had gotten to the point that I was my depression, in itself." But like other kids who experience depression, she feels many feelings that can accompany depression. "Sometimes I feel panic and anxiety. Like, this is never going to go away, and I feel like shit, and you feel disconnected from whatever self you had."

She explains further, "I don't have motivation, energy, anything. I don't have whatever it takes to do it. And having to hide that, it makes you feel worse, because everyone thinks 'Oh, you're lazy.'" She kept it to herself. Every day when she came home from school or work, her parents would ask how her day was and she would say it was OK, fine. "I wasn't coming to them and telling them anything about my life, basically."

Her parents didn't know about anything that was going on. They had no idea she smoked cigarettes in the bathroom at school. They didn't know how old the guy she liked was. "I lied to them about this guy I was dating; he was twenty, and I didn't tell them that." Then she ended up feeling guilty and remorseful for lying to her parents.

She didn't know how to explain that she was depressed to her mom and dad; she didn't feel comfortable going to them. It seemed better to try to figure it out herself rather than having her parents deal with it, since she didn't always like the way they dealt with things. There were some things she wasn't comfortable with her parents about. "I love my mom and I love my dad, he's really cool to hang out with, but when it comes to serious stuff like that . . ." Jamie just figured she would deal with it on her own.

When she's sad she makes sure she is not around too many people and then wallows in her depression. I ask her about this. "Wallowing in it is what you're supposed to do," she explains. Now there are even rules about depression! If she's around too many people, sometimes her depression escalates. This occurs because if she is with people when she's feeling really depressed and someone asks her what is wrong, it bothers her. Then she tells me about anger.

"If you're angry at someone, it's because they're not listening." Jamie tries not to say anything because she often ends up feeling more pissed off. She says she may get frustrated at what they say or do, but if she tells them and they still don't change or respond, that makes it even worse. Sometimes she feels like punching something but she never does.

I ask what she does when she feels angry.

"When I get angry I usually cry. That's how it'll start. I get mildly angry, like you're depressed and just agitated. I don't know what to do. I just kind of stand there and I feel like I'm crawling out of my skin, and I feel like my anger is just like moving away from me. Like my anger is coming out everywhere, and I feel like punching something but I never ever do. It's not like I have to stop myself either. I look at a wall and it's like, hmm, should I punch that? But getting my anger out physically is never something that I'll do." She hesitates. "My voice is kind of funny. My voice is . . ." She stops talking and looks at me, perplexed. "Going hoarse," I say, feeling sad and curious at the same time, hearing her speak with passion and simultaneously hearing her voice dim. She sits up a little and moves into a meditative sitting position, like she's grounding herself. We look at each other; I don't miss the fact that when she is talking about anger, her voice literally fades away.

When Jamie's depression started, so did thoughts of suicide, hovering in the back of her mind. The more depressed she got the more she thought about dying, but not in an impulsive way. She described it as desperation. "I was sick of not getting anywhere and I was sick of feeling so unable to do anything right or be happy with anything. I should be, because I have loving parents, they love me and my sisters and brother. They love me. I love them. And I have a couple of really good friends."

So, like many girls, Jamie thinks there is "no reason" for her to be depressed. Things can get worse if she and other girls decide that they are no good for being so ungrateful. Jamie thought she should be appreciating these things. At first, the suicidal thoughts weren't daily. They just sat in the back of her mind. She thought her own behavior was "pathetic." She was sick of thinking, "I'm sick of you," meaning herself. Constantly thinking these negative thoughts went on for nearly eight months. She didn't like "not ever being able to go through with anything." She bought lots of over-the-counter sleeping pills and for eight months carried them around in her purse at all times.

Valentine's Day approached. "I hate couples. I was having this lonely feeling. I didn't want to go through Valentine's Day. Couples make me sick." Society's emphasis on couples was hard because it made Jamie feel something was wrong with her if she wasn't part of one. She felt left out, alone, a misfit because she wasn't in a couple. It made her feel lonely, and the loneliness was unbearable. So the night before Valentine's Day, she took lots of the pills stashed in her purse. What happened afterward wasn't quite like what happens on TV, where you take pills and peacefully appear to drift away—and then someone finds you. Television doesn't show the throwing up, which is what happened first. Her mom found her in the bathroom and took her right to the hospital.

This brings us to the diary. After Jamie took the pills, her mom read Jamie's diary, and one of the poems she had written made her mom worry that she might have been raped, but Jamie doesn't think so, and her parents want her to have a trauma consultation. Her dad didn't read her diary, so she's madder at her mom. "I trust him not to. I really appreciate him for not doing that. Because when I found out that my mother did, I can understand why she would want to, but it was so humiliating. It was awful, and my mom said, 'Oh, why is it awful? Why is that humiliating to you? Why is it embarrassing?' Those are my, you know what they are, they're just, they're, it's mine! I don't have to share it with anybody or get anybody else's perspective on it. I don't want her perspective on why all this is happening. My diary's filled with a lot of pain that I don't want her to know about. I didn't want to deal with my parents knowing about what I was feeling and having to explain it to them."

"Because?" I ask.

"They're searching for just one answer." That is what she feared.

Jamie is aghast that in her mom's desperation for understanding and an answer, she read the diary to others. "She read some parts to my dad. She read some parts to three other people. She shared parts of my diary with other people, and that's awful. She sees it as 'Well, you hurt me because trust was broken when you tried to kill yourself, so I'm validated in taking your diary and analyzing it' and that's just not right. And I guess she read a lot of these poems I wrote and she said, 'Go and find that poem in your journal and share it with people, share your poems.' And she just interpreted everything, every little thing." Her mom thought that if other people heard or read the poems, they, too, would be worried that Jamie might have been raped.

I gently ask Jamie about the poem. "It was about control—a guy having control over a girl. Maybe if you want to search that deep, it could be about my depression having control over me. So, I don't know, maybe, it was just like the wrong time to bring that up. It's kind of bad timing on her part because I'm not exactly happy with her. And I'm not exactly in the best state of mind.

"And I really feel that I have not been raped, but I'll compromise, and do the trauma consult, because I'm open to it. But," she takes a long pause and sighs, "what gives her the right to share parts of my diary and interpret them and analyze them in a way that's only making it worse? What if I'm kind of scared to find out that I was raped? I'd rather just think it's a chemical imbalance in my brain or I was born different. And I really doubt that I was raped because I don't hang around with particularly violent people. I've only like been passed out like maybe twice." I hear Jamie's fears emerge and feel for her, sensing in many ways that she is frightened. Despite her willingness to compromise and have the trauma consultation, she says, "I just want them to understand sometimes there is no reason."

Now she feels worse that her parents know she's depressed and hurting herself because they keep saying how sad and worried they are, which fills her with guilt. She keeps saying to them, "I'm sorry, I'm sorry." She's getting angry at this point, and thinks they should go to therapy themselves and deal with their feelings about her in therapy, instead of dumping those feelings on her. Her mom cries, so Jamie feels even guiltier.

Her parents think she's not recognizing their pain: "I don't like to think about their pain so much because it's my fault."

Uh-oh, I think. Here comes more self-blame, the vicious cycle, now she's completely responsible for their feelings.

"Is it?" I ask.

"It's nobody else's fault. I did this to them and I'm ruining their lives right now. I'm sick of them telling me every day, 'Oh we're so worried, we're so nervous, blah, blah, blah,' and they go down a list of feelings. It only makes me feel guiltier." She sighs and says softly, "I can't blame them. They just don't know me."

I ask if she feels known by anyone. "Yeah, my friends. My friends try to understand me. My parents don't accept me."

I ask her if she wants to say more.

"They don't hear me at all. Maybe they hear what I'm saying physically, but they don't hear me. They're really not considering me. They're not really taking me seriously as a person. Basically, we never see eye to eye. We both listen to what each other has said but we listen and kind of scramble it, so we can hear what we want to hear. Or it turns into 'You're the bad guy.' I'll take a recent example, of smoking. I'll say, 'I need a cigarette,' and my mom hears 'I want to be part of the crowd, because everybody else is smoking right now.' Then if she says to me 'This is not a punishment, but we're going to send you away to a therapeutic boarding school,' I hear 'You're mad at me, so you're sending me away.' " Jamie realizes that she and her parents need to work on communication.

I ask her what she likes about participating in an adolescent group for teens, and she lights right up. She loves the fact that "you can say anything, you don't have to restrict yourself, you can really just be 'here I am.' "

Sources of Negative Thinking

Negative thoughts about the self originate externally—from things girls hear and see, things that are said to them, such as by Maura's critical and emotionally abusive dance teacher. (They can also come from things that go unspoken.) When critical words come from someone in a position of power and authority, it can be really detrimental. It can be especially devastating if they come from someone a girl looks up to, someone from whom she seeks approval. That shatters confidences, demolishes dreams, disrespects, and degrades. If a girl keeps hearing something negative about herself over and over, it's going to get internalized, the same way something positive can become a part of her vision of herself.

"You can't do anything right." "You're lazy." "You're too slow." "You'll never amount to anything." "Why can't you be like your sister?" "You're nothing but trouble." "You're too fat." "You could lose a few pounds." "What's wrong with you?" These expressions will steer girls to a low sense of self-worth, decreased optimism, and poor resiliency. Such words pave the way to insecurity, lack of confidence, feelings of inferiority, and pessimism. They can lead to the destruction of a girl's very soul. If girls constantly hear what they are doing is wrong, they begin to believe they can't do anything right, and they won't try new and adventurous things. They will be filled with fear and self-doubt.

Teenagers also personalize everything. If someone a girl loves, looks up to, or cares about is busy much of the time, and doesn't have enough time to talk with her or be with her—as is common these days with long work hours and hectic schedules—that subtly says to a girl, "You're not important to me." That can be translated into thinking that person doesn't care about her.

Fault-finding and criticism from other people really can shatter a young person's sense of herself. Girls are constantly trying to adhere to unrealistic images of women, gender role expectations, peer pressure, parental pressure, and academic pressures. Adolescence is an uncertain, unstable time in the life cycle; we've all been there.

Nicole explains, "You're so bombarded by things. How can you look inward when you have to spend most of your energy fending off different parts of the outside world that are coming in, just so you can stand up straight?" Girls end up comparing themselves and feeling they don't measure up. "You're supposed to look a certain way and be pretty. Be what society says is pretty, and if you're not, you're some kind of failure in life." In their malleable teen minds, it's easy to feel like a giant failure, especially when they don't measure up to the standard, which Carrie says is, "ridiculously thin, it's unnaturally thin. It's big boobs. It's long hair. It's light hair, you know, the Aryan look. Blond hair, blue eyes." But girls continue to think they are stupid for feeling sad or depressed for "no reason," if there is no apparent reactive depression event, such as trauma, or someone dying.

Comparing themselves to others, especially to celebrities, brings on the "less than" syndrome, negative thoughts that come from what they are not: I don't look like a model or actress, therefore I'm ugly. I'm not getting straight A's in school; I'm stupid. My teachers say I should try harder: I'm lazy. I'm fat and ugly. They think I'm smart, therefore guys won't like me; Cecilia doesn't want to be my friend anymore; I must be one rotten person.

The Perfect Girl

Perfectionism is another culprit. While it can be wonderful to strive for the highest possible level of performance, when perfectionism takes over and they can't do everything perfectly all the time, girls' thinking can go haywire: their schoolwork has to be perfect, they have to look perfect, dress perfect, have the perfect labels, act perfect, think perfect, be perfect. Whereas some girls may be perfectionists in only some areas, say their schoolwork, for other girls it may be more pervasive. If one thing is not perfect, they begin to think that they are totally awful. See how negative thinking gets started?

The Harvard Project on Women's Psychology and Girls' Development found that girls described the perfect girl as one "who is always nice and good, who never hurts another's feelings, who either lacks or can control hunger and sexual desire, and who contains her feelings, especially anger."[1] For girls trying to live up to these standards, even having a "bad" thought, a "not nice thought," can make them think they are somehow no good. Talk about unrealistic expectations! If, at age twelve, girls think they have to think nice thoughts all the time and that if they don't, they're not good or nice—imagine what could go on inside their heads. It's hard having nice thoughts all the time. Judging their own "bad" thoughts and feelings makes them think: I'm bad because I have bad thoughts; therefore I'm not nice.

If she feels sexual desire and wants to have sex and the word gets out, she's called a slut, so she begins to think she's a slut. Even joking friends can cut to the core. On the other hand, a girl who hasn't had sex because she doesn't want to, because she's not ready, or because it's against her values is shamed and called a prude. So she internalizes that something's wrong with her. One girl told me, "In one of my groups of friends I was a slut, and in another group I was a prude."

Often, girls and women are dismissed and invalidated, not listened to, not taken seriously, which can translate into "nobody listens; nobody cares." If a girl repeatedly doesn't get a response or is subtly ignored, if her requests aren't respected or accommodated, she may think: I don't matter. I'm not important. I'm invisible. And slowly the positive and strong parts of her self begin to disappear.

Locus of Control

Another culprit of negative thinking has to do with locus of control. Your locus of control determines whether you think outside forces (external) or you yourself (internal) are responsible for or in control of circumstances in your life. Having what's called an "internal locus of control" means that girls believe that what happens to them is in their control, which may sometimes, but not always, be the case. They think everything is in their control, which of course is impossible, and when something goes wrong, they think it's "all my fault" and are filled with self-blame. When the locus of control is internal, girls take responsibility for what happens to them, which for the most part is healthy, but for some girls it gets extreme. Girls need to remember that there are things for which they are not responsible. Skyla, for instance, is not responsible for keeping her parent's marriage together. A girl who relies on the internal locus of control may be filled with self-blame. That is one extreme.

The other extreme is when someone believes that her life is controlled mainly by others and outside forces, by fate, by luck. She is relying on an external locus of control. Often, girls with depression and eating disorders have an external locus of control. Girls with too much external locus of control feel helpless and powerless, thinking they have no control, no power, and no agency. They end up thinking, 'What's the use, why bother?' and their self-efficacy can disappear. It's important to find the balance between the internal and external locus of control. After all, that's how life works. I advocate for an internal locus of control because it increases self-efficacy and empowerment. But some girls have too high a dose of it. They need to learn to let go of responsibility that is not theirs and need help in learning to discern the difference.

The Offhand Remark

An external label or an offhand remark can be internalized and turned into a self-fulfilling prophecy. A fourteen-year-old girl I worked with sat in a meeting in which she was being confronted for unruly behavior. She looked at the puzzled professional's surprise, and said quite seriously, "I have oppositional defiant disorder." She wondered what all the commotion was about. Why would they be surprised that she was being oppositional and unruly?

Circumstances can also ignite negative thoughts about the self. Paige entered a private high school and tried out for junior varsity basketball. She didn't make the team. She felt like a big failure. Basketball was her thing, her life. Her friends were on the team. So she attached herself to the couch, watching TV. She thought life was over. She sank further into the couch as the negative feelings went deeper into her psyche. She was a loser—so much of what she valued and thought was good about herself had to do with her skills as a basketball player. Here's how these thoughts take over: The negative thoughts originate externally but then girls internalize them as part of their self and identity.

Ruminating

As we learned in chapter two, girls who ruminate are at risk for depression. Some girls use a more passive internal style of coping with distress and stress, which just makes negative thinking fester; they get stuck in the quicksand of negative thinking. Girls who are encouraged to develop a more active coping style are more likely to do things that refocus their thoughts on something else. They may find ways to actively deal with stress and problems, rather than just thinking about it, all alone. Talking with others and getting involved in outside activities can help. We need to encourage girls to be active, to take the initiative, to engage with the world, lest they become unwitting victims of the silent messages of passivity.

Skyla: Self-Preservation Kicks In

Skyla is seventeen, an honor student, and has large dark brown eyes and shoulder-length golden-brown hair, which she has just cut. I think she's beautiful; I come to learn that she thinks she's plain and overweight. She's wearing a gray-blue T-shirt, bell-bottom blue jeans, and brown leather sandals. She has a bright, warm smile. Shadows of sadness reside in her large brown eyes. I can't help but see it. Her eyes are like deep pools. I feel a lot of love for her. There is a quiet and serious maturity and responsibility about Skyla, an endearing modesty alongside a deep intellect.

Skyla grew up in an upper-middle-class home. Both parents are working professionals; she has an older brother. She adores her parents, and she loves the memories of her childhood. She has a large extended family and they are close. She absolutely adores her dog. Music brings her joy. "It's basically the universal language of emotion." She plays the piano and especially loves playing the guitar. She writes poetry and keeps a journal, describing her writing style as, "the type of writing that Jack Kerouac does, whatever is on your mind just comes out."

A little bewildered, she has been told recently that some of her writing was morbid. "I don't give myself titles. I didn't consider myself to have depression or be depressed. It's just who I am. I didn't consider my writing extremely morbid. It was just my writing." Things in her life began to shift when she was twelve, when she began to see things and people differently. I asked what she thinks it was about being twelve, and she replies, "Maybe one of the added bonuses of puberty is insight." How true.

When I asked Skyla what gives her hope she says, "The possibility of love; the possibility of helping people. A lot of people have helped me." What does she hope for in her future? "I'd like to be with people I love, and then have that love reciprocated. And a good career in the sciences."

The thing she likes best about herself is that she listens well. She says she can tell people are listening to her "by the questions they ask. And, if they change anything as a result." She hates "intolerant, critical, competitive social situations and pointless rules," such as the one at school that prohibits sitting on one side of the lawn but not the other. Sometimes, Skyla quietly sits on the No Sitting–No Walking side of the lawn, just to make a point.

When she's mad at people she ignores them. In social situations and discussions she easily plays devil's advocate to provoke commentary and good-natured sparring. If it's something she feels strongly about and she's actually arguing for a purpose, she's not going to lose sleep over someone disliking her for her opinion. Not losing sleep over an opinion strongly stated is a positive, healthy sign.

Skyla was feeling pretty blue for a long time. She was self-conscious and easily embarrassed. She worried about endangered species, deforestation, the ozone layer, and especially humanity's lack of compassion. Sometimes she wanted to go live "in a cave," away from it all. She often got hurt accidentally. More and more she preferred being alone. When she got really nervous or anxious, she silently counted things around her, or checked things over and over, which are signs of anxiety. Anxiety is often part of depression, or can coexist with depression. She had trouble sleeping—either falling asleep or waking up in the middle of the night. Sometimes she needed to take a nap during the day because she didn't sleep well at night.

She felt easily let down. Disappointments made her wonder why she should even bother to look forward to something, why she should care in the first place. A disappointment began to feel like the end of the world. She felt angry with herself for expecting, for feeling excitement, only to be let down. She felt angry with herself for wanting anything in the first place. She wanted to stop wanting. Nothing ever worked out. Nobody really cared. Everything felt like it was her fault.

When she contemplated death, it wasn't that she wanted to die. That wasn't it at all. She simply wanted to be out of the pain, maybe a time-out for a while, a moratorium on pain. Peace was all she wanted. "A lot of the time—this might sound kind of weird—but it was me getting upset at situations or people, and then getting furious at myself for feeling anything at all. 'Why do you set yourself up like this? Why do you have expectations for anything, when you know that nothing ever works out the way you want it to?'"

When her parents divorced when she was sixteen, she found fault with herself and took responsibility. "Obviously I can't take care of even the people I live with. My parents split up. Obviously I cannot take care of anything and have it go well." They certainly didn't know how to tell her. She got home one day last spring from visiting her cousins and there were lots of packed boxes. Her parents had bought a new house. Instead of the whole family moving, Skyla learned that her parents were divorcing; her mom was going to the new house and so was she, and her brother was going to college. She didn't like the way they told her and she wanted some say about where she was living. She was mad at herself. "I should have known." And angry that she didn't have a say in where she was living.

She had a wonderful childhood. "I love my parents very much. And it was hard for me to come to grips with the fact that I had to teach myself coping mechanisms at a really young age." She isn't referring to the positive coping strategies of writing and playing the guitar and listening to music, all of which helped her express what was inside when she was younger. Instead, she discovered a harmful one as a teenager—cutting. She didn't like to think of herself as someone who had to learn coping mechanisms because things had been rough. It was painful for her, "because I know my parents love me and I know they tried the best they could. It becomes a guilt thing, like my parents did a really good job. Why did I have to develop these kinds of coping mechanisms?

"Speaking about things that matter wasn't encouraged, and anything you said that involved emotion wasn't heard, wasn't responded to," which is why writing and playing music became her mediums of expression. A few days ago, she learned that despite how professionally successful and high functioning her parents were, they both had quiet drinking problems. She never knew that the glass of wine with dinner that turned into a bottle, then two bottles, and the Bloody Marys on the weekends were anything more than that.

"It was tough. I learned that if you get angry or upset, and you say something to try to get it changed, and nothing happens, and no one responds, it's like, it's just a waste of emotional energy."

She got mad at herself for simply feeling anything at all, "for putting myself through an emotional wringer with no results." She began disconnecting from her own feelings and thoughts and started telling herself that she wasn't feeling anything when she actually was. "If something upsets me, but there's nothing I can do, and I'm totally powerless in the situation, it's best if it doesn't upset me. And eventually I got to the point where I wouldn't even notice if I was feeling anything or not."

And she thinks that's where the cutting comes in. When she has an urge to cut, she knows she's feeling something. I ask how the cutting started.

On Halloween two years ago, when she was fifteen and dressed up as a vampire, she and her three friends shared a Halloween kit. Skyla ended up with the fake blood. She mimicked slashing her wrists and something about the visual affected her. She could see the red fake blood; it was vivid, nearly beautiful. She wanted to re-create it. She began scratching herself to re-create the "visual effect."

"For a long time I kept myself together really well. No one could tell that there was anything wrong. But as I began to get more and more upset with myself and with life in general, I wanted to have something on the outside showing people. Even if I didn't say anything, just showing them meant no, everything isn't all right, everything isn't perfect for me."

At first her cutting was in secret, and she thought it was socially unacceptable. She kept it secret for only so long. Scratching led to delicate cutting, which led to deeper cutting. Her parents were going for marriage counseling, which Skyla did not know could foreshadow divorce. She went to several counseling sessions with her parents and dropped hints about herself and her cutting, which the counselor figured out. Skyla was trying to get noticed and get help. Skyla started going to her own psychotherapist. The weird thing was that the first person she told, her good friend, Sue, said she was cutting herself too. Her parents were upset, and she worried that if she cut herself too badly at home her mom would cry or get scared.

I ask Skyla what she thinks it was about visual effect—what seeing her cuts was about for her. "It's an actualization of pain. There are several levels. The most basic is that even if you tell people that something is wrong, a lot of times they won't know how wrong. But all they'll do is see a cut along a vein, and they get the message right away.

"I've basically learned to make it look like everything is fine. But sometimes that can screw you up, because then people won't believe you, that something is wrong. That's where cutting comes in," she says to me as her voice becomes more passionate and strong.

"It's like you can't really use words to deny what I just did. But then when they see it, actually see it, they're like, wow, maybe there is something wrong. Yes, you fucking idiot, something is wrong! I've only been saying it for the last seventeen years. Excuse the little outburst," she exclaims passionately, looking right at me. I tell her she can have as many outbursts as she wants. What was touching was that it wasn't much of an outburst at all; her voice simply became more passionate and heated, and her anger was more alive, and she swore. That's all. I've seen kids have what one really would call a *major* outburst.

She also explains other aspects of cutting—it was not simply about communication. "It was a way to get out the pain that was inside of me. If I'm watching my blood leave me, it was as if that would be some of the pain leaving too." And now she feels like it has become addictive and a way to punish herself.

Cutting is understood to be similar to a drug to which people can become addicted. It even results in a high, because it increases the levels of endogenous opiates in the body. Unfortunately, to maintain the high feeling, you need to cut again. Girls—and boys for that matter—will cut not just to communicate, but also to regulate and change how miserable they are feeling. If they feel numb it makes them feel alive; if they feel too much emotional pain, it shifts their pain into the body. "Having physical pain that doesn't have emotional pain feels better," another girl told me.

Skyla explains, "Cutting is a coping mechanism that has always worked short-term. It's hard to give up something that works." Just to make matters more complicated, people's response to the behavior and the negative associations and connotations about cutting or cutters provides Skyla with yet another way to feel bad about herself. "I think it's a form of manipulation, of manipulating other people, and I hate that. And I hate to think I do that, but I know I do." I ask her what she means by manipulation.

"Motivating people through pity of me. And I hate pity. So it's like I'm doing myself no good by getting the help that way," she says.

"Are you getting the help you need?" I ask.

"Yeah," she says.

"What do you make of that?"

"I guess sometimes you go about things the wrong way to get to a certain point." She says it has to do with people not listening. "Eventually, you learn that you have to do obscure things in order to get what you need. And even if you don't like what you have to do, or wish you didn't have to do those things for those reasons, I guess self-preservation kicks in at some point, and you're going to get the help however you can."

It's not just the cutting that has meaning to Skyla. Every single scar holds a story, its own history. She remembers what she was thinking; she knows what she was doing each time. "If I didn't cut, they wouldn't exist. Because in Greek, the opposite of the word 'truth' isn't 'false' and isn't 'dishonesty.' It's 'forgotten.' So, the opposite of truth is forgotten. Truth is what is remembered."

In her efforts to stop cutting, she says, "You start to miss it after a while. And when it becomes part of who you are, it's hard to give that up. At the same time, part of me hates that it's a section of my identity."

Negative Thinking Can Last a Lifetime

If negative thoughts about the self take root in adolescence, they become a permanent part of a girl's identity. Then she grows up into a woman with a negative identity, a depressed woman who feels bad about herself. This negative identity that develops during adolescence keeps her from reaching her full potential. It's as if she inhaled toxic air that polluted her mind. We all know women suffering from depression with underlying hopelessness and negative identity. They probably started feeling this way when they were teenagers.

When something becomes part of your identity you don't simply outgrow it. I'm not saying it's impossible to change—of course it isn't—but it's a million times easier for girls to grow into confident capable women who believe in themselves if they don't bear the burden of negative thinking that is ingrained in their personality and identity from their teenage years.

A negative style of thinking can become part of how girls approach life. Their youthful idealism and optimism can be replaced with a defeated, discouraged, and negative attitude. Instead of, "If I fall down I have the confidence to pick myself up, learn, and go on," girls may think, "It's all my fault. I can't do anything right. I'm a terrible person. What's the use?" Their self-confidence will be diminished, and they will be less likely to attempt new things, take healthy risks, and keep trying when things are hard. Instead, they will repeatedly question themselves, not enjoy success, and begin to take on a "Why bother?" mentality.

Staying Positive

Having a positive attitude helps people in their journey through this life. It influences how we approach life, how we see things, how we interpret things, and how we deal with disappointments, let downs, and failures (and it even has an impact on our physical health). If girls learn to think more positively about themselves, when something upsetting happens they can take meaning from it beyond a sense of their own failure. Even if it is their responsibility, they can learn from it, grow, find something positive they learned, and try to do it differently next time.

With a positive identity and a positive attitude they will fare far better in the world. We need to encourage girls, not have them grow up discouraged. They need to feel empowered, not defeated.

Positive messages, thoughts, and coping strategies can be internalized just like negative and unhealthy ones. One of my favorite stories about working as a therapist with teenage girls is what I call the breathing story. As a therapist, I always teach kids the importance of breathing. It works: It calms us down, and is available at all times. Breathe in slowly to a count of five, then breathe out to five, then get the count up to ten. Believe me, there are times I need to remind myself to breathe. I always remind the girls to breathe. One would do this adorable eye roll each time. I can recall her terrific laughter at this moment. Another would just look at me. Several of them surely deemed me the "breathing queen." But, lo and behold, I was not merely a broken record—for many, many moons later the girls had stories to tell.

My adorable eye-rolling girl had to unexpectedly go to the ER for medical reasons and they had to give her a blood test. She was terrified of needles and refused the blood test. When they said they would have to restrain her to take it, she completely freaked out. Telling me the story, she says, "I could hear you say, 'Breathe' and I did and I let them take the blood test." Another girl, Jasmin, was with a friend who got scared and began to really panic. Jasmin, without even thinking, said to her, "Breathe," and then said, "I can't believe it. I sound like my therapist." Neither girl probably has any idea how much it mattered to me to hear that my efforts were not in vain, that they had internalized my voice. It's an important lesson to remember: Kids are taking things in even when they roll their eyes as if we're a broken record.

Accentuate the Positive

Teenage girls need to hear positive words about themselves every day. They need to hear from someone who believes in them that they are worthy, valuable, and capable. They need to be treated with respect, which shows them that they are worthy. They need to be treated with dignity and honor. They need appreciation for what they do and encouragement to keep doing it. Tell them you're proud of them and why. Focus on the positive, no matter what that might be, and don't focus on the negative or the things they do wrong. We need to teach them to focus on the positive, too.

They need to hear "I believe in you," "I think you can do anything you set your mind to," "I'm proud of you," "I love you," "You're smart," "I approve of you," "You can do it," "You are capable," "I accept you," and "I care about you." Actions need to correspond with words. Show girls they are important. Sit down and look them in the eyes and say these things. Listen to what they are saying and let them know through your words and actions how much they matter and how important they are.

We don't want to prohibit girls from expressing what they are thinking. It is important to know if they are harboring hidden negative thoughts about themselves, even if they are not indicating them verbally or through their actions. It's crucial for them to name, articulate, and acknowledge self-deprecating thoughts, but they should not dwell on them. Negative thoughts become negative mantras, and we want to get those thoughts out of their heads, not further in. Don't let girls say, "I'm useless" over and over again. Help them replace those words with positive thoughts and words, even if at first they don't believe them. Ask them: "What are three things you are good at doing?" "What are three things you love to do?" "What are three things you like about yourself?"

It's not healthy for girls to joke about themselves in a negative way either, or for others to try to get away with it through "teasing." Putdowns are not OK. They are a subtle way to plant negative thoughts, self-doubt, and inferiority in a person's being. It may appear to be all in good fun, but girls need to be built up, not torn down, not even with jokes.

It's important to spend some time in a group, in a workshop, or in therapy exploring where negative thoughts originally came from, the sources. It can often help girls to understand that these mean thoughts about themselves originate outside of them. It can help them understand how they become their own thoughts. Talk with girls about where the thoughts come from. "I'm fat. I'm a loser." Where does that come from? Whose words are they inside her head? Hers? Or, rather, things she's heard from others that she's taking into her inner thoughts and feelings? Girls need to understand that they're not "bad" or "worthless" and that there is not something inherently wrong with them.

I often give girls affirmations, or we make them together—positive statements about themselves and their lives. I have girls write and say them to counteract these negative thoughts. Some girls are eager; others roll their eyes and sigh. Overall, these affirmations help, although when negativity is entrenched, girls have a hard time saying something positive about themselves. That's why they really need to hear it from others.

A young teenage girl I worked with was filled with self-loathing, and made negative comments about herself, so every day in her journal I wrote to her about how smart and strong I thought she was. I had her write it too, three times a day; at first she thought it was stupid; then her mom told me she overheard her composing and singing a song on her guitar, with words something like, "I'm special, I deserve respect, I'm strong, and I carry on."

Help girls make a big list of all the things they're good at doing.

Make another big list of all the things they love. Affirm the positive. Stow away the lists and look at them in five years. Have things changed? Do they still love roller coasters? Playing the guitar? The beach? Provide girls with plenty of opportunities for success. Teach them that they can learn from mistakes, and letdowns, and that something good can even come from it.

Girls can be encouraged to succeed without destroying their positive sense of themselves. They need help to form a relationship with a person in authority who, unlike the mean dance teacher, encourages a girl to do her best. A girl needs to like her teacher and wants her to be proud of her based on the relationship, not because the teacher has shamed and humiliated her into doing better. In the short term that may bring success, but in the long term it is detrimental. Girls thrive on encouragement, praise, and belief in themselves—as do all of us.

The earlier string of thoughts that opened the chapter can be replaced with these words: I am worthy. I am strong. I am good. I am smart. I am beautiful. I am love. I'm deserving. I'm successful. I believe in tomorrow. I am loved. I have courage. I'm confident. I'm capable. I'm still growing. I am successful. I can do it. Good things happen to me.

As Kristy says, "It's all these little things you can't pinpoint that change how you see things, and that in turn changes how you interpret things and it spirals in on itself." We can reverse that spiral—and we should start today.

In an effort to help girls stay positive, have them name three good things that happened today, three things for which they are thankful. If they don't want to say them, get them a special journal to write them in. Have them say out loud or write positive statements about themselves every day. Also have them name three good things about themselves that don't have to do with looks or body. Make a time to really listen to the girl in your life—maybe at the dinner table. Ask questions or let her ask them, and really listen—don't have everybody talking at once.

The more positive identity we can build in them, the better we can help girls face the trials, tribulations, and tragedies in the world.

5. RISKING LOVE

I n the United States, we remember the shock of September 11, 2001. Trauma and tragedy often strike when we least expect it. When I began writing this book, one of my closest friends, Michael, unexpectedly died. Like many others who loved him dearly, I was devastated, heartbroken, and completely grief-stricken. This was a friend I talked to daily, a friend I could call no matter what time of day or night with any joy, song, prayer, anxiety, or sorrow. He was so excited about this book that he called every day to ask, "How's the book?" When he died, I wondered how I was going to get out of bed, much less write my book, and I knew isolation was not good after loss. I went to my chiropractor. He checked my back and, puzzled, asked, "What happened?" But with faith, prayer, the grace of God, and talking with friends, I got out of bed every day, and even made my way to the computer. I put up a sign in my apartment reminding myself to carry on. I prayed. I re-read "Footprints in the Sand." I talked on the phone with people who were also grieving.

Six weeks later, I went back to the chiropractor and after the appointment, with a smile, he said, "You're out of the slump." With time to grieve, in a month I felt a little better, and with each passing month the acuteness of the pain dissipates. It takes time and I'm an adult. I'll always miss him and feel waves of sorrow, but that unbearable acute grief that feels like it will never end did stop.

Grief slowly subsides, and life goes on. For young people who have experienced trauma or loss, the aftermath of that experience has repercussions. Mental health experts tell us that trauma and loss are major contributors to depression in teenagers. I find this to be true for many girls.

Depression in teenagers is like a chameleon that quickly changes color. When I was a little girl, my little brother had four chameleons. I remember watching with fascination as they changed color, noticing their alertness, how they sometimes darted around, and at other times were very still, no movement, just quietly watching. Depression manifests itself in a wide range of behaviors and activities, and the surface may not reveal the inner despair. The stories of Jessie and Janessa are heartwrenching. Yet we need to hear them and to understand how their shock and sorrow turns into depression, so that we can recognize the many forms deep sadness and longing take.

Jessie and the Horrible Thing

A sweet kindness and sturdiness flow from Jessie. She's perceptive, bright, and optimistic. She has a soft prettiness, long wavy hair the color of dark honey, and big round hazel eyes, and wears a purple T-shirt under a pale pink zippered sweatshirt. Her faded jeans brush the floor, and her silver and lavender earrings dangle delicately. Fifteen-year-old Jessie lives with her mom, dad, and brother in a town on the very edge of a small city. She loves them very much and she never wanted to do anything to upset or hurt them. She likes hanging out with her friends, swimming, and playing pool.

School is a big problem and Jessie never really enjoyed it. She didn't think the teachers liked her as much as some of the kids who made really good grades. She tried alcohol with some kids when she was around eleven. The other kids took it out of their parents' house. Most of the kids she knows began trying drugs at around ten, eleven, and twelve. Jessie is an idealistic and caring girl. She thinks the world would be a much better place if people had more goodwill toward one another. She doesn't identify with a particular religion but believes in God. "Like I'm not a Catholic, I'm not a Protestant, I'm not a Christian, I'm not Jewish, I just believe in God."

The horrible thing happened over a year ago, but remains "in her heart" and hurt her more than anyone knows. She went to a party with a boy she knew from another high school and he sexually assaulted her at the party. For weeks, she wouldn't tell anybody, frozen with shame and fear, and she cried in secret. A few weeks later, her best friend, Jackie, found her crying hysterically and asked, "What's the matter, Jess?"

"I can't tell anybody and I can't say anything," replied Jessie, but in a matter of seconds Jessie ended up telling her. Jackie told her she had to tell. So Jessie told her parents. The boy and his family, they learned, had just moved thousands of miles away, and proceeding legally was complicated because she was too shamed and scared to tell right away. He moved, "and that was that, but like you figure it's all over but it's still in your heart and it hurts you a lot." I tell Jessie how sorry I am for what happened to her and commend her courage in being able to talk about it, and also tell her I understand why she didn't tell at first.

"That was really what started it all because I couldn't think straight, I couldn't sleep, and I would have terrible nightmares, and I have flashbacks" she tells me. Given my clinical training in child and adolescent trauma, I ask Jessie if she has had help for any symptoms of Post Traumatic Stress Disorder (PTSD). She is getting help for it now. Right after she told about the assault, she went for short-term therapy, but now she knows it wasn't enough. The longer-term effects of depression and PTSD were not recognized, and things got worse.

Only recently was she diagnosed with "post-traumatic stress disorder, depression, and subsequent substance abuse." She thinks the assault triggered her depression and heavy drug use. Jess always believed she was and had to be strong, so when she began to be overwhelmed by feelings she didn't know what to do. She didn't feel as though she should let anybody know, because she was strong. She felt terrible in general, was upset, and felt like she couldn't accomplish anything.

Haunted by it, she explains, "I couldn't get my mind off it and I became paranoid and I couldn't sleep and I couldn't eat. I didn't want to go outside. I didn't want to go to school. I didn't want to go for walks. I didn't want to be in the town I lived in. I felt like I wasn't good enough." This is a typical kind of aftereffect but it is detrimental because isolation is the worst thing for depression and trauma. People need to be with other people, people with whom they feel safe and loved.

Most of the kids Jessie hung around with were using drugs, so it was easy for her to get started. Getting drugs became her reason for going out of the house. She started using pills, legal drugs like Percocet, Percodan, and other painkillers, and then Ritalin. Then she started using heavier street drugs, and began smoking and drinking. She became friends with the coolest drug dealers. "I started using, like, LSD to try and, like, make me happy and I'd hallucinate and see good things. And then I'd use ecstasy, which made me feel wonderful and then I'd use cocaine, which would also make me happy. I'd use PCP, which made me feel stronger and it was terrible. And I'd be upset, and I would use more. And the more I tried to stop the more the feelings came back. And it was like a cycle, and the more addicted I'd become."

She forced herself to get to school, but didn't always stay there. School made her feel worse about herself. She walked in the front door and walked out the back. She was constantly getting in trouble. Jessie was never a great student, and she thought school wasn't her thing. She wasn't a favorite; she felt she was only average, and was considered a troublemaker because she spoke up and talked back. After the sexual assault happened she really talked back to the teachers. She went to school wasted. She skipped classes and eventually skipped days. She got suspended more than five times for skipping and insubordination. When she was suspended she didn't have to go to school. That just gave her an empty day to do drugs and hang out with kids who didn't go to school or skipped and did drugs. (This is why suspending kids is not the best way to handle school problems; it just pushes them further away and gives them even more time to hurt themselves and get in trouble. We need to be looking out extra carefully for kids who feel they are on the margins.)

Since she had never been one of the "good student" kids, no one at school seemed to notice that she was having so much trouble or to care why. To Jessie, it didn't feel like anyone at her school cared whether she was there or not. A teacher would send her to the principal and she would just leave the school through the back door, never going near the principal's office. No one ever followed up on her. "I couldn't deal with the school 'cause they really weren't even sensitive to my needs. Then I hated the whole place. The only people I was involved with that were in the school were the kids who didn't go to school and the kids who were bad in school. I got a reputation at the school for being a troublemaker so all the teachers really didn't pay attention to me and I figured they thought, 'Oh yeah, she's just going to do what she wants. We'll just take care of the kids that want to do schoolwork.'" Unfortunately for Jessie, this created more alienation.

She was so stressed out that she began picking at her hair, pulling out one strand at time, whenever she felt sad or nervous or scared or anxious or upset, or when her thoughts overwhelmed her.

She asks, "You know how some people cut themselves?"

"Yes," I say.

"Because it feels good. I ripped my hair out 'cause it feels good." She says she does it especially when she is nervous. Sometimes sitting in her room hanging out, she'll do it. Stashed under her bed and well hidden was a bottle of vodka for when she was upset. "I would just take a few shots and pop a few pills and go to sleep."

The principal called in her parents and confronted them and said that they were not doing enough to keep her in school. "I was aware I had problems but I was trying to do it all by myself and I didn't want to say anything. I was just hopeless and in despair and I felt terrible about what I had been doing to my family and to myself and all my friends around me and people that cared about me. I'd deny it 'cause people would confront me and I'd deny it totally.

"It was really hard now because I reinvented somebody that I was." She didn't want to hurt her parents; she didn't want to make trouble for them, which was partly why she couldn't tell them how she was feeling. Now she felt that she was really hurting them, and she didn't want them to feel that it was their fault. Jessie felt like a failure because she thought she had to be independent. Guilt washed over her and she felt saturated by it.

So she vowed to stay in school, to not skip, and to keep her mouth shut, but at this point she had a reputation for being a troublemaker, so the teachers had no interest in helping her. She talked back in an outburst of anger and got suspended. Then she felt a level of pain and self-loathing that she was convinced she couldn't climb out of, so she went home from school and tried to overdose by taking a bottle of Tylenol and a bottle of Advil. After that she went in her room, dug out the hidden bottle of vodka, and gulped some of that down.

I ask Jessie how she felt at that time.

"Like I wasn't even good enough. I was in despair and couldn't do anything on my own. I felt like as much as I wanted to be independent and do things for myself and be as good as I could, I couldn't. And as much as I wanted to be happy, I could never get happy. And the more I was on drugs, the more unhappy I'd be, even though I was happy. I was like a walking contradiction. It was terrible. I decided that it wasn't even worth it to be here anymore. And I figured my family would be better off without me, and, I'd be better off not even living because I had nothing going for me at the time."

Jessie passed out in her room from taking the pills and vodka and then woke up and was sick to her stomach. She crawled to the bathroom and was sick all night. "My parents stayed with me while I was throwing up." She told them she didn't know why she was sick—maybe the flu or food poisoning—because she didn't want to hurt them. Her mom was saying that Jessie had been through a lot. "She wanted me to go to a different school and get a psychiatrist, which I did. I didn't want to say 'Mom, I tried to kill myself because of everything that is going on.'" It was nearly a week before she ate regularly again.

While Jessie was at home during her suspension, her mom was trying to enroll her in another school. But by the end of the week, she craved drugs and told her mom that she wanted to try it again at the old school. That way she could get the drugs the next day. Her mother was relieved that she was willing to try again, and Jessie went back to the school. "The whole thing started again because that's all I knew, the drug culture." She felt terrible and she overdosed again. "I did it out of impulsiveness, just out of this rage." The rage was hard to put into words. She thought her family would be better off without her; that feeling of not being good enough had enveloped her. She thought she had hurt people too much and felt awful about it, and her despair felt unbearable. But she doesn't mention rage about the assault.

Sexual assault is a big risk factor for depression and suicidal behaviors. Even though she was underage, Jessie went to a bar in a nearby town where many of the people were already on drugs. Somebody offered her some, and she took some Percocet and another drug and got into a physical fight with another girl and almost passed out. She went outside and the girl was waiting to fight her. Jessie was mad and started walking. She remembers getting dragged into a car, having her belongings stolen: her money, her jacket, everything. It was winter and it was cold and she was pushed out of the car into the street. She was on the street sobbing and flipping out and some kids she didn't know drove by. They stopped. Jessie was barely walking, but she managed to get in. "The driver is smoking a blunt with some weed in it and I couldn't really function and I was trying to smoke that and then at the light I started flipping out and I opened the door and fell out. And the girl driving said, 'Something is wrong with her.'" Jessie doesn't remember how, but she ended up in someone's house, very sick. She doesn't remember giving them a phone number but her dad magically appeared and took her home. He stayed with her all night. She told her dad she must have been drugged.

The next morning, her dad's brother came over with a box of assorted donuts. She was too queasy to eat but they made her smile. Her uncle Ray gently confronted her about everything that had been going on. Her uncle Ray is in a 12-step program; he goes to AA. "It was too overwhelming, and I just like broke down and spilled everything. I couldn't take it anymore." From there they took her to the hospital. She now has a therapist she really likes and has been going to 12-step meetings and proudly exclaims that she hasn't used alcohol or drugs for twenty-eight days, which gives her hope: "It feels really good, I feel really hopeful, like I've accomplished something. It gives me a lot of strength, like I can accomplish a lot more. My biggest fear is that it could happen again. I think I just need to be as strong as I can be, smart enough not to let my feelings overwhelm me and be able to talk about it, which I need to learn to do, which I had never been used to before. I'm just starting."

"What do you think would help you to be strong?" I ask.

"Self-esteem, more self-respect, more trust in people like my family, realizing that you're not going to be happy all the time and there is nothing that can make you happy. There's no magic pill that will make you happy. There's no magic therapy that will cure your depression. At some point you are the only one that can enjoy your happiness. I just want to find the positive about everything, try to find the best of myself and other people and realize that right now, really, my family is all I need. I don't need to have the coolest friends that deal the most drugs and make the most money. Instead just look out for the ones I love and that love me, and I'll be there for them and they'll be there for me whenever I feel the way I did."

I ask what helps her feel better about herself. Laughing softly she looks at me and she says shyly, "Compliments." She tells me about a group for teenagers she attends: "Everyone gives a lot of compliments and everyone is really supportive. We listen to each other's stories and everyone will cry and then the whole group, thirteen kids are crying, boys and girls, and everyone's giving each other hugs and telling everyone it's going to be OK, and telling them how wonderful they are and how smart and how strong they are and how brave they are for being able to talk about it. When I first started talking about it, that's what they did for me and I just felt so happy and so hopeful that I could, and that there really are people like me out there that I could relate to and it was great." The power of positive peers is what kids really need. They want to be with peers, and peers have a strong influence on them. I think positive peer groups and peer leadership need to be fostered more in our society.

The Aftermath of Trauma

Jessie's story is very upsetting to read, but we need to recognize that it is not unusual for people who have experienced trauma to become depressed. Trauma overwhelms the capacity to cope. Teens who have experienced trauma are vulnerable to feelings of rage, shame, grief, and betrayal, and are more at risk for drug use and self-harm, research finds. Family members and teachers describe them as more rebellious than teens who have not experienced trauma.[1]

Trauma can lead to depression for many reasons. Trauma interrupts our sense of safety in the world and disrupts the sense of self. Often girls become prone to negative intrusive thinking and self-denigration, and the isolation, stress, overwhelming feelings of loss, and loneliness that follow abuse render girls at risk for depression.

The newspapers are full of traumatic events that range from hurricanes and earthquakes, to war and terrorism, to community violence. Many people in our country are still struggling with the aftermath of September 11. Girls are exposed to a lot of trauma in our society: One in four girls is sexually assaulted by age eighteen. Some statistics report one in three, and one out of every five teenage girls experiences dating violence.[2] Abuse, sexual assault, and witnessing domestic violence have an added impact: Relational trauma—abuse from someone you know— not only disrupts one's sense of safety and trust in the larger world, but also trust in other human beings. This is compounded when the abuse is from someone known and trusted. Trauma is often unspeakable—and often unspoken. In cases of sexual assault, girls are afraid to tell. They may be scared because they have been threatened. They feel shame. They are afraid that no one will believe them. They may think somehow it's their fault and if so they are filled with self-blame. They worry they will be put on trial. These are real fears.

Sexual assault has a profound impact on girls' overall sense of self, not just their sexuality. Often they are filled with self-hatred and re-morse, anger, sadness, and humiliation. The helpless and powerless feelings they experienced during an assault can stay with them. They may be left feeling tarnished and tainted, even when they are wonderful, bright, talented girls. Trauma can lead to depression, as it did with Jessie, and the thought "I'm not good enough" evolves into the negative mind-set of depression.

Traumatic situations in which nobody died can still evoke feelings of loss, sadness, and grief. With trauma comes loss—loss of trust, self, innocence, safety, and ideals, among many other things. Loss of the way life was before the trauma, and lost childhood, if trauma comes during those years. Early on, Freud wrote that depression (back then it was called "melancholia") was precipitated by loss, but not necessarily a death. It might be loss of a relationship, an ideal, home, way of life, job, or part of the self.

The experiences I have just described exert an overwhelming amount of stress on an individual. Our bodies have evolved responses to stress that protect us. When we are under threat or stressed, our adrenal glands release adrenaline, which pulses through our body, preparing it to run or fight for our own survival. This is called the fight-flight-freeze response. Sometimes the response involves freezing right where we are—shock, immobilization. We can't move or talk. We're numb from the pain and horror of the situation.

When our body's stress response is activated, our heart beats faster, our muscles get tense, blood flow increases, and digestion slows down so we can run faster or fight harder. Our bodies do this when we are being chased by a bear on a hike, or when we walk into history class to take a test we didn't study for, or when we take a fast, reckless car ride. So we can imagine the level of stress and adrenaline that would fill our system during an assault.

In the stress response, first we feel hyped up, then we feel exhausted. When I do crisis debriefing in schools, we always teach the kids and the staff that it takes three days after a traumatic event for all the adrenaline to leave the body. So it's important to exercise, sleep, drink lots of water, and eat foods with high water content, like raw vegetables.

Stress—everyday or traumatic—causes muscles to tense. Muscles that stay tense too long can cause migraine and stress headaches. Girls end up with headaches, stomachaches, and body aches. Adults know if their blood pressure is too high for too long hypertension can develop. The latest research says that meditation can help teens with high blood pressure just as it does for adults. A little stress and anxiety keeps us productive and motivated, spurring us on. But too much stress with no relief, extreme stress, detracts from mental and physical health.

Girls like Jessie who experience an acute trauma are at risk of developing PTSD. Bessel van der Kolk, one of my mentors, helped us understand that PTSD is a biologically based syndrome, and not just psychological. In response to a reminder of the trauma, the body's entire stress response system, or a trauma response, becomes activated.[3]

PTSD is characterized by two phases, one wherein girls feel overwhelmed by intrusive thoughts, images, and feelings and the other in which they feel numb, dazed, and in denial. But these can happen simultaneously, which Lenore Terr describes as "frozen watchfulness."[4]

On Alert with Instant Replay

When experiencing the intrusive phase, girls are overly alert—not just vigilant, but hypervigilant or "hyperaroused." They are in a heightened state of alert because their stress response system has been overactivated and put on guard. Girls with PTSD can become watchful, fidgety, jittery, overexcited, jumpy inside, and subject to angry outbursts, flashbacks, insomnia, and nightmares, just like Jessie. Intrusive thoughts, often scary or disturbing, may go through their heads over and over. One girl said that what had happened replayed over and over in her mind "like a silent movie." And she didn't know how to change the channel. In therapy, I help kids learn how to change the channel, so to speak. It's not quite as easy as using a clicker, but they understand the concept and that it is an adaptable way for them to help manage thoughts.

Girls with PTSD they feel as if they're drowning in a flood of feelings and they don't know how to swim; they do not know how to manage and regulate the intensity. It's as if they are on a horse that is running wild and no one ever taught them how to control the reins. To "quench" these intense feelings (hyperarousal) they may do wild and dangerous things, or read terrifying books, or watch horrifying movies over and over again.

I had to slowly wean one of the girls I worked with off scary books and movies. She would read them and watch them over and over and get herself more and more scared—and then not be able to sleep. (For girls who have experienced trauma, there can be a fine line between terror and excitement.) So we had to think of other forms of less scary excitement, safer excitement that didn't leave her awake at night, terrified. She loved amusement parks; on a special occasion we went to an amusement park and rode lots of the rides, like the roller coaster.

With the right help girls can learn to regulate these overwhelming feelings and thoughts without doing dangerous things, or numbing out. But often PTSD goes unnoticed. It has, in fact, only recently been re-acknowledged as a syndrome.[5] If you have concern about trauma, it's important to go to someone who has the appropriate training.

Sometimes feelings can be so awful girls don't feel anything at all, or talk about their feelings. Feelings are the "f" word. Thoughts are sometimes easier to talk about—instead of "How did you feel?" begin with "What do you think?"

Numb and Spacey

In the other phase of PTSD girls are filled with denial and feel numb, spaced out, dazed, in another world, and forgetful. They may sleep too much, lose time, be unable to concentrate, and quietly overcompensate. Some kids are so numb, or "benumbed," that they don't show any symptoms of intrusive thoughts and feelings, acting as if everything is fine.

Writing about school children who survived a school-bus kidnapping, Lenore Terr says that based on their appearances authorities thought the kids were all right. Alas, the truth is that the children were numb. The title of her book aptly captured this part of PTSD: *Too Scared to Cry*. Some kids who experience a lot of numbing try to be high-achieving and polite, may be hard to get to know, and may have an "I don't care much" response to questions.[6] Some kids will swing from revved up to numbness. Girls who feel numb may cut to feel alive again, to regulate how they feel. Jessie regulates yucky feelings with drugs and drinking, and with pulling her hair.

If a girl has been abused, little things in her everyday life could trigger her body to go into the stress response—a sound, a smell, a feeling, a word, someone's behavior. To you and me it would seem completely neutral, but to Jessie it could set off the body's entire alarm system, and send her into flight or a big fight. When I was teaching on the topic of trauma to college students, Jeff, one of the students, understood it immediately. He told the class that once at a family cookout, someone slammed down the lid of a large cooler. It was a loud, unexpected sound that so startled his Uncle Jay that he dove into the bushes. Everyone was baffled. His uncle is a Vietnam vet. Jeff said, "Now I get why he did that."

A startle response is a common response to the aftermath of trauma. However, many "triggers" or "traumatic reminders" aren't as blatant and readily discerned as Jeff's uncle's. Certain feelings trigger more overwhelming feelings, and those can be hard to pinpoint, especially for kids. But, with help and support, girls can learn to be detectives in figuring out their own triggers and how to manage and cope with them.

The societal force that tells kids they have to be strong, independent, and autonomous makes them reluctant to acknowledge that they need help. Combine this with the denial that sometimes accompanies trauma, and the girls are in a hard place. If a girl has experienced trauma and is depressed, it's important that she get help for PTSD as well as depression.

Janessa: When a Boyfriend Dies

There is a quiet shyness in Janessa's large black eyes, which sparkle when she feels relaxed and interested. A bright girl and careful observer, she watches the comings and goings around her closely, "checking it all out" she says. Stunningly beautiful at sixteen, she looks a little older than her age in jeans, a black T-shirt, platform sandals, and an array of silver bracelets on her left arm. Her nails are finely manicured. A perfectionist, she's concerned about being good.

She lives with her mom, dad, and younger sister in a suburb on the very edge of a big city. She always attended a private school until this year, when she started in a public high school. Her friends are really important to her and so is her family.

Her family is very close. She loves her grandmother especially. She was mad at her mom for taking her rap posters, TV, and DVD out of her room as a form of discipline. They had been fighting about how late she could stay out, what her curfew was, and who she could go out with.

Intelligent, her education and achievement are important to her. She says her teachers and parents told her she could make significant achievements if she applied herself.

Janessa tells me she didn't like to disagree or tell people when they did something that upset her. She was afraid if they got into an argument or conflict, they might not like her anymore. A psychologist told her she was so worried about pleasing people that she had a hard time expressing anger.

She says she needs to learn to be more assertive. She knows she can give people an attitude sometimes, and it's cool to have an attitude, but inside she wants them to like her and care about her. Being assertive is different from having an attitude, she says.

When she's not depressed, she's spontaneous and outgoing; she loves to travel. She likes music and her dance classes and track and field.

Mild depression began when Janessa was around thirteen. Her best friend moved across the country and even though they could instant message and talk on the phone, it wasn't the same. Then, when she was fourteen, she injured her foot and couldn't run or dance hip-hop or jazz, which kept her from spending time with many of her friends. She couldn't practice with the team or go to her dance classes. She started feeling lonely.

When she was fifteen, she started liking a boy named Mark. They went to different schools but they became friends and in six months he was her boyfriend. They were in love and he was the first person she had sex with. She was friends with his friends and spent most of her time with him.

Then tragedy struck. Mark died in an accident. Janessa explains the immediate aftermath to me. "I was already depressed and so it set off a really bad depression. I didn't get out of bed, I wouldn't shower, I wouldn't eat, I felt like I was just dead." Janessa didn't even have to get out of bed to go to the bathroom "because I never ate, I never drank. I like didn't do anything for three days. I heard the phone ring a bunch of times but I never really thought about it. I was too dazed out." Janessa went to the funeral, but because she went to a different high school than he did, she was not involved in any of the school support for his loss.

Her parents were at work during the day, and she stayed in her room when they got home. They were kind to her, and her dad came in and talked to her, and her mom brought her food. They tried to get her to eat, but she was in shock, immobilized. They insisted that she go back to school. She didn't have her team to be on, so she felt very lonely at school. No one at her school had known Mark well, so she was alone with her pain. She knew his parents but they were dealing with their own loss, and she didn't see his friends anymore either. Janessa felt as if the friends she loved had been taken away. It was bad enough when her best friend moved, but Mark's death was beyond her comprehension.

Janessa felt lonely all the time after he died. "I don't like how lonely it gets. When I'm in a room by myself in ten minutes I'll start getting really lonely. I don't like how people get taken away from me, people that I love." She had told Mark everything. He was the only one who knew she was already "a little depressed." She always talked to him "if there was something, like, really bad."

At one point, the longing was so strong she wanted to die so she could talk to him. "I was crazy: I wasn't in my right mind," she explains. She thought about dying, not only to be with him, but also "because of the depression and loneliness." She had no energy. Her friend Bernadette was "trying to take me out to parties to meet other guys and stuff, but I really wasn't ready."

Janessa would cry and was afraid of never stopping. Then she felt numb. She didn't want to go anywhere or do anything. She wanted people to be near her but couldn't get herself to physically move. All she did was think about Mark. She didn't watch TV because she couldn't focus. She couldn't believe that she could never see him or talk to him again, until one day when she got to heaven.

Eight months later she didn't feel much better. She explains, "The depression makes you want to quit doing everything. I wasn't active at all." Then it began to affect her thoughts: "It's like you can't look at anything positively. It's just so negative, so down. It's really bad. It's such a roller coaster, anything can happen. You're barely ever up and just always feel depressed and always lonely."

Within about another four months, she stopped caring about herself. Her behavior became reckless. She got into a car with guys she didn't know, despite her friends' protests. That even scared her, afterward, but at the time she just didn't seem to care.

Sometimes she didn't go home when she was supposed to. Then her mom and dad were worried about her. Without permission, she went to forbidden places and parts of the city. She began regularly sneaking out her window by tying sheets together and sliding down them. (She's not the first girl I've heard of doing that.) She thought she had "chronic fatigue syndrome" so she tried speed. "It helped me escape from reality. I used speed because I got so tired. The speed would help me and energize me. It was like I self-medicated with it a lot."

Grief Is Not Depression

Grief affects us not just psychologically, but also on a bodily, cellular level. People are more vulnerable to illness—not only do we not sleep or eat well, there are cardiovascular changes, abnormal responses of the immune system, and a lowered number of white cells. In the years following the death of a spouse, widowed adults are more susceptible to physical illness. Bereaved people smoke and drink and do more drugs, and that certainly can include teenagers who are often experimenting to begin with. Remember Harmony from Chapter Two?

Grief and depression can be similar. When somebody you love dies it's unbearable. Eventually, however, grief does fade; love doesn't go away, but the acute sorrow does. Psychiatric professionals don't consider someone depressed if there has been a serious loss in the past two months. That's bereavement. The two-month cutoff is a way mental health professionals distinguish grief from depression, because the symptoms are so similar. (We all know that the pain of loss does not subside in two months, but many of the acute symptoms do.) If after two months the symptoms persist, then they call it depression. In some situations, a death can trigger depression. If the mourning process becomes complicated, if a girl is more vulnerable to depression and stress, if she has other simultaneous stress or trauma, or if she was a little depressed to begin with (like Janessa), she's at a higher risk for serious depression. If someone is already depressed when a death of a loved one occurs (like Harmony) she may be more at risk to stay depressed.

There is, however, one important difference between grief and depression. When grieving, people do not have the self-hatred, self-loathing, and decline in self-worth that accompanies depression; Freud noticed the distinction nearly a century ago. Grieving, we may feel that the world is empty and void. But the sense of self is not diminished. With depression, a girl may feel empty and diminished, just like her world.

With grief, as with depression, it's hard for a person to find pleasure in other things because his or her energy is tied up with the lost loved one. For a while it should be. Then, energy, not love, has to be slowly withdrawn from the loved one over time, so that one can use the energy to carry on and find joy again. Girls need to be told that it can take a long time to feel better, and teenagers need extra assurance. Unless they have experienced a death before, they don't know that they will eventually feel better. Girls need opportunities to talk about the lost loved one and to think of the positive memories—maybe draw pictures of the good times they had, or make a memory book.

When feeling acute grief, a girl may not want to go anywhere or do anything. (She does need to go to school, and doing her regular activities is important.) For a couple weeks, this is OK, but have friends come see her. She may feel lonely and adrift. She may not be able to concentrate, not even to watch TV. She may not care whether or not she does the things she usually loves doing. She feels wiped out and exhausted. She may not be able to sleep, may not feel like eating, and may feel angry and alone. Or she may sleep to escape the pain and eat to soothe herself and fill the emptiness inside. She will wonder if this feeling will ever go away.

Teens don't know that things will eventually get better. If it's their first experience with such loss, it may be hard to believe that they will feel joy and pleasure, and have fun and want to dance again. Recently, when my beloved friend died, I had to remind myself that I would not feel bereaved forever, that the worst of it would eventually pass and I would feel alive and alert again. I'm an adult and a psychologist, so if I had to tell myself, "You'll be all right," surely a teenager needs to hear that they will live through it and will be all right. Teens also may not know that something positive can grow from it; they can grow stronger.

If the experience is new, teens will need new ways to cope. If it's their first encounter with death, the finality usually feels like it's splitting the ground right beneath them. Teens feel invincible, but when the shock of a loved one's death stares them in the face, the innocence and invincibleness evaporate, forever. Though some bereaved teens' outward reckless behavior might indicate otherwise, on a deeper level they know that life can be cut short. Look after them especially during this aftermath, as there may be unconscious wishes to be with the loved one, which heightens the risk of putting themselves in harm's way.

About one week after my dear friend died, a friend called and, hearing the tone of my sad voice, she asked, "Are you depressed?"

I said, "No, I'm grieving, I'm sad, shocked, and wiped out. If I sound like this in a couple months, ask me again."

When someone dies, usually people have the most support in the immediate aftermath. It's certainly needed then, but it's also in the days, weeks, and months that follow, well past the first one or two months, that those terrible feelings of missing and loss continue. Girls think about the things they might have done together—holidays, birthdays, and special events all change when someone you love is not there. Grieving can be continuous but can also be intermittent. Birthdays, holidays, special occasions, and death anniversaries are all vulnerable times. Janessa would feel the loss on their anniversary, his birthday, her birthday. Who could she call every day after school, and at lunch? Who would she be with on the weekends? She didn't even want to go to the prom.

The Most Difficult Place

Teenagers who lose a peer, boyfriend, or girlfriend are in a difficult place because they are not part of the family that is grieving. Often they end up isolated while grieving, which leads to depression. It is important to be with other people during the time of grief. It's no surprise that so many ethnic and religious customs gather people together after someone dies. It is important for schools and communities to do something both immediate and ongoing to provide opportunities for teenagers to talk together in groups as well as individually.

It's difficult for Janessa and other teens to lose a romantic relationship in which they were sexually active. As adults we may be too quick to dismiss teenage relationships. I agree that teen relationships can change as fast as New England weather. Sometimes, as a therapist, it is hard to keep up with who is going out with whom. But there are plenty of teenage girls in long-term romantic relationships like Janessa, and we need to take these relationships seriously.

It can be difficult for parents to think and talk about their child's sexuality. As I said in Chapter One, parents may not be comfortable with or ready to acknowledge or want to talk about their teenage girls' sexual relationships. A mom said to me, "I don't want to know." And a dad said, "I have to remind myself she's going to do this, whether we talk to her or not, so I have to try to talk about it even though I don't want to. I cringe inside." It's hard. Thus, someone like Janessa may not be able to share the full range of what she lost because she doesn't have anyone to talk to about it. She may not know anyone who went through a similar trauma—another plunge toward psychological isolation. If others don't know about her sexual relationship with her boyfriend, she might feel shame, guilt, and further isolation.

Some girls may withdraw, frightened of getting close to anyone and getting hurt again, well aware of their own sensitivity, and protecting themselves. Some girls may feel differently and not want to be reminded that they are different because of the death. Losing a boyfriend, sibling, or parent when you are a teenager marks you as unusual, because the event itself is rare. It deviates from the natural life cycle. Grandparents are generally many teens' first encounter with the death of someone they love, and that is hard enough.

Girls who lose a loved one, in their need and longing to be consoled, may seek out sexual relationships or encounters, may "act out" sexually because they need physical comfort. They want to be held close, which is a protection from grief. Some girls may adopt the behaviors, mannerisms, or ideals of the lost person. This is called "introjecting" and is a part of bereavement. It's similar to internalizing. This can happen even if it's not someone they actually knew. Even if it's a celebrity who dies, it can evoke identification or adopting of mannerisms. I was working with teenagers when Princess Diana was killed, and the kids, girls and boys alike, were in despair, really shaken up. Many of the girls identified with her experiences of depression, self-harm, and bulimia. They were making cards and adopting some of her causes. One girl decided to try eyeliner for the first time since Princess Diana had worn it.

The Depression Response

The response of girls to loss may be varied. Everyone is as unique as the loss. Some girls may become too parental and become adults before their time. Some might sink into denial and go along as if everything is OK, but they may be numb and in shock.

Some girls may act out their pain with behavior that is in effect saying, "Take care of me and comfort me." They can barely let themselves know they feel bereft and blue, let alone let others know. If they can barely feel it themselves, that makes it harder to know that they need to ask for help. If being strong is part of their identity, part of their sense of self, it is even harder to ask for help. It's not that girls don't want support; sometimes it's just too hard to ask.

If they become depressed, girls can fail in school, or start shoplifting, which may be their way of saying, "I want the person back."

It may be easy in the face of trauma and loss to miss signs of depression, but that's when they can be staring you in the face. This is a time when an alert should be sounded since trauma and loss can be significant precipitants of depression. We know that the death of a dearly beloved person takes more than two months to come to terms with, of course. But after that cutoff point we expect people to be able to resume functioning with daily life, responsibilities, and self-care. If not, it's a sign of trouble. It's a signal if girls shut down more and more after trauma or loss, or start acting out more, or doing both, or if schoolwork continues to suffer after a few months. If someone dies, remind a girl that the love stays with you. Grief groups with other kids can be helpful. Girls are resilient and, with the right support, can carry on. While no one likes to suffer, human growth and potential can be realized through suffering (remember the story of Buddha). The energy a tragedy has to bring you down can instead be used productively in a way that leads to growth and expression. Creative acts can be born of tragedy and suffering.

Girls experiencing depression and trauma, especially PTSD, need therapy that will address both. An acknowledgment of what happened is important, as is initial focus on helping them to feel stable and safe. One of the most important things with trauma is to first stabilize girls' eating, sleeping, and overwhelming feelings, and then work on teaching them coping strategies to help them manage their feelings and thoughts, so overwhelming feelings and thoughts don't manage them. Then, they should work on building or sustaining a strong sense of self and self-efficacy.

What We Need to Teach Girls

It's very important to educate girls about what is happening with them. Teaching girls about the reactions and responses to trauma and loss is very important. Teach them about bereavement, PTSD, and depression. This will give them understanding and compassion for themselves, and will normalize their experience, so they don't think they are crazy. Knowledge gives them more of a sense of power and control.

Some of the girls I worked with were like junior therapists. They knew what unconscious meant, what a trigger or traumatic reminder was, and knew all the symptoms. Once, a fifteen-year-old girl I worked with told me a girl at school told her to cut herself if she was angry and she would feel better. She tried to do an intervention with the girl, and proudly told me the story.

Teach girls to monitor their own bodily reactions. Help them to be aware of their breathing. If they feel too hyped up, they can learn to take their own pulse. Ask them, "Do you feel anxious?" "Where do you feel it in your body?" Trauma numbs girls, which is why some even cut or do drugs to feel alive. Make sure young teens know names of feelings, to help them articulate what they are feeling. They can draw how they feel. They can draw their anger, their sorrow, their hope, their joys. They can draw a "feelings pie" and divide it into different-sized slices of feelings, depending on the size of a feeling.

Ask girls, "On a scale of one to ten, how happy, frustrated, anxious, excited do you feel?"

Have them draw a feelings thermometer. When angry, many girls draw it bursting.

If grieving and in a time of bereavement, a girl can make a book of good memories using drawings or cutouts of her and the loved one. She can write stories about the good memories. She can find some special pictures and make a frame. She can write the departed a letter. She can plant a tree or a flower in the departed's memory or have a star named after him or her. She can do something in his or her honor.

Sometimes the symptoms of depression are very hard to recognize, and in the next chapter we will meet two girls who just seem to be difficult—they are acting out so much. But as we pay close attention to them, we will see the sorrow that lies beneath the surface.

6. WHEN ACTIONS SPEAK LOUDER THAN WORDS

"If a kid is acting out there has to be some reason for it. You can't just assume they're a bad kid, like they weren't brought up right. Usually if a kid is acting out they're automatically asking for help. And you really need to see it from all directions, so you can get kids the help they need."

—Elizabeth, age 14

When I was training to become a child and adolescent therapist, one of my first kids was a teenage girl, Lily, who was stealing. As always, I eagerly went to my supervisor Blair's cozy little office and sat in my usual spot, expecting to learn some techniques that would help me help Lily.

I remember asking, "What do I do to help her stop stealing?"

"Read Winnicot on stealing," Blair said.

I was taken aback because for some reason I didn't expect her to suggest reading; although there was lots of reading for my seminars in learning to be a child and adolescent therapist, somehow I figured there was a specific thing I would learn to do or say to help a child stop stealing. But, alas, insight awaited me in a book. As a graduate student, I had tons of reading to do. Since I love to read, especially about these kinds of things, I thought, "OK, I don't have the book, but now I have an excuse to buy it." My curiosity was piqued because I was familiar with his work.

D. W. Winnicot, an early child analyst, said that for children and adolescents stealing was about hope. A youngster was rightfully longing for something that was his or hers, often love. The act of stealing is symbolic. The youngster has not given up. Winnicot writes that therapists and adults often miss seeing the act of stealing as a moment of hope because they are just looking at the problem to society or the individual who was stolen from. As adults, we lose a chance to help if we don't see the hope in the act.[1] I resonated with his writing, as this was precisely what I was noticing about girls' acting-out and suicidal behavior. Paradoxically and desperately, it's about hope.

Acting Out

Believe it or not, acting out is a hopeful form of communication. It's reaching out. I certainly understand that it can be disturbing, infuriating, and stressful if you're contending with it, but if times are hard, remember that it's hopeful because it indicates that your daughter remains connected in her own acting-out way; she is not shut down. It's something to work with, which is good news. Behavior is a language we need to decode and understand. When girls do not have words to say what they are thinking and feeling, or if they fear no one will want to hear or listen, or if their speaking voice has not been heard, they will speak through behavior. Indirectly, they enact what they know and want, or how they feel.

If we see acting out as only problem behavior, we miss the point, which may be that girls are reaching out for help. Given the fact that so many girls are shut down and feel prohibited from expressing their thoughts and feelings—especially angry or unpleasant ones—those feelings and thoughts may emerge in some other way. It can be infuriating if your daughter is skipping school, shoplifting, running away, repeatedly missing curfew, refusing to be responsible, out drinking, or fighting with you constantly. This is behavior you simply want to stop, but it is most important for parents, teachers, and clinicians to get to the bottom of it.

The Theory of Masked Depression

In the late 1970s and early 1980s, once it was acknowledged that children and teenagers experienced depression, the term "masked depression" was coined by researchers who discovered that many of these symptoms were covered over, or "masked," by problem behaviors. Standard evaluation procedures (such as checklists and depression inventories) missed this diagnosis altogether. However, when the same children and adolescents were interviewed in person along with their parents, their underlying depression was found.[2] My colleague, psychologist Gil Noam, found a similar dynamic in troubled teenage girls in the 1990s.[3]

I've noticed over the years, too, that sometimes the kids who appear the angriest are the saddest and the ones who appear the saddest are the angriest. The ones who are scaring everyone are scared themselves. Beneath all the trouble is longing and loneliness, trying to communicate and get needs met that they don't otherwise know how to get met.

Lola's story in the next pages tells us how girls aren't always listened to if they are nice, quiet, and sweet. She becomes outspoken and displays an "attitude" in order to be taken seriously. She is both communicating her "icky" feeling (depression) and distracting herself or regulating these feelings by going out to dance, to party and do things young people in their twenties do. Some girls bury themselves in their schoolwork, some cut themselves, and others live on the edge and put themselves in dangerous situations that create tremendous anxiety for their parents. Wild fun, excitement, and the thrill of danger can certainly help girls like Lola feel a lot less "icky."

Lola hasn't sunk into the quicksand of deep depression; she still has get up and go. It's not good that she's putting herself in harm's way and causing her parents unimaginable pain. If we heed girls' signals and can respond sooner rather than later, we help reduce the risk of their becoming severely depressed.

Freedom-Loving Lola

It is a warm, sunny, and sultry late afternoon. Rays of sunshine peek boldly through the leaves of the stately old trees in the yard. Lola, age sixteen, tall, willowy, and lithe, lounges in a large green wooden chair, sunning, in cut-off jean shorts and a white T-shirt, eyes closed, face to the sun, her arms relaxed, outwardly stretched. She's expecting me, she hears my footsteps on the wooden steps, leisurely but alertly opens her bright, twinkling blue-green eyes and looks up at me with a winning smile. Her light brown hair is pulled back into a loose ponytail but isn't quite long enough, and loose strands grace the edges of her beautiful young face. With a gentle movement of her hand, she welcomes me by gesturing to the chair beside her. Her little gesture charms me, and I sit down. Lola is fun to be with. She's bright, quick, and lively, and her sense of humor is marvelous.

Lola tells me she's just finding out, after all this time, that she might have a learning disability, because she reads slowly; she had just been tested, which helped her understand her own learning style and how she learns best. "This testing was actually helpful for once," she says with a sigh.

Lola loves doing things for other people and taking care of other people. Having to say no to people is hard for her, and she feels comfortable expressing anger only to her parents and sister. Lola can turn her "nice quiet sweet little self into a very firm outspoken attitude person that you have to respect and listen to" when she has to make people listen. In school she plays basketball and lacrosse. She loves to work out, and proudly she shows me her arm muscles. She thrives on physical activity, and enjoys working on her parents' big farm.

She loves her parents, gets along well with one brother, terribly with another who has been mean to her since they were kids, and so-so with her sister. She thinks her brother was beyond mean, and beyond picking on her. He used to hit her and yell at her, and she's certain that that affected her, growing up. Her parents did the best they could managing him.

Like many girls, her relationships with family and friends are important to her. Some of her most special friends are "my boys—guys that are of course older." To Lola, that means they range from age twenty-one to twenty-seven. Many of them look out for her, and she knows "which ones to trust and not to trust." I ask her how she knows, and she explains, "From experience or a feeling I get about them. I see them interact with other girls and other guys, and if it's dirty, I know not to trust them. How people treat others is eventually how they will treat you." I like her insight at sixteen, and I love that she trusts her own experience and intuitive feelings. Girls need encouragement and praise for listening to themselves, heeding the intuitive, yet still small voice.

This is not to say it's OK for her to be hanging out with guys so much older, trustworthy or not.

Describing herself, she says, "I'm tall and have short brown hair. I wouldn't say exactly gorgeous. My sister is gorgeous. I love doing things for people. I have the best organizational skills in my whole family. I love to work. I'm very trustworthy and responsible."

She loves the freedom life has to offer, and eagerly awaits turning eighteen, but what she doesn't like about life are society's rigid rules of behavior. She's sick of worrying about what people think. Unwrapping a truffle, she says, "I hate the discipline society puts on people. It's like I can't live a full life. I hate how if I want to do something or have done something, my parents will say, 'You've got to think how that's going to affect us, what people are going to say.' I hate those words—'Got to think what other people are going to think and say.' You can't worry about that. You can't let other people dictate your life in that way."

Lola stopped worrying, she says, because, "It tired me the fuck out."

When she was in ninth grade, Lola was enrolled in a prestigious girls' boarding school thousands of miles from home. She had never experienced such pressure, such stress. She hated it there. She missed her mom and dad, her sister and brothers, even the brother with whom she fought all the time.

She loved the all-girls part about the school because "In a girls' school you can do as much as you want. You get that intellectual learning that in a public school you might not, because the guys will dominate and girls will be intimidated. You don't want to do anything stupid in front of guys. You learn to find your voice and your own reasoning. You're not second in the classroom. You're first. You're respected for your intelligence. You have freedom of voice, and I think all-girls schools are just absolutely wonderful for girls to find their intelligence, have self-assurance. But you see, that's the tricky part—you have to find the right school that will boost your self-esteem, not lower it."

Yes, that is a tricky part. Lola reads slowly and just couldn't keep up, no matter how hard she tried. The school was too big, with lots of people; yet she felt utterly alone. She thought she might be better off in a small school. The pressure mounted. It got worse. It didn't take long before her confidence and self-esteem withered.

"I had about two seconds for lunch, then I had to go to another meeting or to yet another tutoring session. Or another class. They tried everything in their power to set up more tutoring. But they gave me more work. I felt like shit."

She was so stressed out that she lost fifteen pounds. Her stomach shrank so that a mere half a sandwich filled her. Lola loves food and loves to eat, she tells me with a grin, taking a bite of her fourth truffle. It got to the point where she didn't care if she was late for meetings. She felt and looked terrible; she could see it in the mirror. Her jeans that once fit snugly sagged on her, and her legs looked as skinny as rails. Staring in the mirror, she could see that her shape was gone. She was not trying to lose weight. The boys back home don't go for skinny girls. The stress continued, and she felt worse and worse and worse—it was awful.

In the spring, she ran away.

"Where to?" I ask.

"Home," she says. Something about that touched me, and I felt like hugging her. "I took the bus. All that stress—I was feeling so low, losing so much."

It's healthy that Lola knew she was in trouble, was aware that she was losing her confidence and self-esteem. Lola was not thriving, not eating, and she got out the only way she knew how. In her own way, she was taking care of herself.

Lola's parents understood and they did not make her go back to boarding school. Instead, they immediately enrolled her in the public high school to finish the year. She had two summer jobs lined up for the minute school was out.

When she came home after work, though, she couldn't do anything. She didn't have any freedom. She felt closed in, trapped. Lola and her mom, who are very close, started quarrelling. Her mom and dad, understandably, didn't like that her friends were older, that some of the guys were in their late twenties. Her dad's schedule was as hellish as always. Lola thought her mom was overprotective and they were fighting constantly about everything. She hated fighting with her mom, whom she loves more than anything.

After a couple weeks of working the two jobs and having a hard time, Lola thought it was about time for her to have a little vacation. "I just started feeling more trapped and more trapped. I couldn't do anything. I felt so icky so I was like, 'Fuck this.'" She went out one night and didn't come back until the next morning, explaining, "I call it a little trip, but they call it running away. I was coming right back."

Her "taking a little trip and coming right back" phrase captures my fancy, and I think this is a reason I love teenagers. They certainly have a creative way of explaining themselves. But her "little trip," her running away, began a risky and dangerous pattern that would continue all summer. She tells me she was totally irresponsible. Her parents were worried sick, scared, and they feared for her safety.

I've felt a similar fear because when kids I work with and love run away, I'm terrified. I worry about their safety, fill up with anxiety, have no peace, and yearn to go out and find them. Believe me, I've gone out and looked for several kids over the years. I have trouble sleeping because I don't know they are safe and sound. Are they in danger somewhere? It's awful. You're mad at them for putting themselves in harm's way and for the stress they're causing and for the discomfort and helplessness you feel. Yet you also love them and are filled with compassion and care because you know deep down they are hurting and suffering. I always wonder what they are running from and what they are running to, but it's the youngster on the run who needs to begin to answer that. (Some kids, unlike Lola, run from abusive situations and that certainly makes a lot of sense.)

Lola says, "I love my freedom. I worship it, so I just take it. It leads to my running. It's the need for that freedom, the want for that freedom. I'm sixteen going on twenty-five. I want to experience everything and this gets me in so much trouble at this age. It's so hard for me to withstand the discipline, the rules that take me away from it." She loved to go out partying, loved the whole social scene, being with friends, going to clubs all night and "dancing her ass off." She knew her parents were scared of what could happen to her, and she understoods her parents' side. They saw the danger, but she saw the excitement, fun, thrill; she even loved the danger of it. She understood both sides. "I'm very thankful that I have a gift of understanding both sides, the adult side and my side; I have to learn to compromise." She clearly has some perspective, but that doesn't mean she stopped running and partying.

The scheming distracted her from feeling "icky," and was a lot more exciting than feeling misery. This is what happens for a lot of kids.

The wild, exciting danger shifts and regulates feelings, gets adrenaline pumping, changes how she's feeling. Scheming provides a respite from negative thinking, too. Loneliness and pain can be kept at bay if she's running, sneaking, partying, and dancing all night, and sleeping all day. Lola liked figuring out working around the rules if her mom and dad said no. She said she was going one place and spending the night at her friend's, but really they were going to a club to dance all night. Other times, friends would give her places to stay, which wasn't difficult since the people she hung out with were in their twenties. Overnights turned into three days. Her parents began looking for a therapist and a therapeutic adolescent program for her.

I ask a little more about the running and Lola says, "I know in my heart I'm running from something I don't want to face. And that's why I don't think I'm a strong person. If I were a strong person, I would face it. But another part of me loves running because I get to experience new and different things." She sees the various sides and meanings of herself and her experiences, insightfully.

Lola hated that she was fighting with her mom. "It was around the age that conflicts were getting started. I hate conflicts, I hate arguments, I hate fights, I avoid them to the best of my ability." She was also fighting with her brother and wondered if maybe her family might just be better off without her. She took a handful of extra-strength Tylenol. She felt sick from it—nothing else happened. The next day Lola told one of her family friends, a girl her age, that she felt "iffy because I took a lot of Tylenol," but her friend didn't really respond.

Then Lola told her mother, who was extremely worried and immediately took her to the hospital. I ask Lola if she wants to say more about the Tylenol and she explains, "I guess that suicide attempt was maybe a way for my parents to think, 'Oh, she needs help. She's really having a tough time.' Maybe I couldn't find a way to find a moment when I could tell them. So I had to do something. Sometimes I can't articulate my words, so I depend on my actions. My actions for me speak louder than my words."

Lola said she took only a few pills because she didn't want to hurt her family. Also, part of her did not want to die. With a long pause and a pensive look on her face, she tells me, "For those who really, truly want to die, they'll do it. They will find a way; there's no messing around. Other times, it's a half-assed attempt. Which means there's some part of a person that does not want to die."

Her family realized how much she was struggling and how much she needed help. She started seeing a therapist right after that, and was immediately enrolled in a program for a couple weeks. Her dad works less now, and spends more time with her. She's proud that her family "didn't shove it under the rug." It is very important to her.

Lola loves the therapeutic program she is enrolled in and told me, "It has given me more hope. It's really boosted my self-confidence. It's really making me feel the pain and feel the feelings that I need to get out, that I need to talk about. I need to wonder why I'm like this. So it's going to be a rough road. There's going to be many days when I just want to crawl into a little hole and stay there. But they're going to pull me back out."

I ask Lola what gives her hope for the future.

"All the support, all the caring-ness and love of people, the staff at the program, a lot of therapists. They see a kid trying, and they will support that kid one hundred percent. The work I'm doing gives me hope for the future. Sometimes I think it's dragging on and I'm never going to get through it. But you have to push yourself. And it really hurts. It's very painful, but once you go through that little piece you have more hope than you started with."

She worries about keeping both parts of herself—the responsible part of her and the other side, her wild side. She knows she needs to be less impulsive and exercise better judgment, but losing that part of her-self in therapy is something she does not want to do. "That's why I'm scared of doing a lot of the work. Because I'm afraid that the side that I want to keep, that dangerous side, that side of me that loves to have that fun—is going to be diminished. It's like they're trying to steal that side away from me, and put an end to it. So it's a very tricky situation."

Lola says it's tricky to get the help she needs for depression and running away, without then giving up the part of her that loves freedom and fun. The catch-22, as I see it, is that this freedom-loving, running-wild-and-free, dangerous part of her is also the resilient part, where hope, grit, and healthy resistance dwell. This part got her out of the school that might otherwise have stifled her. I would not want her, or any girl, to lose that part. Lola is self-protecting when she runs from the pressure and anxiety that sap self-worth. She's right to be worried. That part of her is not just the part that gets her in trouble, it's also the part that keeps hope alive, the part that all too often gets stolen from women during adolescence. It's the same part of her that is communicating: I need help.

The challenge is keeping that part of her alive and helping her to transform and channel that energy so that it doesn't end up hurting her. Girls like Lola need to value, maintain, and take good care of all the parts of themselves. They need help developing judgment and finding less harmful outlets for experiencing thrill and excitement. Lola says she needs to be encouraged to say what she's thinking, even when it's in anger. She needs to know that the part of her that loves to dance, loves to feel free, the fighting-back part, will not be squashed—"stolen away," as she puts it. Lola herself knows that she needs some taming, but her story brings to mind that wonderful Isadora Duncan line: "You were once wild here. Don't let them tame you."

Despite her dancing and partying, her fleeing and defying the rules, she doesn't like being in conflict with her mother or brother. In fact, that is what led to the suicidal behavior and got her underlying sadness noticed. When girls are running away and making trouble, we overlook their despair and sadness. Girls who try to emulate the tough-girl image and attitude, more prevalent now than ever before, can be very sad underneath. Some kids are just so sad they can't let themselves know or feel it, so they cover it with anger. Because they make so much trouble, we may overlook their pain by simply trying to stop all the trouble they are causing. I was mistaken in thinking that there was going to be a specific therapeutic technique to help stop a young teenage girl from stealing. I needed to understand the meaning of her behavior. Lola's depression was "masked" beneath her running, partying, and wild ways.

Psychologist Gil Noam, in his research, reports that some girls with depression are more likely than others to blame themselves for everything. They worry about other people's expectations about their behavior, thoughts, and feelings, and are concerned about acceptance. Other people's opinions matter greatly to them, rendering them vulnerable to criticism and guilt. They do not blame others for their despair; they blame themselves. Described as "self-blaming," these girls don't show much outward aggression or outward "problem" behaviors. The psychotherapists in Noam's research rate these girls as depressed. Their outward appearance matches what people typically think of when they think of depression. (The girls in Chapter 4 fit into this group).

However, the girls in another group in Noam's research are action-oriented and impulsive. When they feel helpless they direct aggression outward. This group is described as angry-defiant. The therapists in Noam's research did not rate the angry-defiant girls as depressed, but on self-report the girls expressed deep despair and sorrow, sadness and depression. The clinicians in Noam's research rated "self-blaming" girls as sad and depressed, but not the angry-defiant girls. This means that even clinicians can overlook the despair underlying the "behavior problems," and that girls who have been or are diagnosed with oppositional, conduct, attention, eating, and anxiety disorders or PTSD should also be interviewed carefully for depression.

Surly and impulsive behavior such as running away, stealing, and having lots of sex can easily overshadow girls' depression. Or, if there is a co-occurrence of depression with acting out, the depression does not get addressed and gets no help. Girls and their parents may not understand or realize that they are dealing with depression. If they don't know what "it" is, then they can't cope with it or manage it. Before long "it" unfortunately can manage them, as their positive sense of self fades away and negativity creeps in. Soon their identity becomes, "I'm a bad girl, I'm tough and cool, a hell-raiser, a real troublemaker." Isabelle, whom I love dearly, has a story that illuminates how appearing and acting angry, defiant, and tough often communicates deep distress and hides sorrow and despair.

Isabelle: "I Was Ninety-Eight Percent Sad"

Full of life, bright, quick-witted, and beautiful, Isabelle is petite with shiny shoulder-length black hair, huge dark brown eyes, and long eyelashes, and wears black platform boots with high heels, boot-cut faded jeans, a black shirt, and large silver hoop earrings. When she was two days old, Isabelle, who is Hispanic, was adopted by a single working woman from a well-off family. Isabelle's family loves her, but the world around her makes her feel she is at the margin. "I felt different from the time I was a little girl," Isabelle explains. "I'm Hispanic, so my skin color is different, so it made me feel different. I felt different from my family even though they showered me with love and gifts." She explains that ethnicity is important, because it made her feel so different. When she was only about six or seven, kids made fun of her because she was dark and her mom was white. One little girl said to her, "Why don't you jump in a washing machine of bleach so you match your mother?" Isabelle threw a rock at her.

When she was little, she loved riding her bike, skateboarding, and playing with her friends. Cognizant of "girl" stereotypes, she says, "I wasn't as girly. I became more like a tomboy." As a little girl she had "imagination—the best kind you can have." She made a pretend video store in her mom's living room, and she created a bank, and she and her friends "made our own licenses and used our bikes as our cars for the drive through." Playing celebrities was a favorite. "We played celebrities a lot."

Isabelle's family is Jewish, but she tells me, "I always wanted to be Christian. I'd bring home rosaries, and my mom would say 'We're not Christian.' I'd bring home crosses and stuff. She didn't know. I wanted to celebrate Christmas. I think I did everything to provoke my mom. When I was little we would always fight. I would think, 'You're not my real mom,' and every time we got in a fight I would say that—'You're not my real mom.'"

The "concept of adoption" was difficult for her to understand when she was little, so being adopted really bothered her. Isabelle felt neglected by her birth mother, thinking to herself that her birth mother didn't want her. She knew her birth mother was an adult when she had her, that it wasn't a teen pregnancy, but in her mind she wanted to think she was given up because her birth mom was a teenager, so she let herself think that for a long time. "Because I couldn't understand the concept of adoption, I thought that I couldn't trust anyone." Whenever her mom was trying to do things, Isabelle did the opposite and fought with her mom. But she got jealous when her friends hung out with her mom, thinking to herself, "She belongs to me."

Elementary school was hard because she says she had "behavior problems, was too hyper, and was always fooling around." When she was around eight, she was diagnosed with "oppositional defiant disorder" and with ADHD. "I felt I was different so I thought I should act different. I thought there weren't as many expectations, so I can act different. My mom would say 'You're supposed to get good grades,' but I thought, 'I'm different. Why should I get good grades?' I was constantly compared to my cousin, who never got in trouble. 'Why can't you be like her?' We're two different people.

"I thought that I could act bad because I was diagnosed with oppositional defiant disorder and ADHD," she explains to me. "I was one of the first to try smoking. I was nine. I tried to do everything bad, everything my mom said not to do. She was trying to protect me, but I didn't care about anything." Her mother was worried and trying desperately to get the right help for Isabelle.

Finally, being bad would pay off. "People didn't hang with me in grade school," she explains. "But when I got to middle school it was a cool thing to act bad." For Isabelle, heading into her early teen years, pressure mounted: "I was really affected by peer pressure, and changed my image—hip-hop one day, became a skater, wore jeans baggy and cut at the bottom, switched between metal and rap." Simultaneously, middle school pressures affected her already tenuous sense of self. "When middle school hit, I had low self-esteem because I wasn't happy with myself, didn't think I was pretty or anything. I didn't respect myself at all. I slept with different guys. I always wanted to be accepted and it was important to me for people to like me. Even though I wanted to appear violent and tough, I wasn't. I was very insecure. Deep down I wanted people to like me. I was ninety-eight percent sad."

Sexually active at a young age, she explains, "Some girls would feel like a slut. I didn't feel like that. People looked at me like I was cool. I was smoking and having sex. That made you cool—breaking the rules. I was rebellious, and that made me popular. People liked me because of that." Many girls adopt this tough-girl image to achieve popularity among their peers, but if their behavior is extreme, dangerous, risky, and goes on for long, it's not just trying on an image. It's a sign of trouble. Images can hide what's underneath and then cause girls to be misunderstood.

Isabelle started attending a private day school for youth at risk. Until then she had always attended public school. "There was a lot of fighting. I saw bad things." One girl tried to strangle her boyfriend with shoelaces. A kid said "Turn out the lights," and "all you could hear were these choking noises." Isabelle didn't finish the week there. "My mom whisked me out of the school right after that happened. There was a lot of fighting there." She returned to public school, but the private school had really hurt her. "I think it had a bad impression on me and made me act like a tough person. I thought I was untouchable and could kick anyone's ass. Back in public school, I threatened people: 'Leave me alone, or I'll kick your ass.' I got that from the school. That was really bad. It really affected me."

Isabelle and her mom were always fighting, which made her feel horrible. "I would feel so sorry, and would say so, but would do it again. I couldn't understand why she didn't believe me when I said I was sorry, but, then did it again." Usually fighting was about her mom grounding her. "When I didn't get my way, I ran away."

Each time she ran away, her mom called the police. They found her and her mom went and got her. This happened a lot. "I could end up dead the next day and not give a shit. I hated my life. I was really miserable. I was always in trouble 'cause I did bad things. I was always grounded. I always couldn't use the phone." Sometimes Isabelle stashed phones. Her mom took the phone out of her room, "but I'd have another to plug into the socket when she wasn't looking." In the midst of all this external turmoil, Isabelle explains, "I was always sad. I don't ever remember being happy."

Often Isabelle felt sad for no reason at all: "It feels like you're lost, you don't know why you're depressed, and upset, and sad. I don't know what caused it. Most people know why. It was the worst feeling that I didn't know why I was depressed. I would cry and write poems a lot. It felt like I had a bad day. I don't know what happened. It's like my body switched to a sad mood. That's what's so frustrating about it, getting sad for no reason. It really got to me." Once in a while, she talked really fast and loudly. "I would get really excited about the smallest littlest things and wouldn't stop talking and talking and talking, and my mom would be like, 'Calm down.'"

Throughout this time she was going to therapy and she continued to be diagnosed with oppositional defiant disorder and ADHD. Ritalin and other ADHD drugs didn't work; eventually they were discontinued. Her mom was desperately seeking help from the school system. Isabelle lived with her Aunt Melanie, her mom's sister, for a while, but that didn't last long. She entered a new school in a new town. At the new school, she spray-painted in the boys' bathroom, "If you want to have a good time, call Isabelle." She also forged her aunt's signature. "My cousin said she was embarrassed to be my cousin," she says sadly. She ran away from Aunt Melanie's and ended up back home.

She went to a friend's house to a party one night. The parents weren't home, so there was lots of drinking and things got out of hand. Isabelle got really drunk with the rest of the kids. They broke into an abandoned house. Isabelle passed out in the street somewhere near the house. She ended up hospitalized with alcohol poisoning. During the medical hospitalization, she was finally diagnosed with bipolar depression.[4] "I didn't believe I had a bipolar chemical imbalance. I never really understood it till now. I was really lost with it . . . I just didn't believe I had a chemical imbalance."

Isabelle went to a private therapeutic boarding school. She and her boyfriend ran away together but were returned to the school by police. When her boyfriend broke her heart, she gulped down a handful of pills. Her roommate walked in and saw her taking them and then immediately ran and got help.

Isabelle did not want to die; she was devastated over the breakup. It just so happened that her mom was visiting her that weekend. "I knew my mom would save me," she says with a tone of love in her voice that I cherish and remember. Which is, of course, exactly what happened— her mom took her right to the hospital.

A few years later, Isabelle explains her experience of depression to me: "I didn't know why I was depressed. If you're not depressed and you get upset, you know why. But when you have depression, you're upset and you don't know why, it's like a sudden guilt. You feel bad and you have no idea why." Outwardly we saw trouble, but inside she says, "I was ninety-eight percent depressed. I was depressed more than I was manic. I didn't know what it was. I have a good family. I couldn't see it then."

After boarding school she had a very serious boyfriend. "We didn't go anywhere or do anything, it was more about sex. He didn't take me out. The way he was treating me wasn't right. I didn't see it." Her mom did. Taking her mom's advice, she says, "Breaking up with him was the strongest thing I've ever done, but my mom was there for me. She was so mad at how he treated me. It brought me and my mom closer."

Isabelle sees her relationships with guys in a different light now. "I always confused love with sex. I would have sex with guys because I wanted them to like me and to love me. I didn't have a father, and I confused the meaning of love. I wanted a father." She explains, "I realized that I had to work on myself before anyone could love me. I didn't love myself."

Now in a serious and healthy relationship, Isabelle has her hope sustained by her boyfriend, Jalen. "I realized I could be loved. I never realized my boyfriend could love me. I didn't think guys took me seriously. Being with him changed me." She believes having a loving romantic relationship wherein she's taken seriously has helped her tremendously. She believes that's where a big part of her change has come from. She says when she tells people what she did a few years ago they don't believe her. "You?" they say. "Yeah, me," she answers, with a smile and a sparkle in her eye.

We all act out at times in some way or another. If we do not say what we're thinking and feeling, it comes out somehow, often through our actions. Grown-ups need to understand the language of action. Behind the tough-girl facade, Isabelle wanted to belong, find herself, fit in, to feel wanted and loved. Harassed and bullied by her peers since she was a very little girl for skin color, she wants to belong no matter the cost. In middle school, acting out, being tough, and smoking cigarettes and having sex garnered her friends, belonging, and popularity, all of which she had been longing for.

The Language of Acting Out

One doesn't automatically think of a girl who threatens to kick everyone's ass as 98 percent depressed, which just shows how covered depression can be by behavior. On her own, she was miserable; crying by herself and writing poetry, she dearly wanted to be loved and accepted. Her outer appearance—drinking, smoking, and having sex, putting herself in harm's way—did not conform to the popular image of a sad, depressed girl. But she was. People in authority generally would think this girl was an oppositional troublemaker with conduct problems that had to be stopped, rather than a girl who needed understanding, love, and help. Isabelle certainly was oppositional, but she tells me that having been diagnosed with oppositional disorder when she was young served to define her identity, about which she was already confused. She was only a child, only a little girl. Don't grown-ups and doctors know best? She thought "Well, I have oppositional disorder, that's who they say I am. I might as well fulfill the prophecy."

Children and teens are vulnerable to adults' authoritarian descriptions of them. We have to be very careful about labeling developing kids. The same holds true for depression. Girls aren't depression. It's important that they know that they are so much more than that. They are people who are experiencing depression, or symptoms of depression, or an episode of depression. Depression need not and must not define them. All of these labels place a terrible burden on girls.

Where Depression Hides

Recently, researchers have found many girls in the juvenile justice system labeled "delinquent" and "conduct disordered" are actually depressed, yet undiagnosed. Many have undiagnosed post-traumatic stress disorder, too. Both Lola and Isabelle come from families with financial privilege. Girls without that privilege and its advantages are more likely to end up in a state system for child protection, teen jail, adult jail, or some other type of lockdown facility. These girls are more likely to get arrested for minor offenses such as running away, and are quickly labeled "delinquent."

Little Mindy is swift, petite, observant, and very cute with short, straight jet-black hair. She is a little wary about getting to know people, and began feeling depressed when she was about twelve. One night when she was thirteen, she went out with her older sister, who was smoking cigarettes. They went to a party where there was drinking and other drugs, and they went into the woods to keep drinking. Mindy eventually got so drunk that she ended up lying in a parking lot almost unable to move but aware enough to be terrified to go home drunk. Her sister kept yelling at her to get up. A woman heard the commotion and called the police. Mindy somehow crawled her way back into the woods, even more scared. The police found her and took her to the hospital, where she got her stomach pumped. She had a dangerously high level of blood alcohol. "It really, really depressed me because everyone was lecturing me in a way that made me feel bad because I could have died," she says.

Mindy felt guilty and awful because she hadn't intended to drink that much. She did not want to die or hurt herself and did not know that drinking that much could have killed her. So with her already depressed feelings, everything slid downhill. She liked feeling messed up from drinking and doing drugs. When her parents grounded her, like Lola and Isabelle, she ran away. Her school filed a report because she was skipping so much. Before she knew it, the state and the courts were involved with her and her family and she was scared they would put her in a detention center. She was so scared and angry she skipped her court date, which caused more trouble. Her family got her in therapy. They had family meetings and she says it brought them closer together.

It's Hard on Parents

Fights with parents are often over the struggle for independence, not necessarily over separation. Before they can completely manage the responsibility, many girls want to go wherever they want and come home when they want. It's important for parents to start setting limits very early, even when girls are babies, so that they are used to them as adolescence rolls around. (All children need limits; it shows that you care. And once you set limits, follow through from day one.) But separation issues are never far behind. Lola's quarrels with her mom, with whom she was so close, disturbed her. Sometimes it's the closest relationship that becomes the most strained during the teen years. How do you become your own person when you're so close and connected to someone else? Sometimes girls push away and fight so they can deliberately be mad at their moms. The dilemma and struggle is how to stay connected and be independent simultaneously. That may be challenging, and it's often easier to fight and feel disconnected, but fighting is also a way to stay connected. Girls also know that when it comes down to it, their moms are the ones to rescue them. Remember, Isabelle swallowed pills the weekend her mom was visiting: "I knew my mom would save me." She knew her mom loved her and did not want her to die although she was constantly fighting with her.

Lola told her mother she took a bunch of Tylenol the day after she did it. Her mother took immediate action. In many ways, maybe girls are testing—do you still love me? Is the love the same, now that I'm no longer a little girl? Do you love me in the awkwardness of age eleven or twelve, the uncertainty and insecurity of age thirteen, the rebellion and back talk of fourteen? It's hard for a mom, who was once adored and once the center of the world, to be glared and scowled at when she says, "That skirt is too short" or "You have to be home by midnight," "Who are you going out with?" "What will you be doing?"

It feels awful when you're the target of your daughter's anger, but such behavior does say, on some level, that she feels safe to say all these things to you, because she knows you are going to be there for her. That's love, unconditional love, and it's exactly what girls need, especially when they are feeling so insecure in a developing body. It's hard, as a parent, to suddenly take a backseat to friends, who during the teen years are most important. It happens to dads, too.

A friend of mine was mortified and deeply hurt when his daughter, at age fourteen, no longer wanted to have their Friday night dinners, which they had had since she was nine, when he and his wife divorced. He wanted to force her to keep going to dinner every Friday night, but I explained that was likely to just push her away. It wasn't that she didn't love him anymore. She wanted to be with her friends now on Friday nights, which is a very normative thing for teenagers, but he was genuinely hurt, confused, and a little angry.

As we learned in Chapter Two, there's another problem parents face: Young teenagers are still developing the cognitive and emotional capacities to make good choices. Over time, as they grow, their development will improve, but not in time to avoid conflict. Lola didn't like her curfew; she wanted the freedom and independence to do what she wanted, but was not old enough. She wanted to hang out with men much older than she. Her parents were right not to approve; most wouldn't. She didn't realize or didn't care that she could be putting herself in harm's way by doing the things she did. Teens, unless other circumstances have taught them otherwise, think they're pretty invincible, and may not have developed their foresight and judgment. Their cause-and-effect thinking has not completely developed, and they are more ruled by emotion and impulse than adults, because their brains are still developing. Their bodies often reach full development before their emotions and thinking do.

Lola needs structure, needs to know how to manage impulses and delay gratification, needs something to look forward to that she really loves. She searches for balance, explaining, "There's always, you know, a catch-22. You can always have too much of something where it leads to something bad. You can always be so good that you lose the fun out of life. Or it can be so bad that it can get you into trouble. I want balance; I want a little structure. I want to be able to think things through. Not just make snap judgments. Because I know those snap judgments are going to get me in trouble. So I want the risk, but I want to be able to take the risk with some sort of sense. I don't want to lose my judgment so quickly that I end up in a situation I can't handle." Succeeding at school would help build her positive sense of self, so her parents enrolled her in a small private girls' school, which she absolutely loves.

The stormy years that Lola and Isabelle experienced put their parents through hell. It is really hard to keep in mind that your acting-out teenager is really a good kid, trying to express strong feelings. It's almost impossible to cope with the sudden changes, their fury and anger toward you, and their outrageous behavior. But remember that daughters lash out at the people they trust the most, and those are generally the people they love the most.

The Hope in Rebellion

I love the story I heard when I was consulting at a school: The girls' dorm had a mutiny. They barricaded the doors and wouldn't let the staff in. The founder, my friend and colleague, was delighted, exclaiming, "Hooray, the girls are acting out!" He knew that they were communicating and speaking in a way that we, the adults, would listen to. They were trying to say something—they needed something they weren't getting, they were struggling with something. Sometimes girls know what that something is, other times they don't. Acting out is a form of communication we can't help but notice.

If your daughter is acting out, you might need support. You, too, have to find coping strategies for yourself, and someone to talk to, which may mean therapy, a friend, or another mother or father who has had a similar experience. I think one of the most helpful things for parents is parent support groups.

Parents who have been through this tell me their own therapy helps tremendously. Important for parents, too, is to not become isolated: Talk with a friend, a neighbor, a minister or rabbi you trust so you don't end up feeling disconnected. Of course spouses should talk with each other. The important thing is to stay aligned, not split, when it comes to making decisions and setting limits with your daughter. If she is acting out it can end up creating divisiveness. If you disagree, work it out and then send a united message to your daughter, whether you are married, separated, or divorced.

7. THE SPIRAL BEGINS

Like a predator, disconnection and negativity infiltrate a girl's mind, body, and soul, gradually pulling her down. "It feels like you're in a deep dark pit and you're being stifled," one teenager tells me, and Ali says, "It really sucks because you want to be happy, but you're depressed and it's hard to get through those times. You feel like you're worthless and you can't do anything, and you're fat, and it's really hard." Another says, "Sometimes, when you're depressed, you can feel really disconnected from your real feelings."

And fifteen-year-old Kristy explains, "Depression isn't something you can name. It's all these little things, but you can't say what it is. Like when you're touchier about something. When your parents say, 'Do this now,' and you say, 'No!' When someone tells you something that might imply something bad about you, and you immediately take it the wrong way. Those little tiny things weigh down on you. That stuff is depression. It's what makes you sit there. You don't have that vitality in you. It's that extra weight you can't define that is pulling you down."

A girl spiraling into depression may start feeling lethargic, misunderstood, weighted down, alienated, and wounded. Happiness begins to elude her; she starts feeling like she has been losing too long. She doesn't know what is "wrong" with her, she doesn't feel "normal," and that uncertainty and confusion only serve to nurture rather than obliterate her fears.

The slightest hurtful comment or unkind glance—things she usually took in stride—can now propel her into tears. At the corner store, where they usually let Whitney flip through the magazines before buying one, a new man working there yells at her for doing so. She bursts into tears. She explains that the other guys always let her look before she buys, and he yells at her some more. The words, "Why are you being so mean to me?" escape her lips and then she blurts out, "Jerk," and runs out, taken aback by what she said. "Nice girls don't talk back," and she used to think of herself as a nice girl. She wonders, "What's happening to me?" Her mom gives her one cross word or look, and she storms off to her room in a fury, slamming the door, collapsing on her bed.

She's getting sucked into a negative vortex, loathing all that she is or isn't, feeling worthless, alone, dejected, and useless. She knows people care, but it feels like they don't. She berates herself for feeling so bad, for not being able to snap out of it. Nobody seems to understand, no one gets it—not at home, not at school. Her friends and family love and care, but everybody tells her that everyone feels down sometimes, everyone feels this way: "You're a teenager, it'll be fine in a week."; "Teens are up and down, they have mood swings."; "Don't worry, these years are rough."; "Hey, everyone gets bummed out. Chill, you'll be fine."; "Everybody feels that way. It's no big deal or anything."

Elizabeth: The Girl Who Knows Herself

Wearing jeans and a bright white sweatshirt and sneakers, Elizabeth is smart, tentative, shy, quiet—a pensive girl. She has long brown hair, and large brown eyes nestled in a beautiful round face. Underneath the surface, something in her eyes gives me pause, and I wonder if inside is a lively, bubbling girl trying to dance back to life.

Elizabeth is fourteen and lives with her parents, sister, and brother in the suburbs; both parents are working professionals. She has a big, warm extended family and was very close to her grandmother, who died a couple years ago. She loves her parents but wants to be her own person. Her family is what is most important to her—her mom, dad, sister, brother, and pets. "They're my main base, my foundation. They've shaped who I am and who I'm going to be. And unlike a friend or a boyfriend, they're always going to be there for you."

She loved school, and doing well was a source of joy until she was unable to concentrate. She likes being with people she cares about and loves what she calls that "free feeling of being outside, being calm." She enjoys being funny, playful, and having fun. When asked what gives her hope, she tells me, "Seeing my cousin. She dealt with the same thing I have and she's gone on. She has a husband, they have kids, and a job she really likes. And they're happy."

"For you, what would be important to have a happy life?"

"I don't know, just to be with people that care about me. Don't get too serious. Liven up a little, have some fun while you can."

"Do you feel like you're very serious sometimes?"

"Yeah. I'm wicked too serious."

I smile and tell her, "Me, too; I tell myself that sometimes too."

When I asked her to describe herself, she replies, "I don't know, I'm pretty shy and quiet, but once I get to know people better I usually open up more. Around really good friends and family I'm talkative."

"What helps you talk?"

"If I can relate to the person and they're a good person." A good person is someone she can really talk with, not someone who deliberately hurts others by saying or doing mean things. "If it's a group of people I don't really know, or if I'm meeting someone somebody else knows that I don't know" then she feels particularly shy.

"Is there anything you worry the most about in a situation like that?"

"Just making a good impression."

Making Good Impressions

Worrying about making a good impression began when she was eleven or twelve, as it does for many girls, and may have been her first step toward depression. "When I was younger, I just said and did whatever. I didn't really have to worry about making an impression. But as you get older you start to notice other people and what they think about you. You're growing up, and you have to be able to show that you were brought up right and you have respect for people. With people I don't really know, I'll always think about something before I say or do it. I don't know; I'm just really cautious."

I ask if there is something she is most cautious about. She's especially worried around kids her age right now, since friends are so important and "sort of strangers. With somebody like the real popular girl at school, I'll be cautious because I don't want her to think I'm weird. I have to watch myself, and what I do. I want to be liked by her, obviously. So I won't talk that much. I'll talk a little, but I wouldn't fully state my opinion on everything she brings up. I think over what I should say: 'Should I say that? No, that's stupid.'"

If something or someone bothers or upsets her, or if she feels angry, she says, "I really don't want to hurt anybody's feelings or be rude, so if they did something, I'd just kind of keep it inside and I wouldn't really say that it bothered me." But now she's learning: "But keeping it all inside, eventually it's going to come out."

A teenage girl's descent into depression often starts with this worrying about what people think. The constant nag of self-censoring, of keeping certain thoughts and feelings inside, shutting down, burying away, hiding, repressing, dissociating parts of herself, thinking about every move, and every word and the repercussions is draining. Girls police themselves and are policed by other teens. The censoring drains vital life energy and simultaneously submerges the self.

Elizabeth worries, too, about her recent behavior in front of adults. "A few days ago I was in a meeting with a lot of people. It was a family meeting, and there were about five doctors, and I was really upset and angry. So I worried they would think I was wild or something."

"What were you doing?"

"I was crying a little and my voice got louder—yelling, almost. I was fresh towards my parents or sarcastic. But I think every teenager has some of that in them."

"Do you want to say more about that?"

"You're growing up, and you're not always going to believe everything your parents do or say is right. You have to have your own ideas and morals. It's important to be your own person."

"What's it like trying to become your own person?"

"It's a struggle, because you're always comparing yourself to other people and seeing how other people interact. You have to observe everything and see what you believe in and what you want to turn out to be."

Elizabeth pauses for a long moment and takes a big sip of her juice, then says, "And, inside you, when you're a teenager, you're really unsure of yourself, so it's a question—'Should I do this? Should I do that?'"

Elizabeth explains about girls her age. "Everybody is really unsure of themselves and is really self-conscious about everything, and sometimes if they're jealous they'll say things." She thinks people take punches more seriously than words, but believes the pain of words is minimized, too easily dismissed. "A punch is going to hurt for a little bit of time but you'll always remember what someone says. It will be with you longer."

Elizabeth thinks it's important for people to respect one another, treat one another with dignity, be nice. Nice to her means not talking behind someone's back, not saying something to deliberately hurt someone, not being hurtful or mean on purpose to someone's face. When Elizabeth sees someone being cruel to someone else, she hopes she doesn't grow up to be like that.

Like so many girls, she worries about things in the world, and hypocrisy bothers her. "All the hurtful things people do, how there's war, and killings," troubles her. She tells me, "Grown-ups always tell us kids to talk things out instead of resorting to violence, but if they're not doing that themselves then obviously we're going to see that. And we're not going to do it. They should stand up to their morals and do what they said. They want us to do it."

I ask why she thinks this happens.

"I guess it's easier to shoot each other up and not really get to the bottom of the problem, but that's really not going to solve anything. It kills innocent people and ruins families." She looks at me like there is no logic to it, her eyes growing large.

All human beings need friends. "You need friends, friends are so important." As a teenager, she says having friends is more important and more necessary than ever before. She's learning that some friends will come and go, but real friends and family who truly care are important, because they are around during the hard times. Having real friends when you're a teen is important because "it just teaches you how to build relationships that you're going to need throughout your life. You can just let down your guard and be yourself around them. You don't have to worry about 'What if I say this, what if I say that,' making impressions, because you know them so well."

She worries so much about those impressions, explaining, "I don't really have good self-esteem." I ask what "self-esteem" means to her.

"How you feel about yourself. How you compare yourself to other people. How you feel about yourself physically and emotionally."

"Where do you think your low self-esteem came from?"

"I think it's a really big issue about self/body image for girls because of what's portrayed as being beautiful in the media. It's hard to be different, because everybody has this set of things: what's normal, what's not." Other kids can be hurtful she says. "When I was little, the kids used to make fun of my hair because it was different. I grew up not liking my hair because it was different."

After comparing herself to models and celebrities, she started eating less and less. I ask why, and she quickly replies, "Because being thin is promoted so much. I would only eat dinner, because that's the most family meal and I didn't want them to get suspicious. And I didn't really have time for breakfast because you can wake up and get ready and everything. Lunch was at school, so nobody would know if I was eating or not. And I could just throw away the lunch they packed me, or not buy lunch, and nobody would know."

Even having dinner at home, she could cut up the food and just move it around on her plate, eat just a few bites, and then exercise it away afterward. "I was just obsessed with not eating, eating less and exercising. My life revolved around that, and I'd constantly be worrying, 'What if I eat this, what's going to happen? Am I going to gain weight?' I was always worrying about it, and I just wasn't getting enough food to grow and function properly."

Disordered Eating and Depression

Food and eating are big parts of the spiral, in different ways for girls. Not eating, or disordered eating, is usually an aspect of depression. On top of that, depression creates fertile ground for the development of eating disorders—anorexia, bulimia, and overeating. Low self-esteem is a risk factor for both depression and eating disorders. Traditionally, with depression, many girls don't eat because they don't feel like it; it doesn't have anything to do with dieting. They're in a zone and don't have the energy or wherewithal to put food into their own mouths. Food becomes irrelevant. "I hadn't been eating much at all," explains Nicole. "I'd lost a lot of weight really fast. I'd lost over twenty pounds in four weeks. I just wasn't eating. Honestly, I was not hungry. I had an extreme case of loss of appetite from depression. I didn't think I was fat. I wasn't trying to lose weight. I didn't care. The thought of food disgusted me. I did not want to touch it."

If you've been griefstricken or traumatized and unable to eat, it's a similar feeling. I know for some it's hard to imagine being so despairing you can't eat. The trouble is that when you're depressed and eating is irrelevant, this can lead to physical malnourishment and low blood sugar, and that will make you feel even worse.

Depression can stand alone, or it can coexist with an eating disorder. Unfortunately, sometimes the focus becomes too much on food and not enough on the underlying thoughts and feelings that are fueling the depression.

Not eating and compulsively exercising, Elizabeth is headed toward anorexia in this spiral. Both anorexia and bulimia are connected to dissatisfaction with one's body, to low self-esteem and depression. Dissatisfaction with the body leads to a lowered self-worth and depression. Sometimes girls with depression and eating disorders have too much external locus of control, feel powerless and helpless in the world, and are convinced they have no control over external circumstances. How this intermingles with self-blame is complicated.

I have yet to meet a girl with anorexia or bulimia who did not also have mild (or major) symptoms of underlying depression, but because we focus so much on what is visible, it may not get addressed. Girls with depression and an eating disorder may try hard to seem OK, appearing chipper and bright especially in front of their peers. But inside they are miserable. Their misery may be seen at home, which Olivia explains in the next chapter.

Girls who are susceptible to cultural mandates about having to be superwomen, having and doing it all, are more at risk of developing an eating disorder than girls who understand what is realistic and what isn't, according to Catherine Steiner-Adair's research.[1] Here's another reason to start those consciousness-raising discussions with daughters early on. Talk about what you see in the ads and pictures and the world around you and what it means and what it doesn't mean (we'll explore how to do this in Chapter 10).

Food becomes a symbol, but it's about deeper feelings. It's not that girls with anorexia are not hungry; they aren't allowing themselves to eat. In the English language "anorexia" means prolonged loss of appetite. That's a misnomer because anorexic girls don't lose their appetites—they don't want to eat or can't, which can then lead to appetite loss. Some girls think they don't deserve to eat. "Anorexia nervosa" is the official name of the disorder we now call anorexia. Girls suffering from it will often exercise a lot and in secret. Far too many use laxatives and other diuretics. They get dehydrated, too, and need to drink, as well as eat. Watch out for loose, baggy clothes hiding the disappearing body.

As we learned in Chapter 2, depriving herself of food or nutrients makes a girl feel worse, and now her energy is zapped from depression. When girls are at the point where they won't eat, they need to drink protein meal drinks nutritionally comparable to a meal. This is necessary until they are more stable and can resume eating food. Then they should begin with their favorites. When girls with anorexia nervosa begin to gain weight again, don't tell them they look good because for many of them that means they look fat, which could trigger a relapse. When depression coincides with an eating disorder, a girl needs to be under the care of a doctor who specializes in eating disorders, needs to see a therapist, and needs to have a consultation with a nutritionist. Her family should also be involved in the treatment, which could mean family therapy.

Other depressed girls overeat. They fill the emptiness and loneliness with food, which becomes a trusted friend and companion. They slowly add pounds and literally weigh themselves down. They become filled with guilt and self-loathing afterward. The cycle starts again when they feel remorse for eating too much in response to their heartache; they know they are self-destructing by eating too much, then they get angry for doing it, and the cycle continues.

Others will fill up with bursts of binge eating, which can manage anxiety, sad or angry feelings, disappointments, or losses. They eat lots of chips, or ice cream, whatever the favorite may be. If they are dieting they are really vulnerable to bingeing since they have been withholding from themselves and feel deprived. They crave something fun, like buttered popcorn or a hot fudge sundae.

Others might do the same, but after they binge, they throw up, starting the vicious cycle of bulimia. They get no nutrition because very little food stays in their system, but they maintain their weight. Even so, in our culture we praise weight loss in girls, so if it is noticed, it might not be cause for worry, but it is. Girls are always on diets and losing weight. It's been normalized as part of gender and adolescence. Society quietly initiates and condones such self-harm, praising and encouraging it.

Bulimia is secretive and hard to detect. Does she get up and go to the bathroom soon after a meal? Are there marks on her knuckles? Is the enamel fading from her teeth? Watch and observe girls' eating habits. Talk about the messages they get, starting when they are young. Eat with them. Is the food actually going into their bodies and staying there, or simply being cut and shuffled around on the plate? I have a letter from a young woman contending with depression and bulimia. She wrote, "It's all about suppressed feelings—and loving myself more."

Time Goes (Spiraling) On

Amidst not eating, Elizabeth's beloved grandmother died. It was the first time anyone close to her died, and the loss was painful. Before the death, she considered herself "a carefree kid, not really thinking about death, like that's the end, it's the final thing."

Death changes things. Her grandmother was a professor who took a strong interest in what Elizabeth was reading and what she was working on in school. "When I got into advanced classes for writing, she was really proud of me," she explains with pride, fondness, and sadness in her eyes.

She was surprised how different holidays felt. She didn't realize her own birthday would be a little sad without her grandmother, or that the day it was her grandma's birthday would make her lonely. Elizabeth missed her—not only the big things, but the little ones, too, like how she used to call her "Grandma" and tell her what she was doing in writing class.

Then, over a year later, although she had friends and a boyfriend and was in the theater club, Elizabeth felt much worse.

Before her grandmother died, she would have these dismal times but explains, "I'd usually bounce back and it didn't last for a long time and the feelings weren't as deep, as intense." Soon she began "not being able to see things positively."

By now, her lack of eating and chronic exercising had evolved into anorexia, but only Elizabeth knew that. "People didn't really notice. I was more worried myself. I was noticing there's something wrong. When I stopped getting my period, that was a really big concern." With her own health waning, she realized she had to help herself and thus had to tell her mother. This indicated to me how much she wanted help and did not want to slide deeper into pain and despair.

She told her mom she was worried, and her mom said they would find somebody for her to talk to about it. She went to a therapist specializing in body image and eating problems.

She learned that there was "not one straight definition of beauty," that "bodies come in all different sizes," and "sometimes when girls are high achieving and they get good grades and everything is planned out for them, they have to find a way of controlling. They get control of one thing, like their eating."

Most importantly she learned to "concentrate more on who you are, not physically, but how you feel inside. You have feelings for other people, and you care about other people, you're a good person, you're smart. If people start complimenting you on stuff like that, it helps. You realize, 'I am smart.'" *This is a reminder of why it is so important to praise girls for their strengths and talents and not only for their looks.*

The Lonely Breakup Summer

About six months passed, then around the bend came the lonely summer.

"That summer was hard for me because both my parents started new jobs and they'd be away from home a lot more. So I was by myself at home just kind of hanging around, and I was back from camp and I didn't have anything to do. I was going out with this guy, Mark. We had been going out for a really long time, and we started getting in fights and arguing about anything. I was telling him how I felt and he would try to protect me but he wouldn't know how. He didn't know what to say. And when we finally broke up, when he broke up with me, that made everything worse," Elizabeth tells me.

She was heartbroken. Mark was her first major boyfriend, so this was her first major breakup. Elizabeth was sad, and she was also angry. She was angry at being dumped and to top it off, she was furious with herself. I asked her what she was most angry about. "After we broke up I was still feeling like I really liked him and he really didn't like me at all." Since they shared friends she found herself, "growing apart from my friends. Not being that close to them anymore, not being able to talk to them, have fun with them, and feeling so alone."

I asked if she wanted to say more.

"I was lonely because my good friend that I called was away at camp for the whole summer and I had nobody to talk to about it."

"How do you think that would have made things different or helped?"

"If I had somebody to talk to about it and joke around about it, some things wouldn't seem as harsh and as intense as they really were. Everything blew out of proportion." She wished she could have talked to her best friend about "my boyfriend and my family, how I was lonely and stuff . . . I'd have somebody to spend my time with, so I wouldn't feel lonely." She cried over the breakup and her loneliness.

Loneliness often is at the heart of girls' pain. Elizabeth is smart and knows that if she had someone to talk with, to help her keep perspective, to look at some of it with humor, it would have helped her, but her solitude pulled her further into the spiral. On top of a major breakup, being alone and isolated spelled big trouble.

One day, toward the end of the lonely summer, Elizabeth was reading a magazine. Suddenly she discovered what was troubling her, what was wrong with her, why she didn't feel like she usually did.

"I had read an article about depression. I saw this whole checklist and I had every symptom on there and I took it to my mom and I said look, look. She used to be a social worker, so she really would have noticed if something was wrong, so I thought, well, I probably don't have this problem then."

Her mom thought she was just really upset over the end of her relationship, thought it was due to teen mood swings and a really bad breakup. She told her to hang in there, everyone eventually felt better after breakups, it just takes time.

Things started to look up a bit. "And I was talking to this therapist and I really liked her and I felt that I could tell her stuff and she was really understanding. I started to feel some hope again."

Spiraling Down

In September when school resumed, things got worse. "After I went back to school, things started getting tough again and I was just kind of hanging in there, but, after a while I started to really lose that hope. This fall I felt the most depressed I've ever felt. I was having such a hard time I couldn't even get out of bed. Anything would bring tears to my eyes. Getting out of bed was too much for me."

She was feeling terrible. "I could have been depressed for a long time before that. It started around age eleven or twelve. But this fall was when things were the worst for me. I had a hard time concentrating, sleeping; everything was out of balance. I was sinking lower and lower. If somebody looked at me wrong or didn't say hi to me, I assumed they hated me. I was being really critical about myself. Everything seemed so overwhelming. School was this huge thing I was never going to be able to do, and it was building up and I didn't know what to do with it, how I was going to go on and do stuff day to day."

"Was there a hardest part, at school?"

"I don't know, I felt I had nobody to relate to, really. And I was having so much trouble concentrating, and feeling jittery or nervous all the time."

She felt alone and says, "I had a really bad day at school, nobody was really listening to me."

"Can you say more?" I ask.

"I was talking to people about my feelings. The kids and a couple teachers said, like, 'Yeah, everybody feels that way. It's no big deal or anything.' And it made me more mad." The seriousness of her feelings was being dismissed.

That afternoon when she got home from school she was "feeling so horrible" that she went into the bathroom and took more than twelve Tylenol tablets. Her younger brother was outside in the backyard playing with some neighborhood kids. She began to feel light-headed and dizzy. She called her good friend, Emily, and told her what she just did, and Emily said, "I'm coming right over." Elizabeth gasped once she "said it out loud" and realized she "had actually done it and I wanted to die, so I took more." Her misery and panic were so overpowering, she began scratching at her own wrist.

Emily arrived and in such a rush that it caught the attention of her brother, who followed her upstairs, wanting to know what was going on. They told him to just go back outside, but he persisted. Emily said, "Why did you do this? I care about you. How many pills did you take?" as she called the poison control center. They said to go to the ER right away.

At that moment, the girls heard Elizabeth's dad getting home from work. "Emily dragged me downstairs to tell my dad and I was fighting. I didn't want him to know. I was afraid he'd be so mad and angry with me. When we finally got downstairs he *was* mad. 'Why did you do that? Tell me why.'" He called her mom, who met them at the emergency room.

I remember that she said she wanted to die, and I asked gently if she could tell me why.

"I just hated myself so much for some reason and I felt it was never going to get better."

"If you could put your suicide attempt into words, what were you trying to say?"

Elizabeth looks at me for a long time. She thinks and looks thoughtful, then explains: "It was my cry for help. I'd been talking to my mom about how I wasn't feeling normal. I would get so down and I would dip so low. I'd be so sad and I'd just want to die. I couldn't figure out what was wrong with me. I didn't know and I kept talking to her. She was really sure it was just how teenagers have a lot of mood swings, but I said, no, this really feels worse than that. And she said, 'Well, we'll just see.' You know, 'Hang in there.' I was saying, 'This is how bad it is, I really need help.' I just felt like nobody could hear me and how much pain I was really going through."

Reaching Out

Taking the Tylenol was the only way she could make her family, peers, and school recognize that her despair had spiraled beyond teen angst. She called her friend immediately after taking the Tylenol, a signal that she wanted help. Though she wanted to do away with her depression, self-hatred, and misery, she didn't completely want to do away with herself. Otherwise, she would not have called her good friend.

Although suicidal behavior is frightening and dangerous, what is important to know is that Elizabeth did not hit the lowest depths of depression. That happens when girls become completely withdrawn, shut down, and close themselves off to relationships and help. She is actively reaching out; she wants to be with people. She's trying to tell everyone she's in trouble. She's not isolating herself; she knows something is not right with her. Trusting her own feelings is a brave act for a girl who is struggling with doubt about everything she is experiencing. In our conversations, Elizabeth may use the phrase, "I don't know" but every time she responds, "I don't know" she does, in fact, know.

Despite what the other kids say, despite the fact that her mom thinks it was due to the breakup, to normal adolescence, and must have felt reassured because she was seeing a therapist, Elizabeth does know. She takes herself seriously and gets help, the only way she can. It's actually her love of life and not disdain for it that propels her to act. She wants to be out of misery. Knowing she needs help, she actively seeks it.

When people are too depressed, they are often incapable of suicidal behavior. People can be more at risk of suicidal behavior when depression has "lifted." Elizabeth had not hit the low point where she was too depressed to act.

The lesson we learn from Elizabeth is that none of the issues with which adolescent girls contend can be easily dismissed as "normal," especially since we just don't know what they will lead to. "Normal" is hard to define in the first place. In Elizabeth's case, for example, the sorrow and anger she felt over her own lack of self-worth, her grandmother's death, the breakup, losing friends, and being misunderstood at home and school, by family and friends, led to her suicidal behavior. Able to tell people that she was feeling bad, but unable to directly express her anger, she acted out her feelings of frustration and anger instead, and those actions became her form of communication. In traditional psychological interpretations, one might describe this merely as anger turned inward. However, Elizabeth's wanting her parents and everyone to understand the pain she is in shows that hurting herself is also an external, outward plea for love. Embedded in her act of self-harm lies her hope that her mother will connect with her and that others will hear her.

There is still a lot of cultural denial about teens' angst being anything more than angst. As Noelle said in Chapter One, we're conditioned to think of adolescence as a tumultuous time. When we normalize teens' pain, even the little things, we play into denial. For years doctors and researchers didn't think teens got depressed. They used to think it was teen angst. The residue of that thinking remains, but there are other reasons for our denial: We're taught to look for adult symptoms, and there is a huge cultural stigma. In addition, the fact that teen depression has many manifestations can be very confusing. Parents are busy and overworked. If doctors and clinicians can miss it, how can parents be expected to know?

You need to know what to look out for and when to seek professional help. This book is not meant to help you diagnose a child—that is up to a professional. But teenage friendship and romances create very real heartache; don't ever forget that if things are bad with her friends, and a boyfriend, there is likely to be trouble.

Even though depression is reported to be as dangerous as high blood pressure or diabetes, depression carries a stigma. Most people even miss the signals of negative thinking, the pessimism, and the bodily complaints aspects. Some think that depressed girls are being weak and vulnerable, and adults and other kids resort to the "Pull yourself up by your bootstraps" thinking. Then if the girl can't do that she feels even worse about herself.

What Parents Tell Me

A mom explains the stigma she feels: "That's my child. It's a reflection on me. I'm supposed to have a perfect child, and everyone wants a perfect child. So it's hard to see and acknowledge and accept because as parents we always think it's our fault."

"Parents live vicariously through their children," another parent explained to me. "We want to feel good through our children. And sometimes, it's too emotionally hard to handle. We live by label and we don't want the label 'my child is depressed.'" As a parent, you don't want the label."

With labels come shame, blame, and guilt, which no one wants. Those feelings can feed the denial, because if "it" doesn't exist, you don't feel you have to blame yourself. That will just create more distance from your daughter. Tell yourself you are taking responsibility for helping your daughter and yourself, but let go of blaming yourself and the guilt that comes with it. Parents need to know that it's not about blame; no girl I talked with blamed her parents. Sure, they may have been mad at them for something or other, but did not make any such attribution. They feared telling their parents, or hid it from them for the very reason that they knew their parents would blame themselves and be upset.

"As parents, we don't want to see the signals," another tells me. "We don't know our child is depressed. All we know is that our child is unhappy. Then she puts herself at risk, which signals that she is more than unhappy, but we, as parents, don't want to see it."

"We feel shame," says another.

"We panic, we don't want to really acknowledge that our child is unhappy, we don't want to think something is wrong with our kid. The hardest part was to acknowledge it and then deal with it," says another.

"You have to get over the fact that I have a child that has a problem," a mom explained to me. "Acceptance is hard."

"Everyone wants a perfect child."

And one mom reminds others of what we all know: "Most important is to be a parent, not a friend." Another says, "Follow through, stay consistent, and don't set limits you don't keep, or can't follow through on; start talking to them when they are young." And another explains, "Parents need correct information."

Most of all, parents' message to other parents is: "Don't give up, have persistence; with persistence comes hope."

I recently attended a reception in Boston. I walked to the parking lot with a few people, several of whom were parents. Two people turned out to be dads of teenage daughters. We talked, as people do, about the work we did in the world, and when I told them what I did, one said to me that his teenage daughter had just been diagnosed with depression following suicidal behavior. The first thing he thought was "Oh my God, what did we do wrong?"

He said he and his wife felt awful, and he explained that they had to get past that. For his daughter, depression and struggle had a lot to do with her feelings that people weren't listening. I tell him lots of the girls

I've talked with say that. He explains that as a family they've learned to do things differently. For instance, at dinner when she's talking, everyone is quiet and listens. It's her time. Before, with three kids, two adults, and a dog, everyone would talk at once.

What Happened After Elizabeth's Suicidal Behavior?

She was angry with herself for putting her family through so much pain but she has a new therapist who is helping tremendously, and her family is going to therapy too. She wants to go to an ongoing group with other teens. Elizabeth, like many girls, thinks there should be groups in schools, and she says it's not fair that schools don't have enough money. Now she feels it's important to tell people if she's angry or upset or if they hurt her, or if something they did bothers her. "I think most important is not being afraid to tell them when something they do bothers me or upsets me. It's really important to tell somebody because then they have the opportunity to change it. If you don't tell them, they're going to keep doing it; it's going to make you angrier and angrier. You have to realize that actually what you say is not going to hurt them; it's going to be helpful for you both, really. You can't always worry about other people as much."

She thinks all parents need to "slow down a little, really, enjoy your kids and listen to them. You don't always need a solution. Sometimes my dad, when I tell him something, he'll always just come out with solutions right away without really listening. I don't really want solutions. I just want someone to be able to talk to and be able to listen to me."

For Elizabeth, being listened to "means that that person really does care about what you're feeling and saying, that they really want to be able to help you and understand you better."

When I ask what she wants to do when she grows up, she tells me, "I've had experience with depression—a counselor or a psychologist. There's something about helping other people that just helps myself."

"What do you think it is?"

"Knowing you can help somebody out and make their life better in some way. It's gives you a good feeling all around you." The positive transformation that can be born out of her struggle is already becoming apparent.

"Is there anything that you think is important to know about you, your life, and your story, that I haven't asked about?"

"This is an illness that could happen to anybody—any background, any age, any time and place. But there's always the power to get better."

When the spiral gets bad, sometimes girls bounce back, and do something so their parents will hear them.

Sometimes though, they start disappearing.

8. OLIVIA: THE DISAPPEARING GIRL

"My mission was to shrink, to implode, almost. I subconsciously wanted to be noticed, but I really didn't, at the same time. It was a big conflict."

—Olivia, age 14

Most of us are familiar with the old adage: Let sleeping dogs lie. Well, that may be true for dogs and cats, and it may sound tempting regarding teenagers, but it's not a good idea.

When teenage girls begin disappearing, whether emotionally, cognitively, behaviorally, or spiritually—it's a problem. The disappearance may not be apparent at first, but over time you may begin seeing less and less of your daughter. In the face of depression, some girls contract more than they explode.

Melissa, now in her early twenties, tells me the story of a school vacation week when she was sixteen. She stayed in bed the whole week, sleeping most of the time, and she didn't get up. She couldn't. She didn't know she was suffering with depression and neither did her mom and dad. They just thought she was being a teenager. In fact, she says, it was a big relief for them. She was quiet, she wasn't arguing, she wasn't aggravating anybody, she wasn't griping, she wasn't making any trouble or fighting with them. Everything was peaceful in the house. She says she knows her mom must have been thinking, "Thank God she isn't making any trouble. Thank God she's quiet and not fighting with me." Melissa didn't realize she was contending with depression until she got to college.

We have schooled girls in how to be happy and how to hide what they are really thinking and feeling. But deep disconnection and unhappiness are the result of these very lessons. To remain accepted by their peers or friends, girls have to put on a chipper face, at school—they don't want to lose friends, have trouble making any, or be made fun of. "It's hard because sometimes friends can't put up with people who have depression. You can't be around someone who's depressed all the time. I don't even like being around myself when I'm depressed. It's an awful feeling; your friends try to cheer you up, but they can't because you're tapped into this depression kind of thing," explains fourteen-year-old Ali. If she's trying to hold it together at school, home becomes the only place she dares allow her miserable feelings to show.

Is your daughter home a lot? It may seem puzzling—though not as puzzling as when she's drinking, drugging, or engaging in lots of sexual activity—but thank goodness, she is pretty quiet and isn't making any trouble. She pulls back from herself and before long, you begin to see the signs in her behavior, emotions, and daily routines. You notice what she says and does, and also what she doesn't say and do. Feeling misunderstood, she begins to withdraw from herself, friends, family, school, and before long, the world.

Isolation is the worst thing for a depressed youngster, and that's what often happens when mild depression, unheeded, spirals into severe depression. Olivia, whom you are about to meet, told me, "I literally just went straight downhill. I wouldn't move. I wouldn't get out of bed. I wouldn't talk to anybody. I think that's a huge warning sign."

The Disappearing Girl

At fourteen, Olivia is intelligent and lively, talkative and articulate, with straight chestnut-brown hair just below her shoulders; large doe-like, expressive hazel eyes flecked with green rest behind wire-rimmed glasses. She wears jeans, a white cotton shirt covered by a light-blue hooded sweatshirt and sneakers. She's pretty, petite, and wiry. She loves swimming and hiking. Ever since she was a little girl, Olivia was talented at creative writing. She loved writing stories and books. Her talent in creative writing would come back to haunt her later when she would be told she was "melodramatic and had a vivid imagination."

When I asked Olivia to describe herself she says, "That's a hard question," then continues. "Smart to a certain extent, a little creative, very imaginative, which is a curse and a blessing at the same time. Wanting to be independent. I would like to believe that I'm self-sufficient and I'm sensitive, but to a point where it can be troubling, where I can feel too much for other people sometimes. Mature, maybe more so than some people my age but also a lot more analytical at the same time and very self-critical. I have really high expectations for myself and everyone around me, which is hard." She thinks high expectations for herself might have something to do with why she got depressed.

"When I first started to really get depressed I didn't know it and I thought there was something wrong with me. I had a 'fifties' sitcom life—parents who've been dating since their junior year of high school. Three brothers. No really serious illnesses. I have a successful father, nice house in a suburban neighborhood. I had little Mary Jane shoes."

So, given that she had these things, experiencing depression puzzles Olivia. "See, there's nothing posttraumatic in my life. I just think that there were a lot of minuscule events that led up to a lot. I didn't know I was depressed until I look back now. I was convinced it was a defect with me. I think it was much more mild depression for a long time."

For many years, she explains, "I always wanted to be older, and I could never stand it that people would talk to me like such a young kid when I had all these things I wanted to say. No one would listen to me. Even now, people are like, 'Oh, she's a kid, she doesn't know anything.' "

When she was younger, Olivia's intelligence didn't get in the way or cause trouble with other kids, but starting around fifth grade, the taunting began. "There's Olivia the talking encyclopedia." They called her names like "geek." "I was a little more smart and I was teased unbelievably for that. I stopped raising my hand. I stopped passing work in, and I would purposely spell stuff wrong." She felt like she died inside each time the kids made fun of her, explaining, "Little stuff that would get under my skin eventually, and I just lost a lot of self-esteem to that." This is how Olivia began disappearing.

In sixth grade, things got even worse socially. A girl at school told Olivia she was being abused, and Olivia got scared, telling her mom the minute she got home from school. Her mom called the school counselor, which Olivia didn't know about. When the counselor talked to the girl, she recanted and denied it, saying Olivia had made the whole thing up. So rumors spread about Olivia, and there was a lot of trouble. She started getting headaches. She didn't really want to go to school, and some days she would plead and fight with her mom to stay home, because she didn't feel good. This began a pattern.

In sixth grade all the girls started wearing cherry-colored lip gloss. Olivia longed to bypass junior high and go to high school, and thought that maybe in high school it wouldn't matter if her pants weren't the right style. She didn't care about the style, but the teasing and harassment hurt. "I didn't care if I had a guy to dance with at the dance on Friday, but the other girls were really worrying about this. It was so frustrating because I felt so alone, 'cause my emotions and problems were so much deeper than, 'my tank top shrank.'"

Her problems were nothing when she thought of other people who were really suffering, and that made her feel worse about herself for being ungrateful. "I would also make comparisons to war, like I could be a refugee. They are just happy to be alive. I'm sitting here and I have everything every one of them could ever want and I'm still so unhappy I wish I were dead. I mean, I'm such a terrible person. I'm so selfish. I just make everything my fault, which sounds very self-absorbed, which is something depression is." At school, she pretended she was happy. At home, her parents thought she was moody and irritable.

She began to get really depressed because she didn't know what was wrong with her. Having no concrete reason to be unhappy, she would write stories to herself to justify her feelings, like a story about a girl who had a friend who died. She read about depression on the Internet, but thought she had nothing to be depressed about. Depression, she thought, was what happened to kids who lost a grandparent. Not someone with everything she had, and parents who loved her. She should be happy, because she had a good family and was smart, and she would think to herself "I should be able to handle this," but it was too hard.

Then in an effort to have friends, Olivia begin telling stories rather than writing them, finding a way to connect with other kids, "by making these stories up or elaborating on stories that already existed. I would get this 'Oh my God,' all this attention that was so much more positive than anything I'd ever gotten. But at the same time, I would also feel awful about it and then I would get even more mad at myself and tell myself I'm a bad person."

"Did you feel like you had more friends?" I ask.

"I actually ended up feeling a lot more empty 'cause I felt like no one would ever be able to know me. So I felt like I was going to have to live a lie my whole life," she says.

Olivia wanted more than anything to connect, to have friends, to be accepted, to have relationships—so she brought forth a false self in an effort to have friends, to have positive attention, rather than name-calling and taunting. She made up and elaborated on stories in an effort to make a connection. Only it rendered her more disconnected; the lies made her feel worse because she was not being true to herself. She didn't want to disappear, yet.

The Language of the Body

She had terrible headaches. Olivia began noticing that when she felt awful emotionally she also felt physically ill. She discovered the link. The doctors did not.

"They didn't see that I almost got to a point where my mind and my body were so interconnected that when I was feeling bad on the inside, I actually got physical symptoms. I would get sweats. I would feel so awful that I would look bad, and I would say, 'I have a headache' and it was so weird because I ended up getting stress migraines in the back of my head. The doctors kept blaming it on sinuses and I ended up being put on antibiotics I don't think I ever needed." With traces of frustration in her voice she says, "Because it was so much easier to blame it on sinuses." This was a huge missed symptom.

Despite the various antibiotics she was taking for chronic sinus infections, Olivia continued getting headaches, but the doctors didn't look further as to what could have been causing them. At this point, people began to bring up the fact that she was "melodramatic." Olivia is angry that the doctors didn't think beyond her sinuses, and blames them for her mild depression becoming severe. Recently her new doctor acknowledged that Olivia tried the best she could to get help and when she didn't, she spiraled into a deep depression.

Physical suffering, or "somatic" complaints, kick in at some point and are much more common in depressed teenagers than in adults. These ailments are real, and need medical attention but often are not diagnosed as symptoms of depression. Is your daughter sick a lot? Does she frequently complain of stomachaches, headaches, or body aches? Get her to a doctor and get the appropriate medical care. First and foremost you need to rule out medical causes. But if symptoms aren't getting better or are covered over with pain pills, the emotional pain will go untreated. We have to listen to our bodies and encourage girls to do the same.

Western medicine is too quick to dole out a pill, and we don't always take the time to explore where the pain is coming from and how to manage its root cause. The medical doctors did not think about what was going on with Olivia psychologically. Stress, tension, and depression caused the headaches, and eventually led to stress migraines. The headaches were a teen symptom of depression, but not everyone knows that.

In the days of Freud, physical ailments were taken much more seriously as potential symptoms of psychological distress. "Lies make you sick," writes Carol Gilligan.[1] If you're living a lie, or feel like your very core self is lost to a lie, or has become a lie, or your relationships are lies, or if you feel you are being told lies, before long you're going to feel sick. We can only hold so much pain emotionally.

Where's Olivia?

No one noticed when Olivia started losing weight. Small and petite, she didn't stop eating for body-image purposes. She stopped eating because she felt that since she had lost control of her emotions, eating was something she could control. "Anorexia is a stereotype for when girls are unhappy with themselves. They lose weight. They realize 'I can't get people to look at me with words so I'm going to do it this way.' But it's subconscious."

Girls, she says, have very few outlets for negative emotions and consequently they learn to numb their anger and other negative emotions.

"It's not just these body images we see that eliminate our self-esteem. I'm sure it does affect some people, but it's the fact that we have very few outlets for anger and for very negative emotions. And it's not a feminist thing, it's a cultural thing. I have a whole lifetime of anger stuck inside me because I never let it out. I almost see it like sediment with all those layers built up to make a rock."

I ask if she ever let her anger out.

"I would let it out sometimes, but at the wrong people, like at my mom sometimes in the morning when she'd make me go to school. I wasn't really mad at her. I was mad at everyone for not understanding and for making me go to school when I was really feeling so awful. And I was mad at myself for not being able to tell them. So then I would be mean to her and then I would go into school and be mad at myself." She loved her mom and felt guilty and angry with herself all day long at school.

Girls do other things, she explains. "There are more warning signals, like drastic changes all of a sudden, or hanging out with an older crowd, or trying to toughen up their image. Some girls take on the bully approach, you know, 'I'm going to suck the power out of everyone else and when they feel as bad as I do then I'll feel better' kind of thing."

Eating enough or eating too much has a different meaning and symbolism for every girl. For Olivia, "Not eating was not only a new way to get realized, but it was also the whole simple equation, food plus sleep equals life. So my mission was to shrink, to implode, almost. I subconsciously wanted to be noticed, but I really didn't, at the same time. It was a big conflict whether to let my bubble be popped. And I think that the girls, like myself, who go through this don't intend it at all. It's not on purpose, I mean. And society makes it sound like, 'Oh, we're trying to do this because we want to look like we're really teeny-weeny.' It's not something we just do. It's something that we're soaked in for our lives. And if we go against it and try to stand up for what's going on, then we're labeled a 'feminist' and that kind of has a really bad stigma. You're called a feminist, and you say, 'I am NOT!'" she says emphatically. If Olivia says what she's thinking, "stands up," she's called another name, which is more reason to keep her mouth shut. That way she can avoid more labels, more taunts, more harassment, and less belonging, less acceptance, less fitting in.

I ask what's wrong with being called a "feminist."

"That means you're too opinionated." Olivia, ever articulate, pauses. "It means that you believe in such an old notion like on the whole girls are better than guys, like you're stuck way back when. You're not following the media messages. It's out to be a feminist. It's out not to shave. It's associated with my mom's generation." I think of all the body waxing salons, realizing they would not have had such a boom in the sixties. Quietly she says what she really thinks. "Feminism should be about your rights as a whole."

Then she tells me another reason feminism is so out: "It has to do with guys. Feminism is really unattractive to guys now because they're chauvinists. Most of the guys definitely see women as sex symbols. Porn is the biggest industry on the Net. So girls are also stuck with this—boys who are their age who are growing up watching women without any morals and so it's really unattractive to have any morals about yourself at all."

Boys, she explains, have it rough, too. "They're going through a lot on their own. And by the time they're even ten they're already looking through stuff on the Net that's a thousand times worse than *Playboy*. We hear about all this stuff that's going on, and feminism is also people who are anti-sex. I knew people in sixth grade who were already sleeping with other people and it was terrible. They were eleven. That is just unbelievable."

Olivia, unlike some teens these days, does not think sex, at age eleven, is run-of-the-mill. She lets me in on something very private, whispering even though we are behind closed doors. "I don't want to say this too loud, but I'm the only person I know who hasn't had sex yet." She worries that this could make her an outcast. "And my mom and dad worry about me." Not having had sex, she says, is "bad, that makes me a feminist, that also makes me a prude and that means all this bad stuff. It's unbelievable. It's crazy."

It's very different now. Her mom she says learned what sex was when she was twelve. Olivia learned when she was seven. "I heard about sex at school. I was surrounded. It's just a completely different culture, and we are forced to grow up a lot younger, yet our parents are still the same. They still measure everything in the way that everything was. And they were reading books that are written by people who are not living through this, through what's going on now. It's so frustrating because you have this one perspective from the older generation that's supposed to know everything and you have this brand-new generation coming up in a world that is very screwed up."

At this point Olivia adds, "I was lethargic at school, I didn't want to go, I didn't want to be with people, but I could still do it. And I would get happy, but it was short-lived." Then, creeping back again was that let-down feeling, "like the day after Christmas," only it lasted longer than a day.

Then she began to hurt herself in other ways. "Just little things like involuntary pinching when I got really upset, or scratching until I started bleeding." Then she would purposely pinch herself until she bruised because she was so mad at herself. It was "self-punishment" because she was irritable with her parents. She thought they deserved a different daughter, a better daughter, although she still managed to get A's. Once she even tried to overdose on Tylenol. She threw up and she felt sick the next morning, but she didn't tell her mom or dad and just went to school.

When Olivia felt sad she slept. Sleep was pure escape.

She also wrote poems. Writing is a common and wonderful medium of expression for girls and a way to stay connected to one's own knowledge and feelings. But, as Carrie told me, for her, writing helped, but when she wrote too much and all the time it was another way she was withdrawing and isolating herself. So "everything in moderation" is a good guidepost.

Olivia wrote in her journal up in her room by herself for hours on end. She wrote volumes. She could look back over the months and remember. Something told her she should probably never forget this time. In one way she didn't want to remember, but she knew she could never forget. This struggle, this pain was part of her life that she could not change. She wanted something to remind her how difficult it was. Maybe when she was older she would understand it. This is positive: Olivia could see her future, and could see getting better. She may have been disappearing, but she had not lost hope.

Olivia felt guilty and disgusted with herself for being depressed and then she felt even more depressed.

"And the worst thing in the world is to be depressed and have hope."

"Because?"

"It's so frustrating to want to get better and to really be able to see the light at the end of the tunnel and it's like three steps forward, two steps back. It's easier when there's no light, when it's just dark. I'm not going to get anywhere, so why bother? It's easier to look at it that way since you keep trying to struggle for it. Because then you're thinking that there's a reason to live and a reason to try, but you feel so awful and it's easier just to give up."

"Do you think you have hope?"

After a very long pause, Olivia explains, "I think I have hope, but I'm trying to kill it. And I think that I'm mad at myself for hoping. There's almost two parts of me. There's this really pessimistic part that can't see anything going on. Then there's this other part that really wants to be able to see it and really wants the help but doesn't want to have to feel everything. It's like this constant inner conflict between how much to tell and how much to keep secret and the problem is I don't really know what's going on. I'm giving people the opportunity to understand me and I'm afraid of what they're going to say. I'm afraid of what they're going to say is wrong with me or I'm afraid that also gives people the opportunity to hurt me at the same time. I'm completely exposed."

Olivia reads me her poems, and her self-loathing makes me feel worried and sad for her, so I ask Olivia about her wanting to die.

"I didn't want to live. But that was very different to me than wanting to die."

"Can you explain?"

"I didn't want to exist anymore, but it didn't mean that I wanted to just keel over. It meant that I couldn't go on. I couldn't. I used to just joke with my friends that they didn't get it, but I would say, 'You know what, today's just so awful, I wish I could live in a cave. As long as it has cable and I have someone I could talk to I'd be fine.' And then I just really wanted to just disappear in this little corner. Be alone and just not have to deal with any of it anymore."

Some girls want to escape from the thoughts in their heads. Olivia explains, "My mom would say, 'Do you want to go somewhere? What will make you happy?' I would say, 'I wish I could have a vacation from my mind'; I wanted to get out of it. I couldn't hack it anymore," she says. "I could see how I was affecting my environment so I'd start beating myself over the head, when someone in my family would feel bad or when I would hurt somebody."

On a weeklong school outdoor science education field trip there was another incident. Several school districts from several states participated, so some of Olivia's friends from camp were there. But one wasn't—Jan. Olivia found out from the other kids that she wasn't there because she was recently assaulted. Olivia was overwhelmed, upset, sad, and really angry. She felt helpless and there was nothing she could do. It completely freaked her out. She was distraught and she made a comment about wanting to die and leave this horrible world to a couple friends, who then went to tell a teacher. Olivia went up to her cabin with Julie and began crying and even throwing things. "It was years of depression coming out." Julie calmed her down and helped her into bed as a teacher and social worker arrived at the door.

She told them that she would tell them how she really felt, but she begged them not to tell her parents. Olivia was sent home from the trip, and of course her parents were told. What disturbed her further was that the teachers told her to tell the other kids she was not thinking of suicide, but that she was just really upset and didn't know how to handle it. Being told to lie about how she was *really* feeling when she finally spoke the truth made her really angry. She felt like no one cared about her. She felt shamed. She thought about preparing to die. She didn't want to die at all, but she couldn't stand living the way she felt. She was sick of living a lie. "That's when I really started to crash because I was trying to get help the only way that I could and I lost it. I felt like no one understood me."

Her mom took her to a psychiatrist who recommended an antidepressant, but her mom said no because she was worried about the side effects of medication and was convinced that Olivia was being melodramatic and had a vivid imagination. Olivia didn't know what to say to the psychiatrist, didn't know what she was supposed to say. All she knew was that she was scared of the psychiatrist. Olivia didn't know she wasn't supposed to be scared of her.

The rumors back at school were flying. She was mortified. Stories circulated about her: She was in a mental hospital, she had killed herself, she was sent away, she was crazy, she had jumped off the balcony.

If the rumors weren't bad enough, a classroom incident made her really want to disappear. "I had this horrible teacher who was also the environmental factor my family was blaming my unhappiness on—'It was her fault.' She did not help at all. It goes to show how misunderstood depression is. I wouldn't do my schoolwork. I didn't want to. I made straight A's and I was feeling like shit and I thought why should I even bother? I know I can do this, but I can't even see myself alive a year from now. The point of going to school is to go to college. Forget this. So my grades dropped considerably and this teacher calls on me from the middle of the class. She says, 'Where's your homework?' And I said, 'I didn't do it.' And she knew my whole situation and she said, 'Just because you have psychological problems doesn't mean you get to slack off in my class.' It was just so horrible that someone could be that rude to me, could say that something's wrong with me. I'm not like everyone else."

That's when she began wishing she had something visible, something without stigma. If people could see it she would also be seen.

"Even this year, I'm sitting in class and one of our assignment words in history was 'asylum,' to take under your wing, like to care for, hospitality. And one kid said, 'Isn't that where crazy people go?' And the teacher said, 'No, they don't call it that anymore. I forget exactly what they call it now.' And I said, 'Oh, it's a psychiatric ward.' And this kid behind me said, 'Oh, you only know because you probably have to spend all your time there.' Do you say to a cancer patient, 'Oh, I bet you spend all your time in a radiation room?' Are you that insensitive?"

She wished and prayed that something visible was wrong with her, like a broken bone, so she could "be able to look at my X-rays and say what's wrong with me. I didn't even know what the problem was, so how was I supposed to know how to fix it? It was really frustrating—especially for someone who for their whole life has never really had to work hard at their schoolwork. And all of a sudden I don't have any answer."

That summer she went to sleepover camp. She was so miserable and depressed she could barely get out of bed, so she faked being sick. She told the nurse lies, a wild story that she had a friend who had died, which was why she was upset. "It was so hard to be there. It wasn't even like school, where I could be one person at school and then come home and be a complete bitch and go to bed. I couldn't. It was stressful. I had to be happy and ignore my emotions all the time since I was constantly surrounded by people."

She couldn't bear it. "It was so hard to interact with all these people in my environment and I still had to be fake with them." She imitates being happy for me, saying "Hi" in a high-pitched, singsong, breathy, fake happy voice. She looks at me and says, "I would make these dumb jokes. I would all of a sudden be saying, 'Oh my God, you'll never believe who I saw the other day. It was so . . . ' and stuff like that. I'd become what they want and I can't be that."

Olivia is still trying to be real. Every time she tries to act differently to get along and fit in, she can't continue it. "I can't be that." Despite her struggle and despite lapses, she resists conforming. Deep down her sense of self is strong; she never forgets her real self when she is being false, or when her depressed voice tries taking over.

She had feigned happiness at school for years; she couldn't do it around the clock at camp. She was well aware that kids were not going to want to be with her if she was depressed. She knew that put her at risk for being even more alone. "If you had an option of going to the mall with someone who was happy and bubbly or a person who was going through a lot of pain and distress, you're going to pick the other person." On the one hand she couldn't pretend anymore and on the other she was afraid to be left alone. Olivia tells me what she really wanted: *"I was dying for someone my age to understand."*

She had urges to cut and hurt herself beyond her usual pinching and scratching. "I felt this need to go home and I stood backward at the top of this rocky mountainous slope that went all the way down to the lake and I just fell backward and I ended up with a concussion." And that's how she went home from camp.

I asked her if she wanted to accomplish anything by falling backward. "I wanted to be knocked out. I don't know what I really wanted to have happen. I couldn't be at camp anymore. And then I come home and my mom said, 'I can't send you away anymore. Every time I send you away, something bad happens.'"

This time, she got put on antidepressant medication. A month later she went on vacation with her family to Yellowstone National Park. Despite the medication, she couldn't get out of bed. The medication wasn't working. She was filled with self-disdain for being "such a bitch" to her family. "I had to go on a family vacation and I faked being sick just so I could just stay in the hotel room and watch pay-per-view movies all day while they were out. I lost fourteen pounds. I couldn't get out of bed and we were at Yellowstone. It's gorgeous there. And I was such a bitch to my whole family just because I didn't want to get out of bed or do anything. And I was wallowing in self-pity, which is the worst thing I could possibly have done and I think I got a lot worse." She knew she was really badly off, being in such a beautiful place where she could be outdoors hiking, something she loved more than anything, but instead she was staying in the hotel room in bed the entire vacation, isolated, unable to move.

When school started that year, Olivia says, "I was rock bottom. I couldn't even get out of bed. I was unable to move, unable to talk." She would vacillate from complete apathy to trying to block out her emotional pain by pouring herself into her schoolwork. At this point she didn't even think she deserved the help she desperately wanted. She could barely get out of bed in the morning and would plead with her mother to let her stay home. The pleading was futile.

"I wanted to be alone. And I got my wish as of September. I was supposed to go back to school and I thought that maybe now that I didn't have that teacher or that I wasn't in this class that this was my chance to be happy. And the year, it was fine. I had fine teachers and the work was fine, but I was still really unhappy and I actually ended up diagnosed with mono at the end of September. And that meant that I was alone by myself in bed, all the time. And that was just the worst thing that possibly could have happened. At the time it was this huge blessing because I got to be alone all the time. But I was stuck with my problems in a dark room, asleep and alone, completely isolated. I lost interest in everything outside. I would tell my mom that if any of my friends called I was sleeping. I just lost touch with everybody else. Just my mom and me. I was completely alone and loved every second of it. And every time someone would say something about me having to go back to school I would say that I felt awful again. I didn't want to get up and go anymore. My blood tests, in November, came back negative, and they said that what she could have is a little bit of like post-mono, like when you have an illness you can't get past." And the doctors blamed her unhappiness on that.

Catching Olivia

That's when she showed her mom her hidden cuts. "I just couldn't get out of bed. I would get in fights with my mom. It was a struggle just to get up and go. And finally I told my mom about the cutting since that was the only way to try to get her to understand."

Olivia says using positive coping strategies, such as writing, didn't work as far as getting her help. "You're seen just as normal, yet you're still going through a lot. You don't have any real signs, you're not sure of anything because you're still dealing with it alone but it keeps building anyway. And you can't talk about depression at school because of the stigma that comes with it."

If she had a physical illness, she says people would be sending get-well cards and visiting, "but a mental disorder, depression, everyone around me is walking on eggshells. They're afraid to do anything 'cause it's so taboo in our society to have a mental disorder, because you're associated with the padded rooms. It's so made fun of. And it's awful because there's nothing that you can see. There's no real X-ray that you can pull out and say, 'Oh, this is what it is.'" Explaining further she says, "You can't see what's going on. It's the fear of the unknown because no one really knows what's going on. We'll just not talk about it and pretend it's not there. So then girls have to make a physical existence of the problem, like a skeletal body, 'cause then there's a real problem, then it's visible. Or getting your stomach pumped because then there's a real problem. It's just so hard to have an intangible situation as opposed to a tangible one."

Medication didn't help her. She tried three different antidepressants, and she decided she had "emotional depression not biological depression."

"I was only taken seriously with my mom after I showed her the cuts. That's when she wanted to get me more help. When I'd still been telling her all this stuff in words it didn't matter, but as soon as she saw it, BOOM, she still needs more help. I knew it was there, but when she saw it, it freaked her out. It's not words or subtle messages. You have to hit someone over the head with an anvil before they're going to notice. You can't just tap them on the shoulder."

I ask Olivia why she thinks this is so.

"I think that people in general are looking at their own problems and they're not waiting to see something that's not blatant. It takes a lot for them to get to notice you. No matter what they've studied or whatever. Everyone signals in different ways. As I said before, I have nothing against people from older generations but, when they were growing up, mental disorders were associated with mental asylums, you check yourself in and you're in a locked facility. Awful stereotypes like *One Flew Over the Cuckoo's Nest*, Nurse Ratched and all that stuff. It's awful, and they grew up without knowing anything about it. Because they're over twenty-one and adults and can vote, why does that mean that they know any more about it than we do? And they're the ones that are supposed to help us, yet they weren't brought up knowing to look for anything. We have to hit them over the head with the anvil 'cause they weren't taught to look for the finger tapping."

The cuts she showed her mother made Olivia come back from her disappearing state. Olivia had exhausted all the other tactics she could think of to get the understanding and help she knew she needed. When the medication didn't work and she found herself in that lonely place of isolation, Olivia chose life. Her determination and hope got her out of a miserable—but not unusual—place. Think of the smart, beautiful, talented teenage girl, suffering as she did and contemplating obliterating herself. And be grateful to her connection to her mother and her love of life that she didn't disappear and is here to tell her story.

9. GRACE: A STORY OF HOPE

Few things in life are as scary to a parent as a child's suicidal thoughts and behaviors. Suicidal behavior is a plea for understanding, help, and closer relationships, a desperate attempt to be noticed, to compel response—and, paradoxically, a signal of hope. Most suicidal girls don't really want to die; they just don't want to be miserable. They want understanding, to be "noticed," and they want someone to realize that they need help, that something is wrong.

As compared with teenage boys, whose suicidal behavior is often fatal, girls don't as often kill themselves. It's not that girls attempt and "fail" to kill themselves. Dying is not their intention. Their suicidal actions are actually a way to get help and have more genuine relationships. When pushed to the limit, these girls reach out. It's a dangerous act that people notice. Therein lives their hope, because the act itself expresses the strong desire for help, and for real relationships.[1] Through these actions, they are certainly letting others know how they really feel: They are not hiding; they are not disappearing. They are on their campaign to be heard, seen, noticed, and helped, because something is wrong.

This may help explain why researchers have not found hopelessness to be correlated with suicidal behavior in teenage girls as it is with adults.[2] Nevertheless, all suicidal thoughts and behaviors in girls must be taken seriously.

As I said in Chapter Three, women's depression has been described by Dana Jack as "silencing the self;" but most girls with depression are not silent forever. This is the healthy resistance to silence, disconnection, false relationships, and the loss of self and their voices that Carol

Gilligan discovered in early adolescent girls. Early adolescence is a time of risk, but also a time of resistance to false relationships and pretending. Not all girls are buried away, hiding in their room. And when their hints, words, or actions aren't responded to, they express themselves by hurting themselves. They learn that violence is a language our culture responds to. Although their behavior may be scary and cause others concern, they are seeking help, hoping to get their needs met the only way they can in our culture.

The good news is that the girls are actually seeking closer relationships and better communication with their parents, teachers, and other adults close to them (as well as their peers). Strong relationships are both the best protective factor for a child, teenager, or adult under stress and the key to psychological health and well-being.

Grace's story shows just how far girls will go in their effort to be heard, to be taken seriously, and to have real relationships. Just as important, it shows how critical it is to build a relationship of trust into any therapeutic process involving adolescent girls. For Grace to trust me, for her to speak, for her to tell me what she was really thinking, feeling, and experiencing, I would have to share parts of myself, building a bond between us, a "real" relationship.

Saving Grace

It was autumn, and I was beginning my training in clinical psychology, my predoctoral clinical internship. On a breezy, sunny Wednesday morning when our clinical team assembled for its weekly meeting, the director read a referral that caught my attention: a thirteen-year-old girl, Grace, from a middle-class family, had been referred to the clinic. Her aunt was worried about her and wanted a second opinion. She had lost her parents during her middle childhood, and her aunt and uncle were raising her. They had three sons in college, and one who had recently moved home.

The referral note cited sleeping too much. It described a recent diagnosis of depression and a concern that self-destructive behavior might be starting: she was piercing her own ears even though she could have it professionally done. A bright and academically successful girl, she'd recently stolen the teacher's grade book. This detail caught my attention. Because I'd been a teacher, I appreciated the enormity of the act and I offered to see her. The referral note mentioned another detail about Grace: She had been seeing a psychotherapist for more than six months; however, although she went to her sessions, she had not spoken in therapy. She had remained silent.

I met first with Grace's aunt. The following week, I met Grace. When I came out to the waiting room, I saw a girl—slim, adorable, with short brown hair—engrossed in a book, wearing jeans, a purple sweater, and running shoes. "Hi," I said, "are you Grace? I'm Lisa. I'm happy to meet you." She looked up at me with large green eyes that seemed wary, shy, uncertain, and immeasurably tired. Immediately, I felt concern for her. Perhaps it was the sense of exhaustion she exuded. She chose to come into the session by herself, and we settled into large chairs in a comfortable room with toys, books, and art supplies on a bookshelf surrounding us.

I asked her whether anyone had told her why she was meeting with me, and Grace said quietly, "I don't know." She continued to respond to my questions by saying, "I don't know," until I decided to address the relationship between us.

"I'm asking you a lot of questions," I said. "Are there any questions you'd like to ask me?"

Grace suddenly came to life and sat up in the chair, smiling at me. Her eyes brightened, and she eagerly nodded her head. "Yeah," she said, "are you married? Do you have your own apartment? Do you have children? Are you a student? Who do you live with?"

I didn't try to find out why she wanted to know these things about me, as would normally be the practice of a psychotherapist. Her questions were an effort to form a real relationship with me, a relationship in which we both would speak. So I told her that I was not married, that I had my own apartment, that I did not have children.

"Why did you wonder if I am a student?" I asked, and she answered, "I saw the sign when we came in that said this was a teaching hospital."

"How do you feel about my being a student?" I asked, and she replied, smiling, "I like that. That's OK." Returning to the second unanswered question, she repeated, "Do you have roommates, or do you live on your own?" I answered, "I live on my own."

I asked Grace to tell me about all the things she liked and the things she was good at doing. She talked about soccer, poetry, and swimming. She told me that she was on a school soccer team. She loved school and enjoyed reading and writing. She told me about her favorite characters on television as well as her favorite shows. She left happy, and agreed to come back next week to meet with me.

The following week, in our second session, Grace came in to tell me what she knew. She told me about an incident at school where a boy had made fun of her because she lived with her aunt and uncle. She said, "Sometimes at school I feel like crying but I don't want to cry in front of the other kids." Then she said, "I can't take it anymore," and talked about her current situation at home—when her aunt and uncle weren't home, her cousin Malcolm, who was twenty-two, who wasn't supposed to drink, would start drinking and would call her names and say horrible, mean things to her. There were times when he pushed her and even hit her. She said she couldn't bear to live in the same house with him anymore. There was no sexual assault, but the verbal and physical abuse were unbearable to her.

I reminded her that I am required by law to report this kind of information to the state's department of child protective services (CPS). She immediately replied that she had tried to run away about six months earlier. When the police found her, they made her return home. Workers from child protective services came to her home to check on her, but she said, "They came and talked to me once and never came back. They didn't seem to care much."

"I care," I said. "I'll do all I can to help you." The look of relief on her face was as easy to read as the exhaustion had been earlier. Together we constructed a safety plan. If she felt physically threatened or unsafe in any way, she was to leave the house and go to a safe place; we wrote down the addresses of three friends' houses close by where she could go, and emergency phone numbers she could call.

Her aunt was distraught and understanding of the situation and explained that she felt terrible; she knew Malcolm had had a problem with alcohol since college and was going to therapy, but resisted getting more help. She was beside herself because she couldn't put her own son on the street and yet she worked all day and often into the evening. So did her husband. In fact, her husband's job required that he travel frequently and he was often away from home for several months at a time. She said the school had called her and they had contacted CPS once before over this matter. In tears, she said she had been trying to get help from CPS. She wanted what was best for Grace. I tried to make sure we were all working together to keep Grace safe and, eventually, happy.

When I called the state child protective services, just as her aunt said, they told me a report had been filed about Malcolm in the past. In response to my report, they immediately said Grace was just a "defiant adolescent," who like many other teens enjoyed "butting heads with authority." When I asked why the case was closed so quickly I was told it was because everyone had agreed to go into therapy. In response to my report, CPS decided that the situation merited further investigation.

I worried about Grace and, because I knew she wanted out, I tried to find an adolescent shelter that she could go to. I ran up against a rule that stated that, without a referral from the state, there were no shelters available to girls her age. She had to stay at home: her aunt and uncle did not have the financial resources to send her to a boarding school, and there were no other family members in the area.

In the week between Grace's complaint and the investigation, I received an early evening phone call from her aunt, who was very upset. When she had gotten home from work, she had learned that Grace had just run away from home, and had called the police. There was nothing I could do but call my supervisor, wait for news, say a lot of prayers, and contend with that helpless, terrified feeling you harbor when a child you care about has disappeared. The next morning I called her school and her aunt and I found to my utmost relief that she was there, that she had followed our safety plan. Malcolm had started drinking, saying mean things, and physically threatening her, so she went to one of the friends' houses that we had put on the list.

With permission from her aunt and uncle and her friend's mother, Grace stayed at her friend's house until the state's investigation concluded. With the investigation finally over, the state's investigator reported that Grace seemed as distressed about the verbal abuse as she was about the physical abuse. Despite Grace's obvious "distress," the state investigator concluded that her situation did not warrant removal from her aunt's house. Grace must return home. She responded, "If I go home, I'll run away." The next day, when it came time to go home, she ran away from school. She was found later that day.

The act of running away accomplished what the reports of threats and abuse did not. After she was found, she was placed in a temporary fourteen-day shelter for teens; she was not required to return home for two weeks. Unfortunately, this shelter was very far from my clinic, so I stayed in contact with her by phone because she could not get to therapy. The phone contact may be the key in understanding the rapid escalation of Grace's behavioral demands to be heard and taken seriously.

When she unwittingly broke a rule at the shelter she was punished by losing a privilege: to walk home from school with her best friend. Grace called me, sobbing, deeply disappointed; she told me how much she had been counting on their walk home together. She pleaded with me, "Please get me out of here." I explained that I understood that it was hard not be listened to but that there was nothing I could do about the shelter's rules. "If I can't get out of here, I'm going to run away," she said. When I told her that I would be worried about her safety, especially at night, if she ran away, she hung up on me.

I learned from the shelter staff that Grace did not run that night, but the next day after school she "ran away"—she walked home with her friend and spent the afternoon with her. She returned to the shelter at sunset. I continued to call her and she continued to refuse to talk to me. I left messages, asking the staff to write them down, so she would have a note, something concrete, letting her know that I cared, that I was thinking about her, and that I was working on her behalf.

In her second week at the shelter, Grace was told again that she would have to return home at the end of the week. She expressed her anger, confusion, and disappointment in a poem: "I want to be out of this horrible pain, this horrible life, my spirit yearns to break free, soar free out of this pain." The shelter staff was concerned by what they deemed might be suicidal thoughts and feelings, and a crisis evaluation team was summoned to assess Grace's level of danger to herself. When they concluded that she was not a danger to herself, she was sent back to the shelter with a recommendation from the crisis evaluation team that she go from the shelter to an out-of-home placement, such as a boarding school. The shelter also suggested a boarding school placement; my clinical treatment team concurred. Her aunt and uncle agreed that a boarding school would be in Grace's best interest, but needed help funding it. Despite this impressive arsenal of recommendations, the state's child protective agency maintained its position that Grace had to return home. According to CPS, Grace's situation was not serious enough to warrant removal from her home (CPS's decision was about money; they are not well funded).

Confronted with the realization that she would have to return home, where Malcolm still was, Grace became suicidal. She wrote a note wondering if anyone knew how many times a day she felt like killing herself. She ran away daily, and did not return until well after dark. Grace and another girl ran down railroad tracks at night, in the rain, and got lost. She took off from the shelter and was seen hiding in a nearby graveyard. Alarmed, the staff of the shelter called an ambulance to take Grace to an adolescent unit of a psychiatric hospital.

The hospital would not discharge her home, providing her with free care until an appropriate adolescent boarding school placement could be found for her—one that allowed her to continue to work with me and to which the state would agree to send her. She stayed until she went to boarding school, although she would have never ended up there in the first place.

Grace's risky, suicidal, and dangerous behavior can be understood not just as a cry for help, but also as an active fight to hold on to her self and her voice—and as a sign of hope. When Grace felt that I had left her in a dangerous situation, she literally hung up on me. She then proceeded to dramatize her predicament by exposing herself to danger and potential harm. By endangering herself, she communicated her knowledge that she was in danger and was asking, in effect, if anyone cared. I understood Grace's suicidal behavior as reflecting her intense need to be taken seriously.

I continued to meet with Grace in therapy where, later, we explored the meaning of her running away, her wish to kill herself, and her potentially self-harming acts. When I asked her what she liked about running away, she said: "It got people to listen to me. When they wouldn't listen to me about home, I told them I would run away and they took me to the shelter. When the protective people wouldn't listen to me and I was going to have to go home, I ran away and then I went to the hospital, and now I'm in the school."

Grace's ordeal taught her that the language that is taken seriously and heard in our culture is violence. She discovered that it is a form of communication that everyone understands and also a language that is widely spoken in our society. My speaking on her behalf, multiple clinical recommendations from various agencies, and Grace's own words had had no effect in changing the plan to return her home. When she realized that I was unable to protect her, she became silent in our relationship.

When I asked her about her thoughts of killing herself, she said, "I didn't want to go that far, but I knew it would get them to notice." Grace had learned to speak the language that "they" listened to, but, because she did not actually kill herself, she was dismissed and labeled "manipulative," by some of the people she encountered. As one of the crisis evaluators said about Grace's success at getting herself into a school rather than being returned home, "it was calculated." Grace, once labeled a "defiant adolescent," was then called "calculating."

This catch-22 lies at the heart of the crisis in girls' depression and suicidal behavior: If girls threaten to kill themselves, they will be taken seriously; if they do not actually kill themselves, they risk being dismissed as manipulative and are not taken seriously. As sixteen-year-old Rachel told me, after suicidal behavior, "I think they take me less seriously because they don't listen at all— oh, she is incompetent. She doesn't know what she wants."

Finding a Voice

In his work on suicidal teens, analyst Joseph Laufer writes that in the past, suicide attempts were described, by many distinguished psychoanalysts, as a cry for help. However, he observes that this "very apt term has fallen into disrepute because it has been used in a pejorative way about those who have attempted suicide, implying that they behaved in a manipulative way to draw attention to themselves."[3]

My research with girls shows that dismissing teenage girls' suicidal behavior as manipulation overlooks what may have been the meaning of the suicidal act in the first place. They may have learned to manipulate, but are doing so in a spirit of hope, of getting needs met that have not been met otherwise. The original meaning of the word "manipulative" is "to lead by the hand." When suicidal acts enable girls to get help, it is inaccurate to see these acts as merely "manipulative." Treating them as such can lead girls to give up hope. And then, psychologically or literally, they are more likely to kill themselves.

Teenage girls, by rendering their desire for help and real relationships a matter of life or death, exemplify what the child analyst Erik Erikson called the "meaning of meaning it" and the "voice that means it." In his work as an analyst with teenagers, he observed that they are often wrestling for a "benediction which is to lead to the patient's conviction that he is an alive person, and, as such, has a life before him, and a right to it. For less, such patients will not settle."[4]

For an adolescent, he writes that this is "an adventure in reaching inner rock bottom to find something firm to stand on." Erikson warns that the risk inherent for an adolescent is to "remain at the rock bottom, and deplete the energy available for his emergence" becoming a "lonely twisted tree on the ledge of a stormy rock, or the rock, or just the ledge out in nowhere."[5] He writes that at times, "the eyes of these young people are often lifeless and out of contact; then they suddenly scan your face for its sincerity or even its mere presence; these patients, who according to popular judgment could be said to be 'not quite there' most of the time, are all too suddenly and flamingly there. They can appear as remote, as lifeless, as impenetrable as they say they feel; and yet, there are those moments of mutual recognition when they do seem to trust themselves and you, and when their smile can be as totally present and rewarding as only an infant's first smiles of seeming recognition. But at this point the struggle just begins—as indeed does the infant's."[6]

Carol Gilligan writes, in an analysis of adolescent development, about the tension between exit and voice, leaving and speaking, as alternative responses to unbearable situations. With the onset of adolescence, teenagers now have both the option of leaving (which they did not have when they were little) as well as the option of speaking (remember, speaking can be through their behavior). An important part of her analysis is that, for an adolescent, the option of speaking is more likely to occur in the presence of someone they think is loyal to them.

This helps us understand why girls' suicidal behavior often takes place in close proximity to other people, or they tell someone afterward.[7]

Researchers discovered (as is clear from the stories in this book) that girls' suicidal acts most often occur when they are near a person whom they love or care about, someone with loyalty. The suicidal act becomes an expression of the desire for and test of those relationships. That girls' suicidal acts are often not fatal reflects girls' correct reading of their relationships: that, on some level, the other person *is* paying attention and cares whether they live or die. We need to think carefully and consider our responses to girls' suicidal behavior in terms of relationships that constitute and show loyalty.

The Language of Suicidal Behavior

A subtheme of this understanding has to do with the readiness with which girls use violence against themselves when they discover that people finally take notice. Fifteen-year-old Noelle says, "People aren't listening, teenagers are going to go to the extremes." But observing this phenomenon, we also note that teenage girls may stress the difficulties and disappointments of their relationships and forget, disconnect, or dissociate themselves from the experiences of love that continue to nourish and fuel their hope for real relationships. At the beginning of her novel *The Bluest Eye*, Toni Morrison illustrates and then undoes this form of dissociation. The narrator of the story starts by recalling her impoverished childhood: The house was cold and old, her mother overburdened and distracted, a child's illness became the last straw. Then she stops herself, asking, "But was it really like that? As painful as I remember?" What she had forgotten was love, not an idealized or romanticized image of love, or of mothers, but her memory of "love, thick and dark as Alga syrup . . . I could smell it—taste it—sweet, must, with an edge of wintergreen in its base—everywhere in that house . . . it coated my chest, along with the salve, and when the flannel came undone in my sleep, the clear, sharp curves of air outlined its presence on my throat. And in the night, when my coughing was dry and tough, feet padded into the room, hands repinned the flannel, readjusted the quilt, and rested a moment on my forehead. So when I think of autumn, I think of somebody with hands that does not want me to die."[8]

Amazing Grace

Later in our work together, I asked Grace why she talked to me in therapy after being silent with her previous therapist for so long. She explained, "It's because you talked about yourself. When you asked me if
I wanted to ask you any questions, I was like, 'Yeah!' And I asked you all
those questions!" We talked about her stealing the teacher's grade book
and she mused, "I'm sort of like a rebel, I guess." Sitting back in the
chair, she was pensive and quiet, and then looked at me with a big smile,
and said, "I think that I like that I'm a rebel." I too liked Grace's rebellion against being mistreated, and her insistence on being heard.

Even if depressed, adolescent girls show remarkable spunk. One
of the women at that hospital fondly said about Grace, "That girl has
spunk." Girls also show impressive tenacity. Girls' depression is not as
hopeless as it is in women. Instead, their efforts to communicate and
to cope express their hope for their future. The girls say their hope lies
in "the possibility of love," and the anticipation that they will eventually manage to reach people who believe in them and who don't give
up on them.

Although girls' resiliency is at risk in adolescence, their healthy resistance to fake relationships,[9] to people's ignorance of them, heightens
in adolescence, which is why it is a time of ultimate hope. Girls' suicidal
behavior peaks at ages thirteen and fourteen because that is a time when
girls are fighting for themselves and for relationships that are real.

10. BETWEEN ANGST AND DEPRESSION

"I was dying for someone my age to understand."

—Olivia, age 14

It's hard to tell the difference between normal teenage angst and depression, and that puts a special burden on parents. You don't want to be a worrywart about everything that your daughter is experiencing, but if anything goes wrong, you know you will blame yourself. Reading the stories in this book may have been a bit traumatic for worried parents, because it seemed to take so long before the girls got the help they needed. You can't use your own anxiety about her as the guide, because she needs the room in her life to explore, to experience joy and sorrow, and to grow. But do listen to your inner voice, your intuition, that instinct, the gut feeling that we often dismiss. It's a difficult balancing act that parents of adolescents go through. But the big message is that while many teenage girls can get depressed in these years, they work hard to find ways to signal their distress and get help. In adolescence, the rebound from emotional wounds can be quick—if the problems get proper attention. And girls are doing a lot of signaling for help.

Much of the wisdom I gleaned from my work with teenagers applies to all teens, and so anyone who reads this chapter will get tips on how to strengthen one's relationship with the girls in their life, how to help inoculate them from the dangers surrounding them, how to notice the signs of trouble, and how to help.

Again and again throughout this book, you have heard stories in which the trouble began when a girl shifted schools. Sometimes it's a family move, but most often, it is the change from elementary to middle school, or from middle school to high school. School transitions are particularly hard on teenage girls, and it's an important time to be attentive. "Middle school was rough. Everybody picked on everybody, no matter who you were, but basically they picked on the weaker people. I've been picked on. I hate it. It's just sad. It makes that person feel better, but look how many people they're hurting. That's partially where I got my depression from. I don't want any other people to end up like me because people make fun of them," says fourteen-year-old Ali.

Every girl I've ever worked with disliked the move from a small school to a large one, where she suddenly became anonymous and cut off from friends. "Middle school separated everybody. Bruce and I were best friends from the soccer team, and in sixth grade we were in the same math class, but then we got split up. Middle school was really hard because everybody made fun of you, and I started getting depressed around then," says Victoria.

And just when they have figured out the culture, cliques, and groups of middle school, and the different ways of teachers, they move to high school, and they have to start all over again. All teenagers go through these changes, but these transitions may be a time of heightened risk for some girls. Relationships with friends get disrupted, their ordinary routines of study have to change, they may not make the same sports teams they were on in middle school, and the older kids in the high school present a great cultural change to young teenagers.

These are vulnerable but hopeful times. We need to be on the lookout for relational disruptions, as friendships go through radical shifts and romantic relationships add to the uncertainty. Each school year brings something new—both exciting and stressful. A day makes an enormous difference in the life of a teenager, so daily communication is even more critical than before.

So that all parents, teachers, and clinicians can benefit from what I've learned from girls, here are some good tips about what you can do to shore up girls' strength whether or not they are in crisis. Doing these things might even help them ward off the toxins that lead to depression.

The most important things girls need are a sense of belonging, solid relationships, and a strong and positive sense of self. Talk with the girls in your life about how adolescence can be challenging but fun; tell them that you understand that there are a lot of changes that can feel like intense pressure; say you understand only if you really do. Teenagers sense authenticity.

Coping with Change

If you know these many changes can become stressors to a girl, start working on coping strategies early. Make sure she is enrolled in some type of regular and consistent physical activity; this is important to keep her connected to her body and to keep her endorphins up and flowing. Exercise is considered one of the best protectors against depression. A study found that when girls participated in aerobic classes three times a week, symptoms of depression decreased more readily than in girls who didn't go to such a class. It was also a place providing that necessary sense of belonging. (Be careful with girls who have eating disorders and are overexercising and not eating; compulsive exercising becomes another way to lose weight.)

Making sure your daughter feels like she belongs, especially to a peer group at school, is one of the best things you can do. So often girls give themselves up to belong to a peer group. Research tells us that, in early adolescence, parental relationships can help buffer girls against the changes of adolescence that act as stressors. So your love, your presence, your attention, and your care matter even if she doesn't let on that they do. If you're going somewhere as a family, and she doesn't want to come, let her bring a friend along. Bringing a friend along really helps in two ways: She's happier with a friend, and the stranger often helps diffuse family tension—at least as long as the outing goes on.

Research shows that maintaining a regular spiritual or religious affiliation helps. It can be a source of strength, hope, and belonging. When I was a kid, church and Sunday school, youth group and junior choir were important to me and are for many kids. Harness their idealism. See if there's a shelter program they would like to work in, or an assisted-living facility they can visit. Encourage them to get active in local politics, and encourage them to act on their worries about the world—there's plenty of opportunity to help heal the world. This is especially good for teens because the people they help are so grateful and affirming. They get a good sense of their ability to make things better, and a perspective on their own troubles. The arts, and especially the performing arts are excellent avenues of expression for girls and work wonderfully.

Mostly, a girl is going to want to be with her friends. Though some of the activities or suggestions in this book can be done solo, they can also be done with others, and it's important to recognize that possibly *the* most important thing for a girl is her relationships. Above all else, ensure that she's getting enough interaction with other people, especially with kids her own age.

At this age, you want girls to develop coping skills to contend with the changes they are experiencing. Coping skills from childhood may no longer be as useful, because girls face new challenges. Start helping the girl in your life build new coping strategies. For example, you can say, "When I'm stressed out I can think of three people I can call and talk to. I can put on some music and dance. I can put on some music that makes me feel good and psyched up and empowered or calm. I can exercise. I can do yoga. I can run. I can read. I can write to a friend online. I can draw or paint or make a collage. I can write. I can pray. I can do volunteer work. I can intern."

Increase Family Time

As far as family goes, increase the connection and time spent together as much as possible during this period. This is another preventive measure. It's hard, I know, because girls want to be with their friends—not with their family. You don't want to interrupt that, so just try to be present. I know you're thinking, "Well, she's always in her room." Visit her room, or be present when she isn't in her room. As I was writing this book, my sister-in-law, Peggy, was in town for her annual June hiking trip in New Hampshire and a tennis match in Wellesley. I was anxious about my deadline, and said, "I can't spend any time or do anything. I'm writing my book." She said, "I just want to be with you, Lisa, I love you." And she stayed with me like she does every year, in my tiny studio apartment. As I sat at the computer writing while she quietly watched tennis, her presence was soothing. Here I was worried that she would be bored and I would be distracted. Being present means a lot. Sometimes when you sit around the room, your teenager might look up and say something. Without the stress of directed conversation, some kids relax and tell you what's going on with them.

Your daughter knows you love her, but say it sometimes. Give her a hug. Leave her a little note saying you love her and are proud of her. Focus on the positive. Give her space and time to talk about the hard things. As Rachel said, "You have to be ready to talk when they are." They may not say it, but they want to be most important to you.

How to Deprogram Your Daughter

By talking with the girls we love or work with about what they will encounter in the world and the meaning it has to them, by raising their consciousness about gender roles, and by deprogramming them at the end of each day, parents and other adults can help give girls the chance to survive their preadolescent and teenage years relatively intact. Without that connection, they're in quicksand. Deprogramming means talking with your daughter after her day, asking questions, letting her ask you questions, having a conversation about what she encountered in the world, in school and after school, in her relationships. Who is saying what? What is the source? Who are they? What messages did you see and hear? How did you feel, what did you think, really think? What do you feel inside? Whose truth do you listen to? Do a reality check together. Every day, focus on the positive things she did; have her tell you positive things about herself that don't have to do with her looks.

I have found that talking with girls when they are young about how women are portrayed in advertising and the media is critical. Because of the intensity of advertising and how women are displayed and exploited, we need to make girls critical consumers of the culture by teaching media literacy. Begin talking with girls about it when they are young, in an age-appropriate way. Look together at programs and ads on TV, in magazines, on billboards, and on the Internet. Talk with your daughter about the fact that ads are exploiting girls and women and sending messages. Talk with girls about how women are depicted. Are there stereotypes? If so, what are they? What is the real message they are giving? Are they trying to make you feel "less than"? Not perfect? How do you feel watching the commercials? What do you think? Do the ads make you feel good about yourself?

Talk with girls about how they are being manipulated by the advertising industry. What roles are women in? Who is in what role? Raise their awareness about how women, men, and people of different ethnicities are portrayed. Talk with girls about the effects of such messages and how they don't just affect their bodies but also their insides, their self, and the way they behave. Make a poster of positive strong images of women, and talk about the differences between those and the sexually subordinated images prevalent in the media. We need to let girls see positive images, hear positive things about themselves and their capabilities. When my friend Jane was a girl, she read every book she could on Eleanor Roosevelt. Who was your heroine? Help your daughter find hers.

Let them know you understand that it may be hard to talk about some things now, but that you want to listen and will not be judgmental. However, if you say that, you need to really mean it and follow through. It's very important to teenagers that you keep your word. And as a parent, teacher, therapist, coach, friend, or relative, relational qualities such as respect, consistency, taking them seriously, and keeping your word are important to them during their passage to adulthood.

Middle school is a good time to be in some type of self-esteem-sustaining and -building group for girls. When I led girls' groups, I taught media literacy and coping strategies, which included breathing and calming exercises. This was a group for girls who were not suffering from anything in particular; rather, it was proactive because this is the age at which girls' resilience is at risk.

Building Self-Esteem and Self-Worth

I created a curriculum and conducted self-esteem and self-worth building groups for middle-school girls. Some groups met twice a week, others once. The girls loved these groups; we did activities such as writing down all their strengths, all the things they liked, and all the things that bugged them. We discussed how to problem solve; we drew pictures and made maps of their hopes and dreams; we made collages of the self. We worked on assertiveness and self-efficacy, discussed how to say things to people that were hard to say, talked about how and when to have another support you when you have something difficult to say. We talked about how to handle all the stimuli that were coming in and bombarding them. We examined what they meant to them, how they made them feel about themselves. Difficult topics came up, of course. The girls in one group discovered that several of them felt uncomfortable with a swimming coach, so they discussed what to do, and who to tell. We ate together—snacks, juice, water, healthy stuff, a little bit of not-so-healthy stuff—and talked about the differences in foods' nutritional values.

Girls could ask about sex in the group; they had one another and an adult. Kids need an adult to talk to. Sometimes at this age, though, some feel awkward and embarrassed talking with their mothers. These were ten-week groups. The girls loved them and begged and pleaded for their group to continue when it ended. Sometimes a weekend group works for early adolescent girls as well.

Chloe, now twenty-one, says she talked to a neighborhood mom. "There were just some things you couldn't talk to your own mom about but needed an adult to bounce things off of, to vent to, who you trusted who wasn't going to tell everything you say." It wasn't that she didn't want her mom to know these things, but she felt awkward revealing them. Sometimes there is an aunt, or a friend of the parents, with whom a girl feels comfortable. Let your daughter talk with her, but continue to make an effort to talk with your daughter yourself. You are the most important one, so don't feel hurt or threatened if she talks to other adults.

Mother Still Knows Best

It's impossible to do all the things I have suggested at the same time, so parents need not be overwhelmed by this long list of to-dos. The most important thing is to work as hard as you can to strengthen your communication and relationship with your daughter. It means looking past the typical tantrums of the angry teenage girl and not feeling personally attacked when she lashes out at you, the family, and everything you stand for. That's to be expected in this society. Think of a newborn baby whose only way of communicating is by bellowing. Keep up the communicating, and keep up the love, even when you are seriously angry with her and thoroughly disapprove of her behavior. Dealing with an adolescent can be like parenting a "terrible two." When your child is two years old, you can control her environment. When she's twelve, you can't do that, so it's important to keep your decoder at the ready.

What do I mean by a "decoder"? Well, girls at this age may display a series of signs that they are getting into trouble, that they are disappearing. These signals are not direct, and they are hard to distinguish from angst, but there are patterns of communication below the surface, and it helps to be aware of them.

One summer when Shelly was about fourteen she began a little pattern of sitting in the rocking chair listening to music with a headset. After a couple days, her mother said, "That's it, out you go. Go do something. No more sitting in the chair, tuning out the world like that." At age twenty-three, Shelly thinks that might have been a huge intervention. Her mom is a nurse, she says, and maybe she knew. "My mom was watching me in that rocking chair, and got me out of it fast."

Is Your Daughter Disappearing?

What are the disappearing signals and behaviors? Is she burrowing her way into a cocoon? Like the signals of negative thinking, signals of disappearing can manifest through words, what she does and does not say; through behavior, what she does and doesn't do; through the balance of daily routines and rhythms, her body, posture, health, self-care, even the light in her eyes. Are her daily routines of life out of sync? Every girl's experience is unique, but there may be similarities in behaviors that you see and don't see, in things that you hear and don't hear.

Does she appear different, not from the changes of adolescence and puberty, but in how she holds and carries herself? Posture is something to notice. Is there a decline in physical movement, physical activity? What does she seem to communicate through her body language? Is she slumped over? Are her shoulders hunched over, caving forward? Is her head down all the time? Or does she stand tall, shoulders back, as upright as when she was a little girl?

Does she look alert? How are her facial expressions? Is she dazed? Do her eyes look constantly sad or brimming with the fire of anger? Does she genuinely look happy? Could she be pretending?

Clothing and hair are huge forms of expression. Girls' clothes and hair can begin to match their moods, their thoughts. Is there a drastic change in appearance? Is she looking drab? Does she look miserable and depressed? Is she wearing only black? Does she have excessive body piercing? Tons of tattoos? Is this somewhat out of character? Is she piercing herself in the bathroom?

Sometimes in winter girls don't dress warmly enough. One girl I worked with had to be reminded to wear a heavier coat. She often forgot her gloves and never wore a hat, and it was very cold. On the other hand, is a girl wearing a turtleneck or a sweatshirt on a swelteringly hot day?

Are there rope and stretch bracelets around her wrists? Is there anything under them?

The best place to start is with the basics of eating, sleeping, exercising, and bathing—the acts that we perform routinely and without thought, but that girls may not be able to bring themselves to do. Is she eating well? Is she sleeping? Is she exercising? Showering? Making sure basic needs are being addressed is a good way to stay connected. It sounds so routine, but it is important. These are the little things you can look out for to help prevent a decline.

Modeling Healthy Behavior

If your daughter has stopped doing any of these things, help her. If she's depressed, just knowing that someone is there who cares about her, who feels she's worth taking care of, helps lift a girl out of her depression enough to take care of herself. Though these things are habitual rituals for most of us, for someone who is heading for depression or is depressed they require enormous effort. For example, I bought Laurie some special shampoo, body wash, and lotion. She loved that it smelled like strawberries (her favorite), and it was just what she needed to feel perked up enough to get in the shower again.

It's also important for parents and adults to model good health habits. Are you eating well? Are you offering her the right foods? Is the house quiet at night? Is there herbal tea or some other ritual you might introduce to help her sleep? Rituals are good. Maybe she can write down three things she was happy about today in a little book—three good things about herself that don't have to do with looks.

Extreme Teen Behavior

Is she taking unnecessary risks—not buckling her seat belt, or jaywalking? Is she increasingly reckless? Having lots of accidents? Does she end up in bed frequently from being injured or sick?

Has she gone from being reasonably calm to overly nervous and anxious? When I was asking Olivia how adults would know if a teenager was depressed, her reply was "Anxiety, really fidgeting." Some girls bite away their nails and cuticles, chewing away the self. However, you can't expect a girl to give up something that helps her cope until you help replace it. Taylor, at age fourteen, arrived at a school and she bit her nails so badly that they were going to put gloves on her. She became hysterical, and I explained to the staff that she needed something else to do, to help her cope. Some girls pick at their scabs so that wounds remain, unable to heal. One girl successfully picked every piece of lint off the blanket she had wrapped around her as we talked during a dorm meeting, maintaining eye contact and the conversation the entire time. I watched, fascinated. But that was much better than chewing or picking at herself, which she once did.

Many of the signs of disappearing into depression are typical teen behaviors gone to the extreme. For example, Olivia tells me, "Sleeping all the time is a sign, but that's a stereotype of teenagers. So, it's hard to distinguish." Then again, other depressed girls can't sleep. So look for unusual duration and intensity in typical teen behaviors. And talk to them; communication is key.

Depression can come in waves, or can be low grade, chronic, and gradually worsening, like Maura with dysthymia from Chapter Four. Are there spells wherein your daughter seems moody and irritable, then seems OK, only to have that sullen spell return later? Is she cranky, unhappy, bored, and restless? It's easy to think that she's just being a teenager and to feel convinced she'll simply grow out if it.

Has her communication pattern changed drastically? Does she chronically ignore questions? Does she respond with one-word answers over and over? Does she answer at all?

Has she become silent and stopped talking? Does she have outbursts on a very regular basis? Is she agitated? Is she pessimistic? Does she see only the negative side to everything?

Does she constantly say, "I don't know, I don't care, whatever" about everything? We may recognize that as part of typical teen dialect, but these phrases—particularly "I don't know"—signal a loss of voice, a disappearing of the self, a reluctance or hesitancy to say what she thinks and feels.[1] If she's says "I don't know" all the time, take notice. Ask more questions. Tell her you are there for her when she wants you to be. If a girl says, "I don't know" she may in fact know. It can become a rote response. Remember Elizabeth? She always said, "I don't know," but she did know. When she has to constantly monitor herself, she might lose touch with and stop expressing what she knows and feels.

Does she feel misunderstood? Does she repeatedly think you don't get it, that you never, ever understand? Olivia says, "This is another thing that is normal for teenagers, constantly saying, 'You DON'T understand.' Because if you're saying 'You don't understand,' it means that if you really didn't care that they didn't understand you'd just say fine, but you're trying to tell them something. So if you say that they don't understand, it means that you want them to. So something's wrong." What Olivia is saying is that she does want you to understand.

Teenagers may not want you to know everything they are doing, but they want you to have empathy for their struggle and pain. Even though there may be deep ambivalence, on some level they want you to understand what is going on with them. They may not have the words to say that they're scared, shamed, or embarrassed, or feel ungrateful because they have a good home, yet still feel depressed. They want to please you and others though it may not always seem that way. Girls don't know that they are experiencing depression, which creates anxiety.

What to Look For

Are you frustrated? Is your patience wearing thin? Think back to when you were fourteen or sixteen or seventeen or twelve. What did you worry about? What scared you? What were your fears? What frustrated you? What helped? What didn't? What did you want to hear? What brought you joy?

Has your daughter stopped talking about friends and other kids? Does she have friends? Does she talk about school? Does she talk about anything—what she wants to do? Where she wants to go? Where she's going?

If she does talk to you, what does your gut tell you? Do you sense a growing absence? Is she always in a bad mood? How often does it come and go? Are you getting surly remarks every single day? Is she telling you she's miserable? Have her grades dropped? What are her teachers saying? Is she spaced out in the classroom, not engaged the way she once was?

Girls begin to withdraw literally, psychologically, and physically for many reasons. In a matter of time, their selves feel snapped away, their relationships feel false, and their energy is sapped. And when the real person inside begins disappearing, who and what is left is not happy.

Girls see that others prefer the company of upbeat, positive people. Who wants to be around someone who is pessimistic and negative all the time? It can be draining to be around a chronically depressed person. Girls know this, so some of them pretend to be happy when they aren't.

Is your daughter sullen, irritable, and snappy? Does she silently look right past you or through you, passing you by, not saying a word? Is she too quiet? Is she moping, cranky, and sullen most of the time? Is she always lying on the couch or never out of her room? Do her crying spells go on forever? Does she seem bland? Lifeless? No energy? Displaying no emotion, seemingly numb? Olivia did not want to cry: "It's this huge thing to have self-control, to not cry, to sit there and bear it." She doesn't want to cry because, "It's showing vulnerability and it's showing my real emotions."

Does she plead to not go to school? Is she avoiding other kids? If so, why? What is going on at school? Is she alone and being picked on? Who are her friends? Are mornings awful? Is getting out of bed a huge feat, repeatedly?

What about eating? Does she show up for dinner, or say that she had cereal after school? Carrie proudly told me she hid her depression so well that there was never one single signal anyone would have ever noticed. She said no one knew she was starving herself because instead of coming to the table for dinner, she would say she had eaten cereal after school, or at a friend's, and was too busy doing her homework. "Aha," I said, playfully joking, "so there was a sign, but one that not too many people would get." I'm a child psychologist and steeped in and teach about girls' troubles, so I could see it. Her absence from the dinner table was a signal, but one most parents wouldn't think of because she was diligently working away on her homework, trying to get into a good college, saying she already ate.

Will your daughter come out of her room for dinner? Do you see food going from her plate to her mouth? Does she disappear into the bathroom after meals or frequent the ladies' room if you're out to dinner?

Does she say she has to stay home because she doesn't feel good, or she has too much homework? See how these could be reasonable explanations for not wanting to be with people, but if they're chronic, you want look deeper. Is she engaging with others at home or isolating herself? Is the phone ringing?

A prominent indicator that depression has hit hard is the loss of pleasure—she no longer does the things she loves, things that brought her joy. Instead, she's hiding in bed. She's disappeared. She doesn't venture out, crawling further into her cocoon. If she doesn't want to go out and do something she loves, it's a big signal.

Does she still want to wear her favorite clothes? Are they shoved away in the back of a drawer or closet, or in some heap on the floor? Are there drastic changes in the way she dresses? Does she seem distant? Is she listening to her favorite music? Pay attention to whether or not she has the same interests, and is engaged in them.

Interests can involve both other people and self-expression, and when she doesn't partake in these things it creates further disconnection from others as well as from herself. For instance, a team sport or a dance class provides an opportunity for both belonging and self-expression, so if she drops out she loses both.

Is she withdrawing from peers and school? Her friends? That's really something to be on the lookout for.

Does she bury herself in schoolwork? This is an easy way to hide, an acceptable way to disappear. Sooner or later schoolwork can suffer too. Olivia eventually stopped doing schoolwork. First she shut down to hide her intelligence from the teasing and taunting classmates, then apathy took hold. The pleasure she once felt doing well in school faded away and she no longer did her homework.

The most important advice I can give parents is "Don't give up." Do whatever it takes to stay connected—or to reconnect—with the adolescent girls in your life. Here are some basics that a parent can do: Increase the time spent together and make it quality time. Encourage authenticity in relationships, so that girls can discuss and explore the full range of their feelings. Give them permission to do so by making your open-minded acceptance clear. Raise their gender consciousness. Talk with them about the cultural gender rules around anger, sadness, success, and sexuality. Bring them out into the open. To be successful in the treatment of girls' depression, parents have to move beyond scrutinizing their daughters and take a look at themselves as well. Making sure that both words and actions convey messages of love, support, and caring is critical. Parents have to heal themselves along with their daughters and they have to follow through once girls identify changes that could help them.

The Joy of Good Friends

It's common knowledge that a friendship gone awry or the lack of friendship can precipitate depression in girls. But friendships can also be their biggest blessing; I've seen many girls whose friendship with someone kept them from falling over the edge. So first, make sure the girl in your life does have some friends. What does her social circle consist of? What does she do with her friends? Because the adolescent social world can be so hostile these days, make sure there's a friend around whom she can trust. Again, because relationships can be so difficult, help her diversify her peer group. Is there a community activity outside school she can become involved with? Is there an extracurricular activity within school that will expose her to a different group of kids? Help her broaden her network of friends, even if some of those friends happen to be adults. Provide opportunities for her to be with other teens struggling with similar issues. We see the power of the peer group in teens. We need to harness and make more use of positive peer leadership in a constructive fashion. Programs in which teens are helping other teens are very effective.

Like friendships, romantic relationships have incredible power over girls, and sometimes these relationships can be unhealthy. Adolescence is a time when girls are struggling to develop and maintain a sense of self, yet all too often this sense of self becomes completely wrapped around a boyfriend (or girlfriend). Then what happens if the relationship ends? Help the girl in your life maintain a sense of self, independent of her relationship. Make sure she maintains her friendships, even as she's focused on her relationship. Take the relationship very seriously. Romantic relationships are often a precipitant of depression and suicidal thoughts and behaviors. Help her see that it's OK if she's not in a romantic relationship. Teach her what does and does not constitute a healthy relationship: how to tell if she's being exploited and abused, what the difference is between communication and intimidation. Many girls think that if a boyfriend is jealous or controlling, that's merely an indication of love. Talk with her about respect and the difference between love and control. When a boyfriend get possessive and checks up on her all the time, a girl may think that's a sign of affection, but it's actually a sign of trouble. Make sure she knows what a healthy romantic relationship is and what it isn't.

Lonely in a Crowd

A girl can be with friends, family, and loved ones, but if she's hiding her real self, her real thoughts and feelings, if her real self is disappearing, she can feel profoundly alone. When she begins to hide physically, she not only feels alone in the company of others, now she is doubly alone through isolation.

Teenage behavior and depression can be hard to discern; there are ways it shows in relationships, as Olivia explains: "Girls getting involved with a really bad crowd, or getting involved with bad people they don't really care about and withdrawing from people that care about them is a sign of depression."

Relational attunement is very important. Pick up on girls' rhythms and patterns. There is a synchronicity in relationships. We are social beings, and when we feel despair and are consumed with negativity, we need others the most. Cutting herself off is the worst thing, because it is her connections that link her to love, to life, to health.

I ask thirteen-year-old Jade, "How would adults know if you were depressed?"

"I sit and I isolate," she replies matter-of-factly. Olivia answers the same question. "Isolation is a big one."

Be alert if a girl's personality seems to flatten out. Does she somehow seem bland? Is there general apathy?

It can be very scary when this happens, and parents can feel overwhelmed. Make sure you have support for yourself as well as for your daughter. Most parents need the support of therapy if their child has dipped low. It's very stressful. Parent support groups are terrific. What do you do to de-stress?

It can feel like she is gone, checked out and, petrified, you will wonder if you will get her back. Don't let fear immobilize you. Take action. Girls can and do get better. Even Olivia had hit rock bottom and was surfacing when I met with her—she was lively and bright a few months after she was bedridden with mono and serious depression.

If she is really isolated, invite family members or friends to visit. Make sure her sleeping and her eating get stabilized immediately. Make sure she gets regular exercise. (Remember that girls with depression and anorexia/bulimia often overexercise to lose weight, so each girl's specific needs will depend on her own circumstances.) If she's buried away in bed in her room, she won't get any sunlight. Do familiar things, things she likes to do.

Is there a family member she feels comfortable talking to? Remember how Jamie said that sometimes it was easier to talk to her mom's best friend? Remember how Jessie's parents had her uncle come over and she told him everything? If there is a kid who has been through a similar experience, get them together. I can't tell you how many girls say that making friends with other kids gave them hope. Other kids helped them to know they were not alone, which they said was very important to know, because often they think they are the only one with troubles. Knowing other kids who had been through it helped them think they were going to be OK, and that they, too, could make it.

Girls who think there is no reason for them to be depressed, who do not have something tangible that happened to point to, may be more likely to hide than girls who can point to something concrete. What the girls aren't consciously aware of is that their self is being chipped away. Sometimes girls who are scorned or harassed by other kids are hurt and it leads to depression, but they don't consciously make the link to that being a reason to be depressed. Meanness is becoming normalized as part of the typical peer culture.

Friends to the Rescue

Carrie and Nicole are both girls who thought they had no reason to be depressed and so worked hard to hide it. But careful observers noticed. Let's join Carrie's story when she began not eating. At home the mornings were a rush, and everyone was out so early that it was easy to skip breakfast. Lunch was at school and Carrie would sit with one group of friends, and someone would say, "Aren't you going to eat?" And she'd reply casually, "Oh, I'm going to grab something with so-and-so toward the end." And then she would tell so-and-so that she already ate with Beth. Then at dinnertime she was up in her room doing her homework. It was an easy routine.

Her mom would call up the stairs, "Carrie, time for dinner,"

"I had cereal after school," she would call down from her closed-door room. She hid her weight loss well under her loose clothes. She hid her feelings. She knew how to act like a happy girl, but someone at school was carefully watching. She had a close friend, Scott, who became her boyfriend. He began noticing during lunch. He observed that she never actually ate lunch with anybody. He never saw her eat. He also knew that she loved chocolate, and every day he put a chocolate cookie on her desk, and she ate it. She began telling him about herself. She went to his house after school sometimes and they would sit down together and he would pour her a bowl of cereal, and would sit with her at the kitchen table until she ate it. The longest was an hour and a half.

Soon, she told Scott everything. "The way I got help was I only told one person about my problems and what I was going through. I had one confidant, and he told me I had to get help or else he was going to tell somebody. So I wrote my school counselor a letter. I dropped the letter in her mailbox before my English class, and she was waiting outside my English class door after class. She pulled me out of class and we had a long talk, and she set me up with a clinical counselor, and I started meeting with her every week."

This is a story about the power of relationships, of a friend and adults taking girls seriously. Scott took seriously what he saw and gave Carrie an ultimatum. Then there is the wonderful example of how schools can respond, what can be done when they have resources and put them to good use. This was a terrific counselor who took a girl's note seriously and immediately took action.

Nicole: The Girl Who Had Real Friends

Nicole's story is similar; her friends notice and facilitate an intervention. In the long run, as you will see, it helps her mom, too.

Nicole tends to keep things to herself. In eighth grade, she knew that she was going to be sitting all alone because of the way things were with her group of friends at the time. "I remember walking along, thinking, looking up at the little posters, the little thing that says what day it was in the front office. Just walking along and thinking, 'Do I really even feel like these people would care all that much if I wasn't here at all?' It wasn't necessarily 'if I'm dead,' because that attracts a lot of attention. But if I left—if I died, if I moved somewhere, if I disappeared, would there even be a bump in the road? Would it mean anything to them?"

She made new friends but the bad feelings came back again and again. Then Nicole explains, "Through my different cycles of depression at one point, in tenth grade, my depression was finally called to the attention of other people, like adults. I had a bunch of friends that I had been close with that I wasn't close with anymore, because I wasn't talking to anyone. They watched me. I'd tried to do it so they wouldn't notice, but it's kind of hard to disappear from a group of friends and have no one notice, if you actually are friends with them. I would sit off by myself. I was tired all the time. I had no energy. All that." She pauses and tells me it's a long story, asking if I want to hear, and I say "Yes." Here it is:

"So these friends, specifically my very best friend, she'd been trying to be there for me. She was amazing. She was above-and-beyond-the-call-of-duty kind of amazing, even more than you would think a friend would be. She was completely amazing but nothing she was doing was helping. I wouldn't snap out of it. So eventually I think she had a conference with some of my other good friends, and they thought, 'We don't know what to do, but we're scared.'

"So they went to one of the guidance counselors at the high school, who said, 'It sounds like your friend definitely needs help, but this isn't really my specialty, so we need to go talk to the school's clinical counselor.' So they did. They were excused from class and went and met with the clinical counselor who deals with that kind of stuff at the high school. She wanted to talk to me.

"For most of this time, I didn't know what was going on. Then I was quietly sitting in a little corner next to a window, writing something or checking homework. It was a free block between classes, because I wasn't doing a club or activity. They walked up, a whole bunch of them, kind of in a line. I just knew, I was like, 'Oh shit, they did something, didn't they?' They said, 'Nicole?' I got up and tried to walk away. I started walking around the school and they were power walking really fast after me, 'Come back here! We need to talk to you.' I ran away and sat somewhere else and wouldn't listen to them, because I didn't want anything, any attention, anything. Eventually one of them stayed around to keep an eye on me to make sure I didn't try to leave the school building, because they were afraid I was going to run away." The girls were very insistent on helping their friend.

"The other ones went to the clinical counselor and said, 'We can't get her to come meet you.' So the counselor followed them to where I was sitting, which I wasn't expecting or I probably would have done something. She said, 'You have to come and talk to me.' It was an adult, and as much as I wanted to I just couldn't get myself to say, 'No' and run away. I knew I was trapped, and I figured it might make things worse if I ran. So I said, 'OK, fine, whatever.' I went with my friends and sat down in this big old office. It was my best friend and three or four other friends at that point who were all involved. I sat down and a bunch of them sat on the floor. There were little bean-bag cushions. Two of my friends immediately started crying. I don't cry. I never cry. I just don't."

Nicole goes on with her story. "So I was sitting there thinking, 'Oh God, how the hell am I going to get out of this? How am I going to pull this off? I don't know if I can.' My best friend was sitting next to me.

The counselor was talking to me, kept asking me questions. I would an-swer with half-truths. I always half downplay everything. I'd say, 'Nah, it's really not that big of a deal. Yeah, OK, I have thought such and such.' My best friend knew everything about me. I never told her specifics because I didn't want to tell anyone anything, but she kind of knew because we were really, really close. So every time I tried to dodge something, she'd say, 'No, that's not true. I know it's not. I know you. You said something like this to me once.' She sat there and confronted me. So I was thinking, 'Oh boy.' There were plenty of things to talk about, too, because not only was I depressed, I was suicidal, but no one really knew that. My best friend suspected. She knew because she felt it, but I never talked about how much. I had not been eating much at all. I'd lost a ton of weight fast. I wasn't trying to lose weight. I had loss of appetite from depression.

"I was saying 'Really, it's OK, I'm fine. I'm still here.' They said, 'Yeah, barely.' And I had begun secretly cutting, and some of them knew that. Well, they all knew at that point because they'd been talking about me. They didn't all know it beforehand, but my best friend told them. That's when they said, 'Oh my God! That's it, we have to take her in.'"

"Friends who are actually your friends" are the friends who noticed Nicole beginning to withdraw. These smart fifteen-year-old girls did a courageous and significant intervention. Their genuine friendship and love for Nicole is apparent. They didn't just notice her withdrawing and merely infer, "Oh well, that's that with her." They cared, they knew her well enough to say, "Something must be off, this is not the Nicole we know." They did not think "She's a jerk, she's snubbing us." They risked losing her because they loved and were concerned about her. Nicole saw that and was not mad at her friends for trying to help her. These are the unsung heroines we never hear about on the news; these stories aren't on reality TV. But this is a real story.

Nicole didn't want her parents to know. I asked her why.

"They would take it really personally. Parents think it's either some-thing they did wrong or something they didn't do that they should have. Some of the time it's issues that can affect kids, but a lot of the time, it really has nothing to do with the parents."

The school counselor did call Nicole's parents because of Nicole's cutting and suicidal tendencies. She said her parents were terrific. "My parents never really said or did anything wrong in the first place. It wasn't that. If they had somehow known to say more things to try to talk to me more about all that sort of thing, I would have pushed them away; it would have annoyed me more. It wouldn't have helped me at all. It wasn't going to work that way. There wasn't anything they could do. When they finally knew, my parents reacted very well. They were sad, of course, but said, 'We love you, and we'll do whatever we need to do.' To me, that's the only thing a parent really can do: Say, 'We'll do whatever we can to help you and to help us. Whatever you think, whatever people think is best. We'll do whatever we can because we love you.' You could ask for nothing more, in my opinion, from parents. I didn't need my parents to regulate me more now or give me a lot more rules and restrictions. That would just make me feel more suffocated and angry. That would perpetuate the whole cycle."

Sometimes it can be stressful when a child is having trouble, and parents can develop depression; or sometimes parents can have low-grade depression and they don't even know it. Now here is the part of Nicole's story in which Nicole's experience helped her mother.

Nicole and Her Mom: The Circle of Help

"One of the great things is it broke all those barriers for my mother. She said, 'I realize now when I'm not feeling so great, that it's OK to not feel great, and there are ways to deal with it.' So just because you don't feel OK doesn't mean it's a bad thing or it's wrong. You don't have to shut it off and pretend that you're happy. My mom grew up in a traditional family, so whatever it was, you sucked it up and put a smile on your face, it didn't matter. It took her into her forties and many years of that to realize that it doesn't have to be that way."

" 'As horrible as it is,' my mother said to me, 'in many ways I'm glad you brought attention to it, and now we're all taking care of things we didn't even realize were quite problems, but we're all so much better for it.' Even though it's horrible and you wouldn't wish for someone to be depressed, there were a lot of good things coming out of me getting help.

"We did some family therapy, which made my parents much more aware of psychology, how it worked, that there are things that you might think are normal feelings but might not actually be. So after a while my mom started seeing a therapist. Just once every two weeks, just to help her talk through some of her concerns about me that she didn't want to talk about in front of me in family therapy. And the counselor was talking to her about my mom going on some medication because my mom was starting to think about the way she'd felt for so many years, especially in the winter—nothing really extreme but low-grade. Because of everything that was going on, she was becoming aware of the fact that maybe that's not where she should be. She went on medication. It worked for her, but not me. You could just see it in the first couple weeks. She was really OK if all the laundry wasn't folded before a friend of hers came over for tea. She started to lose some of those things a little bit and be a little more relaxed, and enjoy herself a little more without worrying so much. As time went on she was able to smile more casually and felt more comfortable. She still worries about a lot of things, just like she always has, but now it's just something in the back of her mind that she knows she has to do, but it's not in the forefront of her mind, taking away from her ability to enjoy wherever she is at the moment. It's made a remarkable difference."

"My mom looked at me one day and said, 'You know, Nicole, I never really realized that that was my default setting. I always thought I was a quieter sort of person. All along that wasn't really me. It was depression. With therapy and medication I feel like I can be more myself.' She was so happy. If I remember correctly, she had tears running down her face as she realized that this weight had been lifted from her that she didn't even realize was a weight. After that, she kept talking about it, and eventually my dad went on an antidepressant too. It wasn't an extreme case. It didn't make a huge difference for him, but it did make him feel kind of better. Both my parents started feeling so much better about themselves and so much more comfortable. They understood so much more of what I was going through—in a small way. That made such a huge difference for all of us to go through that together." Nicole says that a lot of good has come out of the experience for her and her family.

"For me the beginning wasn't clear, but over the years it's more about me. It's about figuring out who I am. Who you are is an important part of how you deal with the things you encounter, and the signals that you get. Everything that comes into your system is who you are and how you deal with that, how you interpret it, what you do about it, all of it. It's mostly about me and how I handle and look at the world, how I looked at myself, how I am with myself and with my friends, what I wanted, who I was. It's incredibly personal. That's what depression is to me, more than anything else; it's an incredibly personal experience, which is why it's hard for people to talk about."

No plan of prevention, action, or intervention will be the same for each girl. As I said before, each girl is different, and will need different levels of attention, and different types of activities to help her. However, there is great consistency in the areas of a girl's life that need special focus. Parents, teachers, counselors, doctors, friends, boyfriends, and girlfriends are all part of a girl's world, and all aspects of her life need to be considered. The girls themselves are the best authority when it comes to developing a plan, because it has to work for them. For example, you can't tell them the song to play when they want to get cheered up. They have to pick their favorite song. You can always try this:

The Emotional First-Aid Kit

Have a girl make a little kit. It's fun to make it with someone, and then she can always add things. Use any kind of box. It can be decorated as a collage, or painted. Inside it she can put the things she needs to help her feel better. This is not just for girls in crisis. It can help anyone learn that there are things they can do if they start feeling pressured and stressed.

Inside the box, they can write on a little card the names and numbers of friends, family, or others they can talk to if they are feeling bad. A CD with their favorite songs is also helpful. Girls can learn to say to themselves, When I feel stressed I can listen to this song to help me de-stress; when I feel sad I can listen to feel better. It's not that we don't want girls to learn how to bear and be with these feelings, it's just that they need to know they can manage their thoughts and feelings and not have their thoughts and feelings manage them.

In their kit, they can also put on little cards three or four positive affirmations about themselves: "I am important"; I am capable"; "I can do it"; "I am loved." Each affirmation, like the other things in the kit, has to work for them and be their own choice. An inspirational poem or quote can help too. A few pictures of loved ones and friends, of positive moments, are also useful. Also, include the name of a favorite childhood book, story, movie, or song.

A soothing, good-smelling lotion, a miniature one, might be nice. A squeeze ball or silly putty, something squishy for tension and anxiety, would be useful. Gum as a substitute for chewing nails. Lots of girls I worked with like aromatherapy or other oils. A small vial of a favorite scent might be calming.

Small special mementos can be included, as can a little card with the names of a favorite movie, book, and TV show. A list of all the things they love will keep them connected to who they are and remind them of the positive things about themselves and their lives.

Other Things That Help

Being creative and doing things to express herself helps. She can make a collage representing her self. She can make one that represents the depressed parts of her, and another one that symbolizes the parts of her that are not depressed. She can make one integrating both. Have her make a collage of things she loves, affirming the positive.

Have her keep a scrapbook. It is a simple and timeless way to help her keep connected to her self and her life.

We all need to be more involved in helping middle and high schools develop educational programs for teenage girls at risk, including creating groups and space for kids to come together, which is most often not part of school-based intervention programs. Schools can also initiate success-oriented curricula, so that the pressures and heavy criticism that define academics can be assuaged. Girls care if their teachers care, which can be a real source of either encouragement or discouragement. Schools need to have programs that educate kids about depression. When money is low, though, these sorts of programs fall by the wayside.

Therapy is another important tool in helping depressed girls. Adults can be the best protection against the risk of disconnection and psychological dissociation. An adult's ability to speak from her life experience is important in forging relationships with girls.

What is of vital importance for successful therapy is that a girl feels comfortable, safe, and in a trusting relationship with a therapist. If the trust isn't there, the therapy won't be effective. There are different kinds of therapists with different kinds of training, and many that will integrate different approaches. Parents need to ask: Does the therapist have experience with children and adolescents, specifically with adolescent girls? Consider what attributes would be important to a teen. Is s/he open? Is s/he too rigid? Rigidity and authoritarianism will not work with teens. Is s/he willing to balance power? Does s/he take teenagers seriously? Does s/he understand girls' development? The gender of the therapist, whether s/he has hours after school or on weekends, his or her education and training, what kind of therapy s/he does—all of these constitute areas to inquire about and discuss. If feasible, a girl should have a say in choosing her therapist, a solid first step in establishing successful treatment. The bottom line will be trust.

Cognitive-behavioral psychotherapy has proven to be effective with depressed teens, so a therapist who knows and integrates that style will be important. Relational-based therapy, which is therapy that emphasizes the importance of the relationship between a girl and her therapist, is extremely important for girls.[2] Look for talk therapies—relational or cognitive-behavioral—that don't center around just doling out medication. The FDA has issued a warning on the safety of antidepressants for children and teenagers, and some antidepressants can have the adverse side effect of increasing suicidal behavior.[3] So if you are trying medication be extremely careful. And I have found that with teenagers there are some days you sit in the office and some days you take a walk. Some teens may feel more comfortable talking about things in a less intimate setting. I've gone with girls for an ice cream or a slice of pizza. I've gone to CVS with a girl to help her pick out shampoo. I've been to cemeteries. I have proudly watched girls' graduations, and performances in chorus, theater, and sports. Some kids don't need this and some therapists don't do it. It all depends on the girl and her unique situation.

11. A SHINING LIGHT

"That's one thing about us girls, we're resilient."

—Kristy, age 15

"I am sixteen and I like to sing," announces Rachel, who has straight blond hair right below her shoulders, clear, bright shining brown eyes, a beautiful face, and a winsome, beaming smile. Wearing blue jeans and a white oxford cotton shirt, she remembers being depressed since about sixth or seventh grade. One minute she can appear serious and the next she's running and laughing with her friends. Her best friends are David and Kayla. She did well in school until recently, but her real love and joy is singing. She also loved to dance and do gymnastics before she broke her ankle, foot, and arm last year. And even before she jumped off the chair lift skiing, which caused those injuries, she wasn't that into dancing and gymnastics the way she had been, but she still loves to sing. Now nerve damage from the jump prohibits her from dancing and doing gymnastics.

Rachel has a brother and sister; her brother is away at college. Her sister, Abby, is still at home. They are different but love each other very much. Rachel says with a grin, "She would be upstairs doing her homework and I would be downstairs singing. It would piss the hell out of her."

Sometimes Abby would barely give her the time of day. Rachel says Abby teased her, which could make her feel stupid and inferior. When Rachel mentions singing she lights up; her beauty just seems to radiate at the mere mention. I ask if she's doing any singing now. "Not really," she whispers.

Rachel is very close to her mom. She clung to her mom when she was little. Her parents divorced when she was young. Though she lived with her mother after the divorce, around puberty she missed her mom in a way she couldn't quite put into words. It felt as if they were growing apart. Rachel started to think her mother didn't have time for her because she would get home from work and would often say, "I have to do some work." Rachel loves her mom, but at the moment is annoyed with her. She is, however, even more annoyed with her dad.

She felt her dad had abandoned her. At first, after the divorce, she saw him a lot, but within a couple years he remarried. After he remarried, their time together grew inconsistent. "We started not seeing each other and then we saw each other a lot, and then we didn't see each other. It seems like he sets it up so he hurts me." She thought it was "bad" for her and that it changed her relationships with guys, explaining, "Well, I'm always afraid they are going to hurt me. I either hurt them before they can hurt me, or I just get hurt. I'm afraid that people aren't going to like me."

When I asked what she wanted her relationship with her dad to be like she said, "I don't want to see him anymore, even though I love him. I am sick of him. I don't want him to hurt me anymore. I am just sick of all the pain he has caused me and all of the bullshit I have had to put up with." She didn't dare tell him she was angry, though.

When she's sad she says, "I isolate and swim in my depression. I do that negative self-talk."

"What do you do when you are angry?" I ask.

"I never get angry. I hardly ever get angry," she informs me. (She sounds like the rest of the girls, doesn't she?)

"Why do you think that is so?"

"I think if I get angry people aren't going to like me anymore so I bottle up all the anger and I lash out at one person who I know will always love me, which is my mom." But she also got angry with her mom—who wasn't giving her the freedom and independence she wanted. Sometimes, she says, her mom is "overbearing."

Then she says, "My mother puts up with a lot of shit from me."

"Do you feel safe expressing your anger to her?" I ask Rachel.

"Yeah, I know she'll always love me no matter what I do," she says, steadily holding my gaze. Knowing that her mother will always be there for her will keep Rachel emotionally safe in the world.

Rachel can't stand for people to be mad at her. She worries about people liking her or not liking her; if she's mad at someone, she doesn't want to tell them. "I'm afraid they'll get mad at me. They won't understand."

I ask, "Do you worry that you will be alone?"

"I'm afraid of abandonment."

She remembers feeling sad when her mom and her fiancé broke up when she was around eleven. They were engaged for three years. It was like her dad leaving all over again. "Too many adults have left me. I don't trust any of them," she says.

Things built up. One day skiing with a few of her friends, they were riding the chair lift and Rachel jumped off too soon and broke her ankle, foot, and arm. Her mother took her straight to a psychiatrist.

Laid up at home in bed, on crutches and lots of painkillers, she became more isolated and started withdrawing. She couldn't move around so she couldn't go out with her friends. One day, she was feeling "emotional"; her dad was due to take her for dinner at 4:30 to 5:00 P.M. At 3:30, she took lots of her pain medications—Percocet and Tylenol—then went in her room and called her boyfriend, Jeff. She started crying, telling him what she had just done. Her eyes began to swell up, and she could hardly see. She felt heavy and when she tried moving or leaning back, she couldn't. She tried to get up, and fell. Her mom heard the fall, and bounded up the stairs. She could not imagine telling her mom the truth so she said, "I feel really sick." Her mom immediately got a thermometer and took her temperature. Rachel started throwing up.

Her dad was late, showed up at 5:30, but it didn't matter. Rachel was sick all night. The next morning, without any appointment, her mom took her to her psychiatrist, who asked her if she had overdosed, and Rachel said no. They figured it was a bad reaction to the painkillers and discontinued them. She told only her boyfriend. A few days later her mom read her diary and discovered it was a suicide attempt. Of course Rachel was furious at her mom.

Around that time everything began piling up again. She was worried that her best friend, David, might be moving to another state, far away. He was her closest friend and she depended on him. They understood each other and always knew how to make each other feel better and laugh. They hung out a lot and had tons of fun.

She broke up with her boyfriend, Jeff. They had been going out for over a year. Though David was her best friend, if she mentioned his name in conversation, Jeff told her she couldn't talk about him. "Basically he wanted me to choose and I felt like I couldn't live without David and that was upsetting because I still loved Jeff. I know it is stupid for a sixteen-year-old to love someone, but I love him." I asked why she thought it was stupid. "I don't know. Most adults seem to act like you can't fall in love when you are that age." I told her I was once her age and certainly thought she could fall in love. She was upset because now Jeff wasn't speaking to her at all.

School was making her feel inferior. Behind in school from the accident, she was supposed to write an essay over the weekend to turn in Monday or else she was going to have to stay after school. She was sick over the weekend with a fever and could have gone to school Monday but she hadn't finished the essay. She felt panicked. She was upset with herself that she was not keeping up with her schoolwork. It was third quarter and she still owed things from second quarter. Now she was falling behind in third quarter, too.

She tried to open up and be honest in school but was called names and felt judged and ridiculed. "If someone is depressed and they are trying to open up to you and the teacher says you are just doing it for attention they are going to close right up like a clam and never talk to anyone," she says.

Trying to explain how depression feels when it gets bad and thoughts turn suicidal, she asks me if I saw the movie *Girl, Interrupted*, and I say yes. "Remember when she is lying in bed with that guy Toby, and she is talking about suicide? She says, 'Once you are suicidal it is all you think about. I spill a cup of milk, I want to die.' It's just so right. Everything that goes wrong, you think about it, you think about wanting to die." When she thinks about dying it's not about wanting to die. Rather it's about finding a way not to have to deal with all the stressful situations and difficult people. But, she acknowledges, those thoughts can and do pass with a little time.

At 11:30 P.M. that Monday night, Rachel took an entire bottle of Tylenol. Rachel was on the phone with her best female friend Kayla when she started taking it; Kayla asked what she was doing and she said she was drinking water. Rachel was crying because the conversation was upsetting her. She didn't tell Kayla she took the pills. Her sister came home and saw her crying and asked what was wrong, and she said she was talking to Kayla. Her sister went to bed. Rachel didn't think the Tylenol was working so she took some more. They got off the phone at 1:30 and she realized it hadn't worked, that she would, in fact, wake up tomorrow. But she then began to get really sick. Her mom heard her, asked her if she had taken anything, and she said, yes, then no. Her mom called an ambulance.

Coda

Two years later I'm unexpectedly sitting in the front row at a performance of *The Wizard of Oz*. Because of traffic, we arrived just in the nick of time. As the actors take the stage, I recognize a face and a voice—a teenage girl, growing into a beautiful young woman, and the star of the show, singing "Somewhere Over the Rainbow" in a strong and stirring soprano voice, dancing away! No one but maybe I know she once had a broken ankle, foot, and arm. Despite the lighting, our eyes instantly meet and lock, filling us both with wonder, surprise, and joy. It is a powerful moment. Her eyes glisten as she sings and dances. Mine fill with tears that joyfully trickle down my face, for there in front of me sparkling like a ray of light is hope, resilience, and strength bundled into Rachel, now eighteen, who when she was sixteen wanted to die.

Intermission arrives. Rachel immediately finds me. Now both of us are crying and we're holding each other tightly. "I'm so proud of you," I exclaim, taking her face in my hands. Beaming, clearly proud of herself, she smiles that bright winsome smile of hers and says to me, "Oh my gosh, I was such a mess back then. How's the book?"

12. GIRLS' WISDOM

I concluded every interview with the girls, time permitting, by asking them for their advice to parents and others who want to help, and ways schools can help too. I also asked them their advice for other teenagers who may be feeling depressed. Here are their gifts—nuggets of wisdom from brave and strong girls. I decided to present their advice without commentary, because they speak so clearly and plainly. You may recognize some of the girls. Because so many girls talked about listening being the most important things adults can do, I began asking the girls: **How do you know someone is listening?**

They're making eye contact, they're not slouching or looking the other way or saying, "Excuse me for a minute I have to go do this," or "What did you say again? I didn't hear you." It's giving full attention and asking you questions and returning your answers with questions and having comments for what you said. Not just "Yup, uh-huh, OK." —Ali, age 15

You know by the questions they ask and if they change anything as a result. —Skyla, age 17

If I don't think someone's paying attention, I'll just stop talking. Or I'll just say "Yeah." —Mindy, age 14

What can adults do who want to help girls who feel depressed?

Sit down and talk to girls and get to know their experiences as well as you can. You have to be open-minded about everything, too, because a lot of people are one-sided. I think that's probably the most important thing. Most of all, you have to be totally open to listening.

—Noelle, age 15

Be compassionate. Be empathetic. Listen, but also don't take on the real adult-child separation. Try to relate more on a person-to-person level. Don't be scared. We're already scared enough of ourselves. Don't let us know that you, the adult, are scared. Then we'd think, "I guess I really am fucked, because they're scared of it too."

—Skyla, age 17

Really listen. Don't give out advice until you know what's really going on. If they cut, then help them figure out exactly why they cut. It's really important, because you won't get anywhere if you don't know why. Help them make a list of all the good things about cutting, and all the bad things about cutting. And then take all the good things and think of things that you could substitute and take all the bad things and use them as excuses not to do it. And then give them lots of support. Make sure that they always remember that they always have somebody to talk to when they want to cut. Make sure that they definitely have strategies whenever they're feeling that way. That's like me saying what I would want.

—Harmony, age 17

Figure out what happened in their life that they don't like. Or what's going on now that they don't like. Think about the things that have happened that they want to change. Just really listen to them. Just listen. Don't say anything. Don't criticize them. And don't say, "I think it's the marijuana that's doing it." That just makes me more aggravated. Help them figure out what they want to do in life that they would really love. Help them get a sense of hope, and sense what they can accomplish. Make sure that they have somebody to talk to all the time. Give them your beeper number. Take them out to lunch once a week, so they can talk, so they know that there's somebody there.

—Harmony, age 17

In some ways you have to revert back to a kid. If a kid sees that you're so much of a grown-up, all about authority and "I know best," they will not connect to you well. You have to be very understanding, and show that you can put yourself in their place. Revert back to being a kid. Kids always connect with other kids better than with an adult. Try to do something that they love doing. Take them dancing, out to dinner, or to the beach. Sometimes it's hard for grown-ups. Maybe they've been an adult too long that it's very hard for them to convert. But you have to, if you want to help that child, that adolescent. —Lola, age 16

Give them time. Be as encouraging as you can. Be as sympathetic and empathetic and kind and hopeful. Show how much you care. They might think you're corny, but they really like it, they do. They really like to hear that people care. As much as they might try not to believe it, the more it sticks in their head, the more they think, "Well yeah, maybe there are people that care and they're OK." Tell them you care. Show them, tell them, and stress it to them. That works. —Jessie, age 15

Just listen. Basically see what's going on and think of ways to help them. Hear them out. Because most people ignore or they don't listen to everything a kid's trying to say. —Jamie, age 15

Listen better. Each situation is individual. Adults have to listen more to what kids say, what comes out of their mouth, what they are talking about. That's the most important thing.

—Ali, age 14

Talk to kids more. —Jade, age 13

What do you want to tell parents?

I think it was important to really be able to trust your parents and to talk to them. To know that they really love you and care about you, and they're there forever, to give you all the support you're ever going to need. They're not going to give up on you. Just that they're there. —Jessie, age 15

Make time, no matter what you are doing. I don't care if you are making dinner or saving the world. Well, if you are doing that keep doing it. Make time no matter what you are doing. I don't care if you are doing your own work. You have to put it down. Make time, because it will get worse and worse and worse.   —Rachel, age 16

People are so concerned about work and many teenagers are left by themselves. Parents just don't see the signs of what's going on. They're too quick to punish a kid for coming home drunk. Sit down and ask them, "Why are you drinking? What's making you want to drink?" Don't sit there and say, "You're grounded." You'll just get the kid rebellious and make her want to walk out and say, "Screw you." It's going to make them drink more. So sit down and say, "You know what, you're drinking. You're going to cause yourself a lot of problems." If they keep coming home drunk, then take a step up. Put them in a program, a hospital program. I understand people can only do so much, but I don't see people doing enough.

—Crystal, age 16

If you have alcohol in the house, lock it up. Make sure it's locked. Some kids are just like, "Hey, what the hell? It's in the house."

—Mindy, age 14

You've got to take them seriously. Be open. Listen to what they have to say and try to understand it from their perspective.

—Jamie, age 15

Are there other ways parents can help?

Be available for face-to-face conversation. Sit down, look your child in the eyes. Focus on her and her only—not the mail, not work, not dinner, not school, not phone calls.   —Crystal, age 16

Ask questions. Don't just give suggestions. Questions that show you are listening and are interested in knowing more.   —Janessa, 15

Don't judge; don't criticize.   —Jamie, age 15

Let them know they are not in this alone. You will not be scared or appalled or disappointed. That you won't be able to handle it if something is wrong, if she is sad, lonely, empty, been assaulted, got drunk, messed up, wasn't perfect, wasn't "good." You believe in them, you will not give up on them. You will get them the additional support they need, but you won't just turn them over to a clinician. You will do your own work, too, your own therapy.

—Crystal, age 16

Parents could try their best to understand the motivation of their daughter's behavior instead of automatically thinking the parents are the cause of it.   —Maura, age 14

How can schools help?

Have guidance counselors or teachers call on kids more. Try to stop all the clique-ing going on.   —Ali, age 14

Try to see it through their eyes. Schools don't do that.

—Cyrstal, age 16

Schools should have a group with a bunch of kids who have either made suicide attempts or have been diagnosed with depression.

—Elizabeth, age 14

You can really learn from people who have already gone through what you're going through. And they can really make you hopeful that if a lot of other people out there in the same situation as you have gone through it and they're OK, then you can too.

—Elizabeth, age 14

Schools need to be patient. Give kids space and time.

—Janessa, age 15

Don't go to the parents. Go to the kid and talk straight up like adults about it. Talk to the kids adult to adult. Don't be patronizing, because if you do talk to people like you are superior then they are not going to say as much because they are feeling inferior and dumb.

—Rachel, age 16

Never ever claim kids are liars or say that they are trying to get attention. Because if someone is depressed and they are trying to open up to you and you say that, they are going to close right up like a clam and never talk to anyone. It's horrible when they say that. You are trying to get help and you are trying to open up.

—Rachel, age 16

You have to find the right school, one that will boost your self-esteem instead of lower it. You have to click with the school. You have to find one that you feel good at, where you know your work is going to be applauded, and that you're going to get helpful criticism. One school put so much stress on me that I lost fifteen pounds. I was more recognized at a small school. A lot of the teachers recognize achievements of students and really applaud them. They would definitely find time and help you if you had any questions. They would work one-on-one. I had one teacher who knew that one-on-one was important to me. After that session, I would just really pick up. If I were having one trouble spot, after that session, I would just be breezing through it. So I got an A-.

—Lola, age 16

My school really wasn't very sensitive to how I felt. They basically told me to suck it up. We don't care about your excuses; we don't care how you feel. This is school. Every kid has to go through it, and if you don't go through it, we'll have to file a report on you. And your parents obviously aren't doing their job. My teacher knew that I'd come into class really high and pilled out sometimes, and they'd send me out to the principal. I'd leave.   —Jessie, age 15

An early sign would be if they can't really focus in class. If they're really constantly not there, constantly skipping classes, always skipping school, having anger management problems like flipping out, swearing, or misbehaving.   —Mindy, age 14

It could be anything. It could also be really being really quiet all the time.   —Mindy, age 14

They have to be strict, but smart and accepting.   —Ali, age 14

Let the kid tell you what's going on. Just listen to every single word and if you really don't understand, don't say, "OK, I feel bad for you." If you don't feel bad, just say, "You know what? Like, I really don't understand what you're going through. I don't know what to say to you." Don't just say something because it sounds good.

—Crystal, age 16

What do you want to say to other teenagers who may be struggling?

Try not to escape negativity with drugs and running away. Just deal with it because eventually the outlook and the situation will get better. —Mindy, age 14

If you can, just hang on a little longer without hurting yourself. Things really will get better. If you kill yourself you're really not giving yourself a fair chance to work things out and have the life and the happiness you deserve. Also, you're not alone. A lot of people go through this and if you commit suicide you never have the chance to talk to somebody else and realize, wow, I'm really not alone in this. It's something a lot of teenagers go through.

—Elizabeth, age 14

Remember that it's an illness, and very serious, like cancer. You need help. Maybe you need medicine. You need therapy; you need people to be able to talk to to really get better. It's an illness that many people have gotten over and gone on to have successful lives and so can you. —Elizabeth, age 14

If you are depressed, don't isolate because it will make it worse. Don't not think about it—think about what is making you depressed.

—Rachel, age 16

Try not to be negative about things, don't say everything sucks, life sucks, I want to die, that won't make anything better. —Ali, age 14

Be strong. Stand up for yourself. Do what you know is right. Realize that drugs aren't everything. They're not going to make you feel good for long. They just make you weaker in the long run. They aren't healthy for you. —Jessie, age 15

The first time you feel suicidal, get help, because it is just going to get so much worse. You can ignore it all you want but it will always come back. —Rachel, age 16

The healthiest thing is to be good to yourself. Try to find the best in everything. Go to school because a life of drugs and depression is nothing to look forward to. If you're going to be on drugs all the time, you're going to be stuck. What are you going to have in the future? If you don't go to school because you're messed up, you'll end up with no education, no job, no money, nowhere to live. You'll probably end up living on the street or dying, which is really sad.

—Jessie, age 15

If you can't talk to an adult, talk to peers, to positive peers you feel close to. Call a hotline; you won't even know that person, which will make it easier for you. —Jamie, age 15

Stand up for yourself. If someone disrespects you in any way, if you feel uncomfortable with what someone is doing to you, stand up for yourself and say, "I really don't appreciate that or will you please stop, you're making me feel uncomfortable." —Jessie, age 15

There are behaviors that many girls don't realize are self-destructive—having sex and being promiscuous, doing a lot of drugs to drown out your problems or just taking high risks. Self-destructive behavior involves how you feel about yourself and your self-esteem. So you have to learn to feel better about yourself. —Noelle, age 15

Be around other kids who have been through depression. You feel good from the close relationships that develop and then you feel good about yourself and you get a lot of good self-esteem from that.

—Noelle, age 15

Don't look at yourself in the mirror in the morning and say, "I'm ugly, I'm not worth anything, or I'm stupid." You're not; you're beautiful, you're smart, you're strong, and you can do anything you put your mind to. Realize that everyone's like that. Treat others the way you'd like to be treated. —Elizabeth, age 14

It all goes back to your self-esteem.   —Noelle, age 15

I know what you're going through. You're not the only one out there. You've got to tell somebody and try to get a therapist. You need to do the best for yourself, so you can get over it and you won't feel so bad.   —Maura, age 14

It's really hard in the beginning, but as you go through it you start getting better. You start getting used to it and it helps you. You need help, or you'll always feel like crap. So basically, stay in school; don't do drugs.   —Mindy, age 14

I used to give myself advice. When I wanted to kill myself I thought of all the people who cared about me, and that took away my suicidal thoughts. I didn't want my grandmother to die from depression or a heart attack after finding out that I killed myself.

—Jade, age 13

I know how many people care about me, I know that they're going to be really depressed and sad that I'm gone and I shouldn't have to torture other people just because I want to die. That's wrong.

—Jade, age 13

Think of things that are important to you in your life—your parents, your brothers, your sisters—anything like that. If you go and kill yourself, imagine how many lives you're going to be affecting. You won't just affect yourself, you're going to affect a lot of people who care about you.   —Jade, age 13

Get comfortable asking for help. If you're not comfortable asking for help, then you just got to be stronger.   —Jamie, age 15

Try to keep busy. The depression makes you want to quit doing everything. I wasn't active at all. I'm going to start swimming again and I'm going to be out with my friends a lot. I'm going to try to keep really busy and active and have a social life.

—Janessa, age 15

When it's severe like mine is, you may need meds.

—Carrie, age 18

If you are in an abusive relationship, get out of it. —Kaliza, age 16

If you're going to a therapist, make sure that you agree with the therapist. Some therapists say, "Are you comfortable with me?" and it's kind of hard to say, "Well no, I'm not." So talk to someone about it. If you don't, then you should get a different one.

—Janessa, age 15

I've had a lot of therapists I haven't liked at all. They would say, "Well, so when do you want to meet again?" And I'd say, "Well, I don't know. I'm busy then." And they'd keep asking and I'd say, "I don't think I need therapy, OK?" 'Cause you don't know how to say, "I really dislike you and I don't want to see you anymore." Find a therapist you like.   —Crystal, age 16

Don't be afraid of it—depression. If you're feeling like you want to die, a lot of the times it's completely normal with depression. You feel shitty but you'll get through it. If you really think about suicide every day, let somebody know in some form.   —Jamie, age 15

Just know that there are hundreds and thousands of kids who go through this every day. And don't feel ashamed, it's not worth it, because everybody has their problems. You just try to keep your head up.   —Elizabeth, age 14

Talk to someone immediately. People do want to help you. And no matter who you are, you have a voice. And, sooner or later, someone will pay attention to you. You have to be out in the open about it and everything.   —Noelle, age 15

You're not alone. There are a lot of kids out there hurting.

—Noelle, age 15

Take care of yourself. What doesn't kill you makes you stronger.

—Kaliza, age 16

ENDNOTES

Introduction

1. The statistics in this paragraph come from the following sources:
   Angold, A. and Rutter, M. (1992). "Effects of Age and Pubertal Status on Depression in a Large Clinical Sample." Development and Psychopathology, 4, 5–28.

   Marcus, S. M., Flynn, H. A., Young, E. A., Ghaziuddin, N., and Mudd, S. (2001). "Recurrent Depression in Women throughout the Lifespan." In J. F. Greden (editor) *Treatment of Recurrent Depression* (Review of Psychiatry, Volume 20, Number 5; Oldham J. M. and Riba, M. B., series editors). Washington, D.C.: American Psychiatric Press; The National Institute of Mental Health; 2000 Boston Youth Survey Report; Girl Matters, The Girls Coalition Of Greater Boston Newsletter Fall, Volume II (1) 2004; Commonwealth Fund Survey of the Health of Adolescent Girls, 1997.

2. Deykin, A., and, M. McNamara, 1985; Velez, C. and P. Cohen, 1988; Angold A. and Rutter, M. 1992; Kovacs, M., Goldston D., and Gatsonis, C. 1993. I also want to call attention to language: saying that girls are attempting suicide implies that we know that their intention was to die. It's not as though girls are failing at what they are doing; some do not want to die. The language is gendered. Boys and men are more likely, in the United States, to commit suicide, which was once called a successful or completed suicide. Girls "attempt" more often than boys, but don't die as frequently, which means that maybe they are "attempting" something else.

3. The statistics in this paragraph come from: Largesse, the Network for Size Esteem (*http://www.largesse.net/*)

4. *The Boston Globe*, December 29, 2003.

5. The Girls Coalition Of Boston Newsletter, Fall 2004 (*http://about-teen-depression.com/depression-statistics.html*)

6. Rutter, *Depression in Young People*, 1986.

7. Marcus, S. M., et al., 2001.

8. Gilligan, C. (1990a). "Joining the Resistance: Psychology, Politics, Girls, and Women." *Michigan Quarterly Review*, 29(4), 501–536, p. 512. During the decade of the 1980s, Carol Gilligan and her colleagues at the Harvard Graduate School of Education studied the psychological development of girls and founded a feminist research collaborative, the Harvard Project on Women's Psychology and Girls' Development (the Harvard Project). For more than ten years, the Harvard Project, of which I was a member, conducted longitudinal and cross-sectional studies of girls ages six to seventeen at a variety of school and after-school settings. This research involved girls and boys from public as well as private schools, including girls from economically privileged families as well as poor and working-class families. Central findings from this research have to do with observations made at the time of adolescence that offer an explanation as to why at this time girls' resilience is at risk. Books from this research include, but are not limited to: Gilligan, C., Ward, J. V., and Taylor, J. M with B. Bardige (eds.) (1988), *Mapping the Moral Domain*. Cambridge, MA: Harvard University Press; Gilligan, C., Lyons, M. P., and Hammer. T. J. (eds.), (1990) *Making Connections: The Relational Worlds of Adolescent Girls at Emma Willard School*. Cambridge, MA: Harvard University Press; Gilligan, C., Rogers, A., and Tolman, D. (eds.). (1991). *Women, Girls, and Psychotherapy: Reframing Resistance*. Binghamton, NY: Harrington Park Press; Brown, L. M., and Gilligan, C. (1992). *Meeting at the Crossroads: Women's Psychology and Girls' Development*: Cambridge, MA: Harvard University Press; Taylor, J. M., Gilligan, C., and Sullivan, A. (1995). *Between Voice and Silence: Women and Girls, Race and Relationship*. Cambridge, MA: Harvard University Press.

9. Pioneering studies on the psychology of women by Carol Gilligan (1977, 1982), Jean Baker Miller (1976), and Nancy Chodorow (1978) explicated the centrality and importance of relationships in women's psychological health and development. Carol Gilligan's developmental research (1977, 1982/1993) together with Jean Baker Miller's clinical observations (1976/1986) revealed that although relationships were crucial for women's psychological health, the centrality of relationships created a relational paradox for women. Within Western, patriarchal culture, women's expressions of anger, desire, power, and sexuality tend to be restricted; conventions of femininity or "good woman" behavior espouse goodness, selflessness, and self-sacrifice. Thus, many women find that expressing their true thoughts and feelings in their relationships leaves them vulnerable to losing those relationships. The alternative for women is silence—to silence themselves—that is, keep their true thoughts and feelings unexpressed and

out of the relationship. Yet, by silencing themselves, women take themselves out of the relationship, for the very sake of maintaining it. Subsequently, many women experience the psychological consequences of feeling disconnected from themselves, their feelings, their bodies, and other human beings. See Dana Jack's book on women and depression: *Silencing the Self*.

10. Gilligan, C. 1990a. A prominent finding in Carol Gilligan and the Harvard Project's research was that girls have healthy resistance to fake relationships, being unable to express the full range of their thoughts and feelings, and the resulting disconnection from self and others.

Chapter 1: Entering Dangerous Territory

1. Erikson, E. (1968)
2. Many teenage girls say they maintain their virginity and they won't get pregnant performing fellatio, but rates of STDs are rising in this age group, as are rates of AIDS among heterosexual women. Many girls also say that they feel empowered performing fellatio on boys, and that it gives them high status and popularity with their peers. Sexual acting-out can be correlated with a sexual abuse history, and girls who have been sexually abused may be more vulnerable to objectification.
3. A friend who teaches middle school English told me that he is worried, as there seems to be a new trend: When he lets kids write about any topic they want, often the boys pick cars or sports but there has been a concerning trend that the girls are writing about sex and sexual activity, and subsequent feelings of pressure, distress, and depression.
4. Durkin, S.J., and Paxton, S.J. (2002). "Predictors of Vulnerability to Reduced Body Image Satisfaction and Psychological Well-Being in Response to Exposure to Idealized Female Media Images in Adolescent Girls." *Journal of Psychosomatic Research*, 53, 995–1005.
5. Recently, a friend told me that teenage girls are prostituting themselves at the Mall of America to get money so they can buy Gucci and other expensive designer clothes, purses, and other accessories.
6. Here I am referring to Carol Gilligan and the Harvard Project research on girls, which I discussed in the introduction; see also Introduction endnote #9.
7. Despite society's impulse to attribute the spike in girls' depression to the biological and hormonal changes of puberty, that's not the whole story. Neither the hormonal nor the biological changes of puberty account for the dramatic rise in adolescent girls' depression; rather it's psychosocial factors. Estrogen, which increases with puberty, actually helps mood and affects the brain in a

way similar to an antidepressant. Girls should be feeling better, not worse, at puberty. Marcus, S. M., et al. 2001; Angold, A., and Rutter, M., *op. cit.* (1992). Brooks-Gunn, J., and Warren, M. P. (1989). Biological and social contributions to negative affect in young adolescent girls. *Child Development*, 60, 40–55; Miller Buchanon, C., Eccles, J. S., and Becker, J. B. (1992). "Are adolescents the victims of raging hormones? Evidence for activational effects of hormones on moods and behavior at adolescence." *Psychological Bulletin*, 111, 62–107.

8. American Psychiatric Association. (1994). *The American Psychiatric Association Diagnostic and Statistical Manual of Mental Disorders Fourth Edition* (DSM-IV) Washington DC: American Psychiatric Association Press.

9. Michael Miller's research is reported in *Newsweek*, December 8, 2003.

Chapter 2: Hurricane Watch

1. *Time Magazine*, May 10, 2004. p. 61.

2. Ibid. p. 61.

3. Nolen-Hoeksema, S. and Girgus, J. S. (1994). "The Emergence of Gender Differences in Depression in Adolescence." *Psychological Bulletin*, v11, n 3, 424–443.

4. Many bright girls with dyslexia or learning difficulties may be more at risk now especially if they have not been noticed before; they may have been called stupid or lazy, but these are bright kids who do not appear to be living up to their potential. The change from elementary to middle school may make things even harder, and girls who slipped through may show more trouble in school now.

5. Gilligan, C. (1990b). "Teaching Shakespeare's Sister: Notes from the Underground of Female Adolescence." In Gilligan, C., Lyons, M.P., and Hammer, T.J. (eds.), (1990). *Making Connections: The Relational Worlds of Adolescent Girls at Emma Willard School*. Cambridge, MA: Harvard University Press.

6. Girls who ruminate as a style of coping are susceptible to depression. There is a significant difference between reflection and ruminating. It is important that we teach girls to reflect. Reflection can help kids think: What can I learn, what can I do differently, how am I growing? Rumination, on the other hand, is focusing attention inwardly for long periods of times, in a negative way, and thinking about the same thing over and over and over. Talking about things helps; ruminating doesn't. Girls call their ruminating "obsessing." Boys, in general, are encouraged to be active. If they are upset, they do something. We need to encourage more physical activity in girls, because physical activity is a way of decreasing tension and stress, as is talking. Physical activity not only makes you feel better, it also takes your mind

off things. Having a balance of what we think of as feminine traits and mas-
culine traits decreases the risk of girls' depression. Young teenage girls who
are involved only in activities typically cast as feminine (such as hairstyling,
cooking, and sewing) have higher rates of depressive symptoms than girls
who do things like playing games or sports. S. Nolen-Hoeksema and Girgus,
J.S. 1994.

7. If a parent is depressed or a girl knows someone who committed suicide, such
as a friend or close family member, she may be at increased risk.

8. Fredrikson, K., Reddy, R., Way, N., and Rhodes, J. (2004). "Sleepless in
Chicago: Tracking the Effects of Sleep Loss over the Middle School Years.
Child Development, 74, 84–95.

9. Neurotransmitters are "messengers" that enable the brain cells to communicate with one another. B vitamins are necessary to make these substances. For
example, vitamin B_6 is necessary to produce the neurotransmitter serotonin,
which is responsible for feelings of well-being. Stress creates the need for
more B vitamins.

10. May, R. (1969). *Love and Will*. New York: Norton. p. 31

11. Carol Gilligan, 1986; 1990a; 1990b; Brown and Gilligan, 1992; Taylor et al.,
1995

12. Rutter, M. Brown, L., and Gilligan, C. 1992; Taylor et al. 1995.

13. Logan, D.E., and King, C.A. (2002). "Parental Identification of Depression
and Mental Health Service Use Among Depressed Adolescents." *Journal of
the American Academy of Child and Adolescent Psychiatry*, 41, 3, 296–304.

Chapter 3: Who Am I?

1. Carol Gilligan, 1990a, p. 512.

2. Carol Gilligan, 1990b.

3. Carol Gilligan, 1990a, 1990b.

4. Gilligan, C. (1991). "Women's Psychological Development: Implications for
Psychotherapy." In Gilligan, C., Rogers, A., and Tolman, D. (eds.), (1991).
Women, Girls and Psychotherapy: Reframing Resistance. New York: Harrington
Park Press. p. 23

5. *The New York Sunday Times*, January 1, 2004.

6. Bernardez, T. (1988). "Women and Anger: Cultural Prohibitions and the
Feminine Ideal." (Work in Progress no. 31). Wellesley, MA: The Stone Cen-
ter. p. 4. See also: Miller, B.B. 1976/1986; Brown, L.M. (1998) *Raising Their
Voices: The Politics of Girls' Anger*. Cambridge, MA: Harvard University Press.

7. For an in-depth exploration of adolescent girls' sexuality, see Tolman, D.
(2002). *Dilemmas of Desire*. Cambridge, MA: Harvard University Press; see
also Fine, M. (1988). "Sexuality, Schooling and Adolescent Females: The
Missing Discourse of Desire." *Harvard Educational Review*, 58, 29–53.

8. Kidd, S. M. (2002). *The Secret Life of Bees*. New York: Penguin, p. 9.
9. Carol Gilligan, Harvard Project Papers.
10. Jack, D. (1991). *Silencing the Self: Women and Depression*. Cambridge, MA: Harvard University Press. See also: Jordan, J. The "Self in Relation": "Implications for Women and Depression." In Jordan, J., Kaplan, A., Miller, J. B., Stiver, I. P., and Surrey, I. (1991). *Women's Growth in Connection*. New York: Guilford Press; Stiver, I. (1988). "From Depression to Sadness in Women's Psychotherapy." (Work in Progress no. 36). Wellesley, MA: The Stone Center.
11. See Gilligan, 1990a; 1990b; Brown and Gilligan, 1992.

Chapter 4: I Must Be Doing Something Wrong
1. Taylor et al., 1995, p. 25.

Chapter 5: Risking Love
1. Eth, S., and Pynoos, R. S. (1985). Developmental perspective on psychic trauma in childhood. In Figley, C. (ed.), *Trauma and Its Wake*. New York: Brunner/Mazel; Eth, S., and Pynoos, R. S. (eds). (1985). *Post-Traumatic Stress Disorder in Children*. Washington, D.C.: American Psychiatric Press.
2. Silverman, J. G., Raj, A., Mucci, L., Hathaway, J. (2001) "Dating Violence Against Adolescent Girls and Associated Substance Use, Unhealthy Weight Control, Sexual Risk Behavior, Pregnancy, and Suicidality." *Journal of the American Medical Association*, 286, 5, 572–579.
3. van der Kolk, B. A., and Saporta, J. (1991). "The Biological Response to Psychic Trauma Mechanism and Treatment of Intrusion and Numbing." *Anxiety Research*, 4, 199–212. van der Kolk, B. A. (1994). "The Body Keeps the Score: Memory and the Evolving Psychobiology of Posttraumatic Stress." *Harvard Review of Psychiatry*, 1, 253–265; van der Kolk, B. A., and Fisler, R. (1993). "The Biological Basis of Posttraumatic Stress." *Family Violence and Abusive Relationships*, 20, 417–432; van der Kolk, B. A., and van der Hart, O. (1991). "The Intrusive Past: the Flexibility of Memory and the Engraving of Trauma," *American Imago*, 48(4) 425–454.
4. Terr, L. C. (1990). *Too Scared to Cry: Psychic Trauma in Childhood*. New York: Basic Books; Terr, L. C. (1991). "Childhood Traumas: An Outline and Overview." *American Journal of Psychiatry*, 148, 10–20.
5. Herman, J. (1992). *Trauma and Recovery*. USA: Basic Books; van der Kolk, B. A., Herron, N., and Hostetler, A. (1994). The History of Trauma in Psychiatry. *Psychiatric Clinics of North America*, 17, 583–600.
6. Terr, L. C. 1990, p. 84.

Chapter 6: When Actions Speak Louder Than Words

1. Winnicot, D. W. (1984). "Aggression and Its Roots." In Winnicot, C., Shepard, R., and Davis, M. (eds.), *Deprivation and Delinquency*. London: Tavistock. Winnicot, D. W. (1984). "Some Aspects of Juvenile Delinquency": In Winnicot, C., Shepard, R., and Davis, M. (eds.), *op. cit.*; Winnicot, D. W. (1984). "The Antisocial." In Winnicot, C., Shepard, R., and Davis, M. (eds.), *op. cit.*
2. Carlson, G. A., and Cantwell, D. P. (1980) "Unmasking Masked Depression in Children and Adolescents." *American Journal of Psychiatry*, 137, 4, 445–449.
3. Noam, G. G., and Borst, S. (1994). "Developing Meaning, Losing Meaning: Understanding Suicidal Behavior in the Young." In Noam, G., and Borst, S. (eds.), *Children, Youth, and Suicide: Developmental Perspectives: New Directions for Child Development*. San Francisco: Jossey-Bass.
4. See *The Bipolar Child*, (2002) by Demitri and Janice Papolos, New York: Broadway Books. Until recently the field of psychiatry did not think that children and adolescents could experience bipolar depression (what used to be called manic-depression). Demitri and Janice Papolos, in *The Bipolar Child*, write that, unlike descriptions of bipolar adults, children and teens may cycle through moods of being up and down daily much more quickly than adults. Hypersexuality; oppositional, irritable, and explosive behavior; and rapid mood swings from high to low in a day can indicate bipolar depression in teens, which helps us understand Isabelle's behavior. It is important to know that post-traumatic stress disorder (PTSD) can also look like bipolar depression—the hyperaroused part can look like the manic part, and the numbing can look like depression. A careful life history taking is also important as is a clinician able to distinguish between the two and when they coexist.

Chapter 7: The Spiral Begins

1. Steiner-Adair, C. (1986). "The Body-Politic: Normal Female Adolescent Development and the Development of Eating Disorders." *Journal of the American Academy of Psychoanalysis*, 14, 95–114; See also Steiner-Adair, C. (1991). "When the Body Speaks: Girls, Eating Disorders, and Psychotherapy." In Gilligan, C., Rogers, A., and Tolman, D. (eds.), *Women, Girls and Psychotherapy: Reframing Resistance*.

Chapter 8: Olivia: The Disappearing Girl

1. Gilligan, C. (1993). *In a Different Voice*, 2nd ed., Cambridge, MA: Harvard University Press, Letters to Readers.

Chapter 9: Grace: A Story of Hope

1. Machoian, L. (1998). "The Possibility of Love." Unpublished doctoral dissertation. Harvard University; Gilligan, C. and Machoian, L. (2002). "Learning to Speak the Language of Violence." *Studies in Gender and Sexuality*, 3(3), 321–340.

2. Metha, A., Chen, C., Mulvenon, S., and Dodes, I. "A Theoretical Model of Adolescent Suicide Risk." *Archive of Suicide Research*, 4, 115–133; Asarnow, J.R., Carlson, G.A., and Guthrie, D. (1987). Coping Strategies, Self-perceptions, Hopelessness, and Perceived Family Environment in Depressed and Suicidal Children. *Journal of Consulting and Clinical Psychology*, 55, 361–366; Borst, S.R., and Noam, G.G. (1993). Development Psychopathology in Suicidal and Nonsuicidal Adolescent Girls. *Journal of the American Academy of Child and Adolescent Psychiatry*, 32(3), 501–508; Carlson, G.A., and Cantwell, D.P. (1982). Suicidal Behavior and Depression in Children and Adolescents. *Journal of the American Academy of Child and Adolescent Psychiatry*, 21(4), 361–368; Dyer, J.A., and Kreitman, N. (1984). "Hopelessness, Depression, and Suicidal Intent in Parasuicide." *British Journal of Psychiatry*, 144, 127–133; Rotheram-Borus, M.J., and Trautman, P.D. (1988). "Hopelessness, Depression and Suicidal Intent among Adolescent Suicide Attempters." *Journal of the American Academy of Child and Adolescent Psychiatry*, 27(6), 700–704; Noam, G.G., and Borst, S. (1994). "Developing Meaning, Losing Meaning: Understanding Suicidal Behavior in the Young." In Noam, G., and Borst, S. (eds.), *op. cit.*

3. Laufer, J. (1995). *The Suicidal Child*. Madison, CT: International Universities Press, 1995, p. 104.

4. Erikson, E. (1958). *Young Man Luther*. New York: Norton. pp. 170, 198.

5. Ibid, p. 104.

6. Ibid.

7. Hawton, et al, 1982; Rotheram-Borus, M.J. and Trautman, P. D., 1988; Trautman, P.D. et al., 1991.

8. Morrison, T. (1970). *The Bluest Eye*. New York: Washington Press, p. 14.

9. Girls' healthy resistance in early adolescence to fake relationships and losing themselves is a prominent finding in Carol Gilligan's research on girls; healthy resistance is a critical source of girls' strength and hope.

Chapter 10: Between Angst and Depression

1. Brown, L. M., and Gilligan, C. 1992.

2. See the Wellesley Centers for Women series of books and working papers. For example, Miller, J.B., and Stiver, P.S. (1997). *The Healing Connection*. Boston, MA: Beacon Press.

3. A public health advisory has been issued by the Food and Drug Administration regarding the use of antidepressants in children and teenagers. Antidepressants can have the adverse and dangerous side effect of inducing suicidal thoughts and behavior in children and adolescents. Most of these drugs have not been approved for use in children and adolescents. If medication is used, it needs to be very carefully monitored.

BIBLIOGRAPHY

American Psychiatric Association. *The American Psychiatric Association Diagnostic and Statistical Manual of Mental Disorders*. 2d ed. DSM-IV Washington, D.C. American Psychiatric Association Press, 1994.

Anderson, L. H. *Speak*. New York: Puffin, 1999.

Angold, A., and M. Rutter. "Effects of Age and Pubertal Status on Depression in a Large Clinical Sample." *Development and Psychopathology* 4 (1992): 5–28.

Beardslee, W. R. *Out of the Darkened Room: When a Parent is Depressed*. Boston: Little Brown and Company, 2002.

Beck, A. T. "Thinking and Distortion." *Archives of General Psychiatry* 9 (1963): 324–333.

———. "The Core Problem in Depression: The Cognitive Dyad." In *Science and Psychoanalysis*, edited by J. Masseman. New York: Grune and Stratton, 1970.

Bernardez, T. "Women and Anger: Cultural Prohibitions and the Feminine Ideal." (Work in Progress, no. 31). Wellesley, MA: The Stone Center, 1988.

Borst, S. R., and G. G. Noam, "Developmental Psychopathology in Suicidal and Nonsuicidal Adolescent Girls." *Journal of the American Academy of Child and Adolescent Psychiatry*, 32, no. 3 (1993): 501–508.

Brooks-Gunn, J., and M. P. Warren. "Biological and Social Contributions to Negative Affect in Young Adolescent Girls. *Child Development*, 60 (1989): 40–55.

Brown, G. W., T. Harris, and J. R. Copeland. "Depression and Loss." *British Journal of Psychiatry* 130 (1977):1–18.

Brown, L. M. *Raising Their Voices: The Politics of Girls' Anger*. Cambridge, MA: Harvard University Press, 1998.

———. *Girlfighting: Betrayal and Rejection Among Girls*. New York: New York University Press, 2003.

Brown, L. M. and C. Gilligan. *Meeting at the Crossroads: Women's Psychology and Girls' Development*: Cambridge, MA: Harvard University Press, 1992.

Brumberg, J. *The Body Project: An Intimate History of American Girls*. New York: Vintage Books, 1997.

Canetto, S. "Gender and Suicidal Behavior." In *Review of Suicidology*, edited by R. W. Maris, M. M. Silverman, and S. S. Canetto. New York: Guilford Press, 1997.

Carlson, G. A., and D. P. Cantwell. "Unmasking Masked Depression in Children and Adolescents. *American Journal of Psychiatry* 137, no. 4 (1980): 445–449.

Chodorow, N. *The Reproduction of Mothering: Psychoanalysis and the Sociology of Gender*. Berkeley, CA: University of California Press, 1978.

Clark, G. N., P. Rohde, P. M. Lewinsohn, H. Hyman, and J. R. Seeley. "Cognitive Behavioral Treatment of Adolescent Depression: Efficacy of Acute Group Treatment and Booster Sessions." *Journal of the American Academy of Child and Adolescent Psychiatry* 38, no. 3 (1999): 272–279.

Deykin, E. Y., J. J. Alpert, and J. J. McNamara. "A Pilot Study of the Effect of Exposure or Neglect on the Adolescent Suicidal Behavior." *American Journal of Psychiatry* 142 (1985): 1299–1303.

Durkin, S. J., and S. J. Paxton. "Predictors of Vulnerability to Reduced Body Image Satisfaction and Psychological Well-being in Response to Exposure to Idealized Female Media Images in Adolescent Girls." *Journal of Psychosomatic Research* 53, (2002): 995–1005.

Dyer, J. A., and N. Kreitman. "Hopelessness, Depression, and Suicidal Intent in Parasuicide." *British Journal of Psychiatry* 144 (1984): 127–133.

Erikson, E. *Young Man Luther*. New York: Norton, 1958.

———. *Identity, Youth, and Crisis*. New York: Norton, 1968.

Eth, S., and R. S. Pynoos. "Developmental Perspective on Psychic Trauma in Childhood." In *Trauma and Its Wake*, edited by C. Figley. New York: Brunner/Mazel, 1985.

Eth, S. and R. S. Pynoos, eds. *Post-Traumatic Stress Disorder in Children*. Washington, D.C.: American Psychiatric Press, 1985.

Fine, M. "Sexuality, Schooling, and Adolescent Females: The Missing Discourse of Desire." *Harvard Educational Review* 58 (1988): 29–53.

Fredrikson, K., R. Reddy, N. Way, and J. Rhodes. "Sleepless in Chicago: Tracking the Effects of Sleep Loss over the Middle School Years." *Child Development*, 74 (2004): 84–95.

Freud, S. "Mourning and Melancholia." In *The Standard Edition of the Complete Psychological Works of Sigmund Freud*, vol. 14, edited by J. Strachey. London: Hogarth Press, 1915.

Garmezy, N. "Stressors of Childhood." In *Stress, Coping and Development in Children*. New York: McGraw Hill, 1983.

Greden, J.F., ed. *Treatment of Recurrent Depression*. edited by N. Garmezy and M. Rutter. *Review of Psychiatry*, vol. 20, no. 5. J.M. Oldham and M.B. Riba, ser. eds. Washington, D.C.: American Psychiatric Press, 2001.

Gilligan, C. *In a Different Voice: Psychological Theory and Women's Development*. Cambridge, MA: Harvard University Press, 1982/1993.

——— "Adolescent Development Reconsidered. "In *Mapping the Moral Domain*, edited by C. Gilligan, J.V. Ward, and J.M. Taylor, with B. Bardige. Cambridge, MA: Harvard University Press, 1988.

———. "Joining the Resistance: Psychology, Politics, Girls and Women." *Michigan Quarterly Review* 29, no. 4 (1990a): 501–536.

———. "Teaching Shakespeare's Sister: Notes from the Underground of Female Adolescence." In *Making Connections: The Relational Worlds of Adolescent Girls at Emma Willard School*, edited by C. Gilligan, M.P. Lyons, and T.J. Hammer. Cambridge, MA: Harvard University Press, 1990b.

———. "Women's Psychological Development: Implications for Psychotherapy." In *Women, Girls and Psychotherapy: Reframing Resistance*, edited by C. Gilligan, A. Rogers, and D. Tolman. New York: Harrington Park Press, 1991.

———. "The Centrality of Relationships in Human Development: A Puzzle, Some Evidence, and a Theory." In *Development and Vulnerability in Close Relationships*, edited by G. Noam and K. Fischer. New Jersey: Erlbaum, 1996.

———. "Exit-Voice Dilemmas in Adolescent Development." In

Development, Democracy, and the Art of Trespassing: Essays in Honor of Albert O. Hirschman, edited by A. Foxley, M. McPherson, and G. O'Donnell. South Bend, IN: University of Notre Dame Press, 1986.

Gilligan, C., L. M. Brown, and A. Rogers. "Psyche Embedded: A Place for Body, Relationships, and Culture in Personality Theory." In *Studying Persons and Lives*, edited by A. Rabin, R. Tucker, R. Emmons, and S. Frank. New York: Springer, 1990.

Gilligan, C. and L. Machoian. "Learning to Speak the Language of Violence." *Studies in Gender and Sexuality* 3, no. 3 (2002): 321–340.

Gilligan, C., A. Rogers, and D. Tolman. *Women, Girls, and Psychotherapy: Reframing Resistance*. Binghamton, NY: Harrington Park Press, 1991.

Gilligan, C., J. V. Ward, J. M. Taylor, with B. Bardige, eds. *Mapping the Moral Domain*. Cambridge, MA: Harvard University Press, 1998.

Hart, B. I., and J. M. Thompson. "Gender Role Characteristics and Depressive Symptomatology Among Adolescents." *Journal of Early Adolescent Research* 16, no. 4 (1996): 407–426.

Hawton, K., D. Cole, J. O'Grady, and M. Osborn. "Motivational Aspects of Self-poisoning in Adolescents." *British Journal of Psychiatry* 141, (1982): 286–291.

Herman, J. *Trauma and Recovery*. USA: Basic Books, 1992.

Jack, D. *Silencing the Self: Women and Depression*. Cambridge, MA: Harvard University Press, 1991.

Jordan, J. "The 'Self in Relation': Implications for Women and Depression." In *Women's Growth in Connection*, edited by J. Jordan, A. Kaplan, J. B. Miller, I. P. Stiver, and I. Surrey. New York: Guilford Press, 1991.

Jordan, J., A. Kaplan, J. B. Miller, I. P. Stiver, and I. Surrey. *Women's Growth in Connection*. New York: Guilford Press, 1991.

Kaplan, A. and R. Klein. "Women and Suicide: The Cry for Connection." (Working Paper Series, no. 46). Wellesley, MA: The Stone Center, 1990.

Kidd, S. M. *The Secret Life of Bees*. New York: Penguin, 2002.

Kovacs, M. and A. Beck. "Maladaptive Cognitive Structures in Depression." In *Essential Papers on Depression*, edited by J. C. Coyne. New York: New York University Press, 1985.

Kovacs, M., D. Goldston, and C. Gatsonis. "Suicidal Behaviors and Childhood-Onset Depressive Disorders: A Longitudinal Investigation." *Journal of the American Academy of Child and Adolescent Psychiatry* 32 (1993): 8–20.

Laufer, J. *The Suicidal Child.* Madison, CT: International Universities Press, 1995.

Logan, D.E. and C.A. King. "Parental Identification of Depression and Mental Health Service Use Among Depressed Adolescents." *Journal of the American Academy of Child and Adolescent Psychiatry* 41 no. 3 (2002): 296–304.

Machoian, L. *Love, Hope, and Resistance.* Unpublished qualifying paper. Cambridge, MA: Harvard University Press, 1995.

———. *The Possibility of Love: A Psychological Study of Adolescent Girls' Suicidal Acts and Self-Mutilation.* Unpublished doctoral dissertation. Cambridge, MA: Harvard University Press, 1998.

———. "Cutting Voices: Self-Injury in Three Adolescent Girls." *Journal of Psychosocial Nursing and Mental Health* 39, no. 11 (2001): 22–29.

Marcus, S.M., H.A. Flynn, E.A. Young, N. Ghaziuddin, and S. Mudd, "Recurrent Depression in Women throughout the Lifespan." In *Treatment of Recurrent Depression. Review of Psychiatry*, vol. 20, no. 5. J.M. Oldham and M.B. Riba, ser. eds. Washington, D.C.: American Psychiatric Press, 2001.

May, R. *Love and Will.* New York: Norton, 1969.

Metha, A., C. Chen, S. Mulvenon, and 1. Dodes, "A Theoretical Model of Adolescent Suicide Risk." *Archives of Suicide Research* 4 (1998): 115–133.

Miller, J.B. *Toward a New Psychology of Women.* Boston, MA: Beacon Press, 1976/1986.

Miller, J.B. and I.P. Stiver. *The Healing Connection: How Women Form Relationships in Therapy and in Life.* Boston, MA: Beacon Press, 1997.

Miller Buchanon, C., J.S. Eccles, and J.B. Becker. "Are Adolescents the Victims of Raging Hormones? Evidence for Activational Effects of Hormones on Moods and Behavior at Adolescence." *Psychological Bulletin* 111 (1992): 62–107.

Morrison, T. *The Bluest Eye*. New York: Washington Press, 1970.

Noam, G. G. and S. Borst. "Developing Meaning, Losing Meaning: Understanding Suicidal Behavior in the Young. In *Children, Youth, and Suicide: Developmental Perspectives: New Directions for Child Development*, edited by G. Noam and S. Borst. San Francisco: Jossey-Bass, 1994.

Nolen-Hoeksema, S. and J. S. Girgus, "The Emergence of Gender Differences in Depression in Adolescence." *Psychological Bulletin* 11, no. 3 (1994): 424–443.

Obeidallah, D. A., S. M. Mchale, and R. K. Silbereisen. "Gender Role Socialization and Adolescents' Reports of Depression: Why Some Girls and Not Others?" *Journal of Youth and Adolescence* 25, no. 6 (1996): 775–785.

Papolos, D. and P. Janice. *The Bipolar Child*. New York: Broadway Books, 2002.

Peterson, A. "Adolescent Development." *Annual Review of Psychology* 39 (1988): 583–607.

Peterson, A., P. A. Sarigiani, and R. E. Kennedy. "Adolescent Depression: Why More Girls?" *Journal of Youth and Adolescence* 20 (1991): 247–271.

Raphael, B. *The Anatomy of Bereavement*. New York: Basic Books, 1983.

Real, T. *I Don't Want to Talk About It*. New York: Fireside, 1997.

Rice-Smith, E. Group Psychotherapy with Sexually Abused Children. In *Comprehensive Group Psychotherapy*, 3d ed., H. I. Kaplan and B. J. Saddock, eds. Baltimore: Williams & Wilkins, 1993.

Rogers, A. "Voice, Play, and a Practice of Ordinary Courage in Girls' and Women's Lives." *Harvard Educational Review* 63, no. 3 (1993): 265–295.

Rotheram-Borus, M. J. and P. D. Trautman. "Hopelessness, Depression and Suicidal Intent Among Adolescent Suicide Attempters. *Journal of the American Academy of Child and Adolescent Psychiatry* 27, no. 6 (1988): 700–704.

———. "Cognitive Style and Pleasant Activities Among Female Adolescent Suicide Attempters." *Journal of Consulting and Clinical Psychology* 58, no. 5 (1990): 554–561.

Rutter, M. "Psychosocial Resilience and Protective Mechanisms." *American Journal of Orthopsychiatry* 57, no. 3 (1987): 316–331.

————. "The Developmental Psychopathology of Depression: Issues and Perspectives." In *Depression in Young People: Developmental and Clinical Perspectives*, New York: Guilford Press, 1986.

Rutter, M. and N. Garmezy. "Developmental Psychopathology." In *Socialization, Personality and Social Development*, vol. 4. New York: Wiley, 1983.

Rutter, M., C. Izard, and P. B. Read, eds. *Depression In Young People*. New York: Guilford Press, 1986.

Rutter, M., C. E. Izard, and P. Read, eds. "*Depression in Young People. Developmental and Clinical Perspectives*. New York: Guilford Press, 1986.

Simmons, R. *Odd Girl Out*. New York: Harcourt, 2002.

Steiner-Adair, C. The Body-Politic: Normal Female Adolescent Development and the Development of Eating Disorders. *Journal of the American Academy of Psychoanalysis* 14 (1986): 95–114.

————. "When the Body Speaks: Girls, Eating Disorders, and Psychotherapy." In *Women, Girls and Psychotherapy: Reframing Resistance*, edited by C. Gilligan, A. Rogers, and D. Tolman. New York: Harrington Park Press, 1991.

Stice, E. and H. E. Shaw. "Role of Body Dissatisfaction in the Onset of and Maintenance of Eating Pathology: A Synthesis of Research." *Journal of Psychosomatic Research* 53 (2002): 985–993.

Stiver, I. "From Depression to Sadness in Women's Psychotherapy." (Work in Progress no. 36). Wellesley, MA: The Stone Center, 1988.

Stoppard, J. M. *Understanding Depression: Feminist Social Constructionist Approaches*. New York: Routledge, 2000.

Taylor, J. M., C. Gilligan, and A. Sullivan. *Between Voice and Silence: Women and Girls, Race and Relationship*. Cambridge, MA. Harvard University Press, 1995.

Terr, L. C. "Psychic Trauma in Children and Adolescents." *Psychiatric Clinics of North America*, 8 (1985): 815–835.

————. *Too Scared to Cry: Psychic Trauma in Childhood*. New York: Basic Books, 1990.

————. "Childhood Traumas: An Outline and Overview." *American Journal of Psychiatry*, 148 (1991): 10–20.

Tolman, D. *Dilemmas of Desire*. Cambridge, MA: Harvard University Press, 2002.

Trautman, P. D., M. J. Rotheram-Borus, S. Dopkins, and M. Lewin,

"Psychiatric Diagnoses in Minority Female Adolescent Suicide Attempters." *Journal of the American Academy of Child and Adolescent Psychiatry* 30, no. 4 (1991): 617–622.

van der Kolk, B. A. "The Body Keeps the Score: Memory and the Evolving Psychobiology of Posttraumatic Stress." *Harvard Review of Psychiatry*, 1 (1994): 253–265.

van der Kolk, B. A. and R. Fisler. "The Biological Basis of Posttraumatic Stress." *Family Violence and Abusive Relationships*, 20 (1993): 417–432.

van der Kolk, B. A., McFarlane, S. and L. Weisaeth, eds. *Traumatic Stress: The Effects of Overwhelming Experience on Mind, Body, and Society*, New York: Guilford Press, 1996.

van der Kolk, B. A. and J. Saporta. "The Biological Response to Psychic Trauma: Mechanism and Treatment of Intrusion and Numbing." *Anxiety Research*, 4 (1991): 199–212.

van der Kolk, B. A. and O. van der Hart. "The Intrusive Past: The Flexibility of Memory and the Engraving of Trauma." *American Imago* 48, no. 4 (1991): 425–454.

Velez, C. N. and P. Cohen. "Suicidal Behavior and Ideation in a Community Sample of Children: Maternal and Youth Reports." *Journal of the American Academy of Child and Adolescent Psychiatry*, 27 (1988): 349–356.

Winnicot, D. W. "Aggression and Its Roots. In *Deprivation and Delinquency*, edited by C. Winnicot, R. Shepard, and M. Davis. London: Tavistock, 1984.

———. "Some Aspects of Juvenile Delinquency." In *Deprivation and Delinquency*, edited by C. Winnicot, R. Shepard, and M. Davis. London: Tavistock, 1984.

———. "The Antisocial Tendency." In *Deprivation and Delinquency*, edited by C. Winnicot, R. Shepard, and M. Davis. London: Tavistock, 1984.

INDEX

ABOUT THE AUTHOR

Dr. Lisa Machoian taught in Harvard's Department of Human Development and Psychology and was also the director of their Gender Studies Concentration. She has worked for more than twenty years with teenage girls, and her articles have appeared in many publications. She now devotes her time to lecturing, consulting, and conducting workshops for parents, teens, professionals, and institutions including schools, psychiatric hospitals, college campuses, and government agencies. Dr. Machoian serves on the board of Retreat from Violence, an organization that works on preventing teen violence. She holds a master's degree and a doctorate from Harvard and lives in Cambridge.